BRIAN BORU, KING OF IRELAND

failan filius ...rini
failgnad filius failan
fonfailid filius failgnaich
rigne filius fonfailto
rechnerrach fili: rigni

Scriptum in ... ad ecclesiam
mandauit totum fructum
laboris ... ita bab... in
... causam ... elemoysina-
rum distribuendum est apos-
tolice urbi que Roma ce
nominatur apud italiam.
Sic psalm... i beblioten
reotorum ego scripsi
... caluus p... icon
... br...an in...
... ...
...um ...omnib; ...
...

ROGER CHATTERTON NEWMAN

Brian Boru
King of Ireland

ANVIL BOOKS

First published in 1983
by Anvil Books Limited
90 Lower Baggot Street, Dublin 2

© Roger Chatterton Newman 1983

ISBN 0 900068 64 7 case
ISBN 0 900068 65 5 paper

Typesetting Computertype Limited
Printed in the Republic of Ireland
by Cahill Printers Limited

Frontispiece
The page in the book of Armagh
with the inscription
'Briain Imperatoris Scotorum'

Contents

For Etta, Heather and Arthur

Preface

WHO was Brian Boru? What did he achieve and what was his contribution to Irish history? His name is as familiar to every Irish schoolchild as are the names of, say, Alfred the Great or William the Conqueror to an English schoolchild. Brian's death at Clontarf on Good Friday, 1014, is an event as secure in history as the end of Harold at Hastings in 1066. Indeed, one might go further and say that Brian is known as the king who 'drove the Danes out of Ireland'; but on that fiction, and on the fact of his death, his name rests. Harold, William and Alfred have had their biographers by the score, but it was not until 1914 — nine centuries after Clontarf — that a serious attempt was made to analyse Brian's character and accomplishments. The writer who did so, T. J. Westropp in *Brian Boru, The Hero of Clontarf* — a slim volume of thirty-eight pages, first serialised in the *Irish Monthly* — was president of the Royal Society of Antiquaries of Ireland and an antiquarian of formidable stature. While much of his little book is made of the stuff of romance, he was the first writer to penetrate the screen of myth and legend that has separated us from Brian.

A more serious attempt to penetrate the myth was made by Mrs Alice Stopford Green in *History of the Irish State to 1014*, published in 1925. She was one of the first historians to recognise that Brian was not the usurping princeling from Thomond, not the revolutionary despot and certainly not the semi-mythical figure of various popular histories.

'He was perhaps the greatest 'realist' Ireland has known,' she wrote, 'at all times keeping pace with a changing world. His sense of realities taught him how far he could go and when to draw back. Warrior as he was by the hard training of his youth, where any peace was possible his one object was to avoid fighting. The true dignity of his character, and his single devotion to his country's salvation, may be measured by the fact that in all the changing circumstances of his life we do not find a case in which personal humiliation or personal ambition was to him of any account . . .'

That he was entirely devoid of personal ambition, or that in one instance at least — as I attempt to show in chapter eight — personal humiliation had no effect on him, is doubtful, and perhaps rightly so, for we are searching for a man, not a figure from the pages of chivalry and romance as epitomised by Sir Thomas Mallory's King Arthur. But Mrs Stopford Green, herself devoted to the cause of Irish freedom, was generally correct in her analysis, although it was confined to a bare three chapters of her book. An earlier historian, the Hon Emily Lawless, writing *The Story of the Nations: Ireland* (London, 1887), has called Brian an 'unmistakable king', but like most writers of her time devoted even less space to him than Mrs Stopford Green or Westropp were to do.

But Alice Stopford Green and T. J. Westropp set the precedent, and they were followed in 1938 by the Revd John Ryan, SJ, in his long and invaluable essay on the battle of Clontarf in the *Journal* of the Royal Society of Antiquaries of Ireland, and in 1967 with his contribution to *North Munster Studies* — 'Brian Boruma, King of Ireland'. Both essays are referred to frequently throughout this book.

The fact remains, however, that to many people Brian Boru is seen, as Emily Lawless admitted, as a 'sort of giant Cormoran, or Eat-'em-alive-oh! a being out of a fairy tale, whom nobody is expected to take seriously; nay, as a symbol for ridiculous and inflated pretension . . .' I hope that in the following pages this impression is finally dispelled.

It is true that even in his lifetime Brian was regarded by the longer-established royal houses of Ireland as a pretentious usurper from an obscure clan in the south-west of the country. The youngest son of the king of Thomond — a throne in all probability elevated by the most aristocratic family in the island, the Uí Néill, to help maintain their own authority — he was certainly not born to greatness. His leadership of a small band of guerillas, holding out in the wilds of Clare against the Danes of Limerick, brought him into prominence with his own people; and the murder of his eldest surviving brother, Mathghamhain, gave him the thrones of Thomond and Munster. Having come thus far, he went on to displace the mighty Uí Néill on the high throne of Ireland, and in old age established a form of governance that was probably the nearest to a strong central monarchy the conglomeration of disunited Irish kingdoms had ever experienced. He subdued the Scandinavian inhabitants of the island and, having done so, turned their skills in commerce to the benefit of native and Land Leaper alike.

Brian was called Emperor of the Gael by a scribe at Armagh; and although the accolade was accorded him in his presence, and by a lifelong friend and counsellor, he was perhaps the only ruler in Irish history (and certainly the only one in the two or three centuries preceding English domination) who came anywhere near deserving such a title. He never achieved absolute hegemony over the entire island — the Uí Néill at their most influential failed in this — and his reign was not the period of uninterupted peace that some writers would have us believe. But his authority was felt in four of the five major kingdoms and, by the time he was crowned high king in 1002, he held undisputed sway in the south and east and within the Norse city-state of Dublin.

Brian's policies and reforms, unusual when compared with the average politics of his age, were based on a genuine desire to bring peace and prosperity to his realm. He succeeded to a degree; had he been younger he may have achieved far more. Yet, had he not achieved as much as he did, would his name be so familiar today — although it might be said that his death brought him most of his enduring fame?

It is unfortunate that so little reliable source material is available for a student of Brian's life and work. The various annals, in untranslated form, and notably the composition known popularly as the *Four Masters*, are prone to wild exaggeration and eulogistic fancy where particular heroes or villians are concerned. Later amendments and additions, as well as some poor translation or editing in the last century, have further complicated the picture. It should also be borne in mind that many sources were compiled centuries after the events they so vividly describe took place.

Yet, by sifting the probable from the nonsensical, likely fact from undoubted myth, it is possible to gain a considerable impression of the years leading up to Brian's birth and then of the seventy-three years of his own existence. I have referred to the more reliable historians and, I hope, have in some degree succeeded in following their footsteps through the devious maze created by the old annalists. A full bibliography will be found in the Notes at the end of the book.

An explanation should be given of the form of spelling of the names of people and places throughout these pages. Place names still in existence are also given in the English form, to aid identification by the reader; battles fought before or during Brian's lifetime appear in Irish, for as such they would have been known to the combatants, together with the present-day locations. The names of most people must obviously appear in Irish, the most notable exception being Brian Boru himself. It might be thought that if I was to be consistent in style, he should appear as ~~Brian Bórumha; but~~ Boru, the anglicised form, is in common usage, and has been so for centuries. I feel that no excuse is needed for calling a national hero by the name usually associated with him.

Another exception is the use of the term, *Ardrí*, or high king. According to Professor Etienne Rynne, in his editing of *North Munster Studies*, the correct term is *Rí Éireann*, King of Ireland, *Ardrí* not being found in the annals before the coming of the Anglo-Normans. Once again, however, I have decided to use the term that is more generally known. And to help the reader as much as possible, especially with pronunciation, a glossary of Irish words used in the text has been appended.

During the seven years that this work has been in preparation, I have received invaluable encouragement and aid from many quarters. My deepest debt of gratitude is to Dan Nolan, of Anvil Books, Dublin. No mean authority on Irish history, he has not only provided me with important sources for reference — and constantly revived my enthusiasm for the task in hand — but he is publishing the result. It is as much his book as mine.

Dr Pádraig de Brún, Dublin Institute for Advanced Studies, advised in the preparation of the glossary, and for his work and kindness I am greatly in his debt.

The late Professor Michael J. O'Kelly, late head of the Department of Archaeology, University College Cork, placed at my disposal his valuable collection of photographs taken during the excavation of Béal Bóramha, Co Clare, carried out under his direction in 1961, and I am most grateful for his generosity. I must also record my gratitude to his Department for bringing to my attention the late Professor Seán P. Ó Ríordáin's report of the excavations at Garranes (Ráth Raithleann), Co Cork, carried out in the 'thirties.

And my thanks are due also to the board of Trinity College, Dublin, for permission to reproduce the page from the *Book of Armagh* containing the entry 'Briain Imperatoris Scotorum'; to the Very Revd Henry Lillie, MA, Dean of Armagh; to Monsignor Bernard Kenney, private secretary to the Apostolic Delegation in London; Mrs Mette Sunnana and Mr Torbjørn Støverud, cultural attaché, of the Royal Norwegian Embassy, London; Mr Fleming Andre Larsen, cultural attaché at the Royal Danish

Embassy, London; Fr Bartholomew Egan, OFM, librarian at the Franciscan House of Studies, Killiney, Co Dublin; Fr L. C. Coffey, OP, of St Martin de Porres Apostolate, Dublin; and the patient and knowledgeable staff of the London Library.

Miss Nessa O'Connor, Mr Joseph P. Murray, Mr Raghnall Ó Floinn, Mr Patrick F. Wallace, National Museum of Ireland; and Mr Martin Ryan of the National Library, have been extremely helpful and courteous; as have Mr Laurence Walsh, Limerick City Museum; Mrs Brighid Dolan, librarian at the Royal Irish Academy; and Mrs Mary Ireland and Mr C. N. Sheehan, joint honary secretaries, of the Royal Society of Antiquaries of Ireland.

I must thank Bord Fáilte and the Commissioners of Public Works for permission to use photographs and for providing prints; and in this respect am also most grateful to Miss Betty Wilson, film librarian at the Northern Irish Tourist Board; Mr Gareth Hawe of Armagh; the Manx Museum, and the University Museum of National Antiquities, Oslo.

Sincerest thanks are due, too, to my mother, for her limitless encouragement and comments; to my cousin Viva Chatterton-Allison, who first showed me Tara of the kings; and, for various comments (critical and otherwise), to friends such as Freda Wingfield Mundy, Peggie McDermott and Anthony Addison.

Lambay Island in the far distance, and Ireland's Eye

1

The Land Leapers

THE last decade of the eighth century was a dark period for Ireland. Across the waves of the Irish Sea had come the long black ships of Scandinavian freebooters: those Norsemen, Pagans, Galls, call them what you will (1), they descended upon the unprotected shores of Ireland, 'merciless, soure and hardie, from their very cradles dissentious', as the *Annals of the Four Masters* records. Their first appearance in the waters hitherto protecting these islands had been in 787 when, according to the British chronicler, William of Malmesbury, Danish pirates had landed on English shores to 'ascertain the fruitfullness of its soil and to try the courage of the inhabitants'. And although Ireland had suffered no major assault at that date, Irishmen were well aware of the ravages of these soure and hardie strangers.

For the next five or six years the coasts of Northumbria had been regularly visited, and the bands of Irish missionaries who had systematically left their native land to promulgate the faith among the Saxon kingdoms (2) would have had dire misgivings for the welfare of those they had left behind. Their fears were realised with a vengeance in 795 when, after attacking and burning the religious settlement on the tiny island of Lindisfarne, off the coast of Northumberland in north-east England, where a century before the Irish saint Aodhán had established a community, the Norsemen crossed to Ireland, laying waste the island now known as Lambay (3) in the bay later named after the Norse town of Dublin. An Irish bard of the time sang of the miseries foreseen for his unhappy land; words which have survived for posterity and which, in their poignancy, convey a vivid message from those terrible years:

> The bold Norwegians, with a numerous sail,
> Shall try the Irish ocean and arrive,
> Upon the coasts. The isle shall be enslaved
> By those victorious foreigners, who shall place

13

In every church an abbot of their own,
And shall proclaim, to fill the throne of Ireland,
A king of the Norwegian race . . .

The words may be said to have acquired a certain tameness in the process of translation to the English, but the picture nevertheless remains of what was to be the beginning of over two centuries of dissension.

Following the attack on Lambay Island, the raiders in 798 stormed the religious community of Inispatrick, near Skerries, eighteen miles from what later was to become the Norse city-state of Dublin, taking away the precious shrine of St Do-Chonna. Within a few years more Iona, to many Christians the major symbol of Irish missionary endeavour, was attacked and, according to the *Four Masters*, sixty-eight monks were slaughtered and the monastery, founded by St Colam Cille in 563, was burned to the ground. The story was the same elsewhere: the coastal islands of Kerry were plundered in 811, and by 822 the whole coastline from Wexford to Kerry had been subject to visits from those whom the terrified inhabitants called the Land Leapers. Wherever the Norse long-boats could infiltrate the hazardous channels between sea-battered rocks the natives saw in despair their lands laid desolate; their homes in ruins, their cattle and sheep driven off, their churches burned, their sons and daughters led away into slavery.

But what caused the raids, and why did the Irish not immediately retaliate? The answer to the first part of the question is more involved than it may at first appear: it was not that the Norse were simply a piratical race who took ship to lay waste other lands for pleasure — although this adventuring was an essential ingredient in their character. Until the late eighth century the great naval and trading power of north-west Europe had been in the hands of the Frisian peoples, with a commercial capital at Duurstede, south-east of what, today, is Utrecht. For a century they had been in conflict with the expanding Frankish empire, and in 785 were utterly subjugated by Charlemagne.

Until their collapse, however, the Frisians — continental Saxons — had acted as a form of buffer between the aspirations of the Franks and those of Scandinavia — with whom a long and peaceful tradition of trade had been established. But with the coming of Charlemagne, who was obviously not going to halt his march of empire at the Frisian borders, Christianity made its entry into the pagan lands of the Saxons and made itself felt in Scandinavia.

The Saxon and the Norse shared the same gods — indeed, Witikind,

Monastic cell on Sceilig Mhíchíl. The monastery is on the northern pinnacle of the rock, some six hundred feet above the Atlantic

one of the greatest Saxon chieftains, claimed descent from Wodin — and the invaded lands let loose a stream of people who prefered exile to enforced conversion. In the following century, and in different parts of Europe, there was religious persecution, and the countries of Scandinavia shortly found themselves inundated with refugees from Charlemagne's missionary zeal — zeal which to us appears to have been skin deep.

The emperor found the Saxons neither easy to conquer nor to convert; but after his initial invasion and destruction of the pagan temple of Eresbourg, he filled Saxony with priests and monasteries, convinced that the mild doctrines of Christianity could deter the Saxons from their ancient customs. When he discovered his error, he responded to the equally pagan tendencies inherited from his ancestors. Determined to convert the Saxons, and thus to spread his own empire more completely, he chose methods Christianity should abhor. Between 782 and 783 he is said to have butchered four thousand, five hundred Saxons in cold blood, and decreed that any Saxon refusing baptism should be put to death. The numbers may have been exaggerated in the custom of the annalists, but

The Oseberg ship, in the Viking Museum, Oslo

there is no doubt that a pogram was conducted in the conquered land. A secret council was established, its members travelling the country *incognito* to watch the actions and overhear the words of humble folk in village and farm; and those Saxons who escaped death or conversion fled to their kinsmen in Scandinavia. Their deserted lands were given by Charlemagne to his own allies, and in short Saxony was virtually emptied of its original inhabitants, and deprived of its traditions.

Although there is little evidence (4) that before or after the Frankish invasion there was any attempt by the pagans to spread their own religion, and to convert others to the veneration of the old gods, the early refugees must have sworn vengeance on the religion that had displaced their own; and the fjords of Norway could be used as well-protected bases from which to sally forth and attack the harbingers of the new faith. Understandably, Scandinavia became gradually impoverished by the influx of immigrants and the conquest of fresh territories became essential. Later, those territories having been gained in England and Ireland, the independently-minded descendants of the original *emigrés* found the centralising policies of the Norwegian King, Harald Fairhair (872–934), too oppressive, and the new lands attracted yet more waves of permanent settlers.

16

Others found pleasure in a roving life on the high seas between the Scandinavian lands that had sheltered their forebears and the conquered lands to the south; a life in which they owed allegiance to no man, save the leader of whichever marauding expedition they were part. Thus came the Vikings, those warriors of the sea whose name is derived from the Old Norse *vik*, a bay, indicating only too vividly one who haunts a creek or fjord. They were not 'sea kings' as some popular histories would have us believe — in fact, the accent lies on the first syllable, *vik*, with a short 'i' — but the sea was their undisputed highway. And thus came the Land Leapers, a mixture of native and naturalised Norwegians, Danes and even Picts, responsible to no man and masters of all that they surveyed.

By the year 834, over a generation after the attack on Lambay Island, the Viking fleets had left no part of the Irish coast unspared. Inland, their ravages had been more occasional, although no less fierce, due to the impenetrable forests covering much of the country; and those who settled built fortresses, or *longphuirt*, commanding the harbours in which they established themselves. Dublin, Limerick, Waterford, Cork, Wexford and Wicklow — all owe their origin to the conquerors; indeed the very concept of a town, rather than a monastic settlement, as a centre of everyday life, was introduced by them to Ireland, although at first the settlements were strongholds from which the invaders could march out to lay waste to the country or from which, in the event of a concerted attack by the natives, to fall back in safety to the long-boats. The Norman conquest of England saw the south coast garrisoned in the same way, the strongest nobles receiving manors in Wessex and Sussex as a well-defended land channel through which to pass in case of Saxon revolution and the need to retreat to Normandy. And when the Cambro-Norman mercenaries came to aid Diarmaid mac Murchadha of Leinster a century later, their first fortresses were built along the eastern coast of Ireland with a similar idea in mind.

So we come to the second part of our question: why was there no concerted effort on the part of the Irish to repel the first wave of invasion? The answer is that Ireland was by no means a united country. In England, the heptarchy of kingdoms formed after Hengist assumed the crown of Kent in 455 had proved easy for the invaders to infiltrate, with internecine warfare thriving on every side. In Ireland was a similar state of affairs, but on a greater scale so far as the number of kingdoms was concerned. In this patchwork quilt of monarchy lay weakness.

The situation so far as territorial boundaries existed in eighth-century

The Five Kingdoms

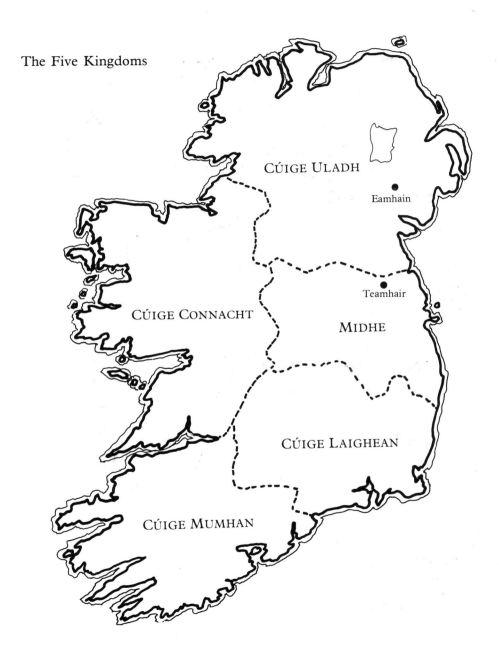

CÚIGE ULADH

Eamhain

CÚIGE CONNACHT

Teamhair

MIDHE

CÚIGE LAIGHEAN

CÚIGE MUMHAN

The Seven Kingdoms

AILEACH

ULAIDH

OIRGHIALLA

CONNACHTA

MIDHE

LAIGHIN

MUMHA

Ireland has been illuminatingly summarised (5) as 'somewhat elastic, expanding or contracting according to success or failure of tribal hostings, and to the chieftain's energy'. The exact boundaries of the ancient kingdoms are today virtually impossible to define, but basically the Iron Age invasion of the Milesians, or Gaelic Celts from southern France and the north of Spain, had resulted in the establishment of four main kingdoms, one of which, Mumha, is a geographical name of uncertain origin, the others, Ulaidh, Connachta and Laighin, being named after the founding tribes. The names are recalled in, but do not correspond to, the present-day provinces of Munster, Ulster, Connacht and Leinster.

Traditionally, the four kingdoms corresponded to the points of the compass, meeting at the hallowed Hill of Uisneach which stands between modern-day Mullingar and Athlone. By the fifth century (6) a pentarchy had been formed, the additional kingdom being that of Midhe (Meath), comprising what is today Westmeath, Longford and part of Offaly. It seems to have incorporated a more ancient kingdom or territory known as Breagh (7), comprising part of modern Co Meath with south Co Louth and north Co Dublin.

But the long-accepted idea of Ireland being divided into fifths, or *cóigeadha*, is misleading and over-simplified. In due course, as we shall see, the rulers of the 'middle kingdom' of Midhe became, sometimes in fact, more often in theory, over-kings of Ireland and historians began to regard the kingdom as being outside the five kingdoms. As a learned contemporary historian has pointed out (8), the 'literati, in order to make five provinces out of four ... invented the theory that the province of Munster really consisted of two provinces ...'

Yet, even so, Ireland did not long remain an island of five kingdoms. Although the aboriginal, Pictish, tribes of what became Ulaidh, Connachta, Mumha and Laighin were subjugated by the Celtic colonisation, in the north at least they retreated east of the Bann and Lough Neagh to set up an independent, but reduced, Ulaidh in what is now roughly Co Antrim and Co Down. And for probably three centuries before the coming of the Land Leapers, the five states had grown into seven, with north-west Ulster becoming the kingdom of Aileach and the area now comprising Co Monaghan, Co Armagh and part of Co Louth being formed into the kingdom of Oirghialla (Oriel).

Within each kingdom there existed a conglomeration of clannish sub-kingdoms or principalities known collectively as *tuatha*. These, according

The catstone on the Hill of Uisneach

to one account (8a), numbered more than one hundred and sixty, but the numbers fluctuated when a powerful ruler invaded his neighbouring territories to establish a *mórtuath* — literally a great territory — under his sole rule.

Each *tuath*, whether nominally subservient to, or wholly independent of, the greater kingdom, had a high level of tribal pride and consciousness of individuality; and this was to survive long after the rise to power of a dynasty who were to be known as the Uí Néill and who were to dominate the Irish political scene for six centuries.

The origin of the Uí Néill is shrouded in the mists of history and mythology — so often in Ireland the two appear to be the same — but it seems probable that they traced their antecedents to the Dál gCuinn rulers of Connacht. Traditionally, the Uí Néill march of empire was spearheaded by Cormac mac Airt, whose reign has been placed (9) as between 227 and 266AD. It is impossible to state categorically that Cormac, if indeed he lived, was the 'nation-founder' who took possession of the sacred hill of Teamhair (Tara) and established the high kingship of Ireland. As a contemporary Irish historian has pointed out (10), the legends surrounding Cormac suggest that both the Dál gCuinn and the Uí Néill came to regard him as such, but it should also be stressed that the partisanship of generations of annalists, by whom such legends have been handed down, makes the genealogy of Irish kings unreliable. Apparently disliking provincialism, the annalists set to work to rewrite, even invent, phases of Irish history that would rival the more mighty dynastic episodes of European history.

Cormac mac Airt may have been nothing more than a powerful chieftain of the Dál gCuinn who, by force of arms, seized Tara from its original lords, the priest-kings of north Leinster. The annalists' determination to make him high king of Ireland, to whom the other kings made some form of obeisance, can be regarded as an attempt to add greater antiquity to the pedigree of the Uí Néill. The king who does appear to have formulated ideas of a centralised, powerful, monarchy based at Tara was Niall Naoighiallach, 'of the Nine Hostages', who died in 405. His ancestry also is uncertain, but the fact that both Niall and his successor, Laoghaire, were kings of, or at least prominent chieftains in, Connacht, and that they were taken from Tara for burial in the ancient Connacht burial ground of Cruachain (Rathcroghan), near Bellanagare, Co Roscommon, suggests that he came from the Dál gCuinn (11).

Whether it was Cormac mac Airt or Niall Naoighiallach who usurped the place of the priest-kings at Tara is immaterial. Gradually the tradition arose, carefully nurtured no doubt by partisan scribes, that whoever held Tara, from which, on a clear day, mountains in each quarter of Ireland can be seen, was 'lord of the four quarters of Erin' (12), and a peer among other kings and princes. The office of high king, or *Ardrí* as it became known, eventually assumed characteristics similar, at least in theory, to those of the English *Bretwalda*, the Welsh *Pendragon* or, in later times, the Holy Roman Emperor. And while those characteristics most probably derived from close association, through trade and religious missions, with the Saxon and German courts, the idea of high kingship as a force (13) can be said to date from the time of Niall Naoighiallach. Certainly it was from him, and not Cormac mac Airt, that his descendants, putative or genuine, took their name — an undoubted mark of distinction and pride.

If Niall hoped to establish a strong, central monarchy with hegemony over the other kings, his ambition was not realised; and it was not until the accession of Brian Boru (Bórumha), six centuries later, that another concerted effort was made in the same direction (14). And certainly for those of Niall's posterity who lacked his stamina, the high kingship was often an empty honour, for upon elevation to Tara the new *Ardrí* had to abdicate power in his own, patrimonial, kingdom.

The *Ardrí*, indeed every king in ancient and mediaeval Ireland, was chosen by election from within his royal house, from the *deirbhfhine* group within which any man whose father, grandfather or great grandfather had been king was theoretically of the *ríoghdhamhna*, or king material, and thus eligible for election (16). Future eligibility extended from the king to the whole *deirbhfhine* descended from him. In the lifetime of the king, one man of the *deirbhfhine* was nominated *tánaiste*, or heir presumptive, to succeed on the king's death; the *tánaiste* was second in authority, and an eighth-century tract, *Críth Ghabhlach*, explains, 'the whole *tuath* looks to him [the *tánaiste*] for kingship without strife'. But, despite the law of centuries, human nature too often prevailed, and one of the *deirbhfhine* set aside by the electors, would revolt against the *tánaiste*, sometimes assuming the throne by force. If the elected successor could be blinded or otherwise maimed, so much the better, for by law a physical blemish automatically debarred a man from kingship.

For a weak *Ardrí*, therefore, to rule from Tara was a means of gaining dubious prestige, but little else. Niall of the Nine Hostages succeeded in colonising the old kingdoms of Ulaidh, and he appears to have carried authority in the western kingdom. But as far as the kings in Leinster and Munster were concerned he was owed no allegiance. From early times (15), Celtic monarchs, the ruler of a *tuath* as much as the ruler of a province-kingdom, were regarded as wedded to their kingdoms, the office being priestly as well as regal. And certainly in the fifth century any outside claims would have been regarded as attacking the sacred person of the priest-king — so long, of course, as that priest-king could resist the aggressor. Less mystically, each king saw himself as *Ardrí* of his own kingdom, although the kings of the north were unable to stem the flood of conquest of Niall of the Nine Hostages.

Until 483, the throne of Tara was held by a representative of the Dál gCuinn, passing in that year to Niall's direct posterity and alternating between the royal houses of Meath and Aileach — in the last, the Grianán of Aileach, a prehistoric stone fortress on the Inishowen peninsula in Co Donegal and seven miles north-east of Derry city, had become the historic capital of the northern Uí Néill whose territories comprised modern Donegal, Derry and Tyrone. Though giving its name to the chief kingdom of the northern Uí Néill, it is not certain that it was ever a fixed residence of the kings of Cinéal Eoghan, but it was a fortress of the highest distinction in the kingdom and the place where the septs met when matters of the utmost importance were to be discussed.

Aileach, royal seat of the northern Uí Néill

The system was still elective, but it gave the Uí Néill a monopoly over what could have been the strongest position in the island. Their failure, over some six hundred years, to produce anything approaching national unity and an hereditary monarchy, shows how titular the rank of *Ardrí* really was, and how little did the other states regard themselves as part of a nation larger than their own kingdom.

The eventual success of Brian Boru in depriving the Uí Néill of the high throne has been viewed by many historians as a clear case of usurpation. And one modern writer (17) notes the 'chaos' it brought 'into an Irish polity which, anarchic though it may have seemed, followed certain inner laws of dynastic hierarchy. He [Brian] showed that any provincial king might make himself king of Ireland by force of arms, and the next century and a half was troubled by eager attempts to learn the baleful lesson . . .'

To claim that Brian's successes brought chaos onto the Irish political scene is absurd. As I will attempt to show, his reign was — once consolidated — a singularly peaceful time for Ireland; and the fact that, in the end, unity could not be maintained was due to the — understandable — inability of other kings to regard themselves as anything other than high kings of their own province-kingdoms. Had the ultimate event of Brian's life, the battle of Clontarf, been accomplished without becoming the disaster it proved to his family, the anarchic Irish polity might have been transformed into the real beginnings of national unity. The Uí Néill had failed to produce unity — why should Brian, with so brief a reign, be blamed for following suit?

24

Aerial view of the Grianán of Aileach

To confuse the superfluity of kingship more, there existed within Irish shores, but owing no allegiance to any Irish king, another state, or more correctly part of a state, known as Dál Riada. Anciently a Pictish kingdom, it had been conquered by the Uí Néill, the natives fleeing across the sea to Alba, later Scotland. In 470 Fearghus mac Earca, ruler of this state which comprised much of modern Co Antrim, crossed over and impressed his sovereignty on the further shore, and from then until Norse invasions became too intense to properly guard both divisions, Dál Riada flourished, not least providing a safe harbour for monkish settlers in the heyday of ecclesiastical expedition in the sixth and seventh centuries. For those to whom leaving Irish shores was fraught with homesickness, even when on a Christian mission bound, the sound of a familiar tongue on Alba's side meant some alleviation of misery.

At length, of course, the marauding long-boats broke the link; Irish Dál Riada became an integral part of Ulster, and the successors of Fearghus mac Earca went on to eventually colonise and rule the rest of Alba. The Picts, like the Norsemen, meanwhile harboured a grudge against those who dispossessed them.

In this atmosphere of disunity, one binding factor appears in the Brehonic code of law, developed through the centuries and carefully preserved by the *breitheamhain*, hereditary judges or arbitrators. The rights of every individual, from the highest to the most lowly, were contained in the code.

An elaborate system of subsidies, tributes and regal rights was paid to the province-king by the heads of the *tuatha*, as token of allegiance. The ruler of the province-kingdom, in turn, paid back to his tributary a courtesy *tuarastal* in cattle, household goods or equipment of use in hunting and hostings. But to suggest that the tribute system extended as far as the payment of stipends from the province-kings to the *Ardrí* — a suggestion made by several generations of historians — is to presume that a federation of states existed, the heptarchs acknowledging the *Ardrí* as absolute head of the federation. And this, as we know, was far from the truth. While a strong *Ardrí* might indeed exercise a degree of power over neighbouring kingdoms, such power lasted only during his lifetime; and the lifetime of an Irish king was often short.

What has been termed (18) 'a very idealised picture of the mutual relations between the kings of Ireland and the high king' appears in the *Book of Rights* (19), a work for long regarded as an historical document consisting of a tenth-century revision of early texts. Purporting to set out the mutual stipends of the province-kings and *Ardrí*, the work opens with the responsibilities of the king of Cashel — otherwise Munster — and the aggrandisement of this ruler can now be seen as a challenge to the claims of the Uí Néill sovereigns in the north. That the book dates from no earlier than the tenth or even twelfth century is the opinion of modern researchers (20), and the possibility that Brian Boru himself had a hand in its compilation is further explored in chapter seven.

But as with the compilers of the various Irish annals, it would be wrong to dismiss completely the *Book of Rights,* or at least its basic contents, as nothing but fabrication or exaggeration. That the tribute system existed in ancient civilisation, and not in Ireland alone, is an established fact (21), but one wonders whether the scribes of other nations equalled, in their vehement partisanship, the claim that the king of Munster was '. . . to be head over all except Patrick and the King of the Stars, the Emperor of the World and the Son of God — save for them he is entitled to supremacy . . .' Even the acknowledgment that the king of Tara, otherwise the *Ardrí,* was 'the noblest of all the host of fertile Ireland' becomes insignificant beside such magnificence.

As Munster is to be the scene for so much of this book, it may prove of interest to illustrate the tributary system as claimed by the *Book of Rights* to operate in that kingdom with the *tuarastal* paid by the province-king. It must be pointed out that in attempting to give the present-day locations of the petty kingdoms — shown in parenthesis — one is treading over bottomless chasms of difficulty, the elastic nature of those territories, as well as the arbitrary spelling of the scribes, making only an approximate identification possible (22):

> A seat by his side in the first place, and ten steeds and ten dresses and two rings and two chess-boards to the king of Dál gCais (ruler of the kingdom of Tuadhmhumha, alias Thomond, of which more in the next chapter); and to lead with him an expedition into another territory and to return at the rear.
>
> Ten steeds and ten drinking-horns and ten swords and ten scings (part of the trappings of a horse) and two rings and two chess-boards to the king of Gabhrán (the king of Osraighe, now the barony of Upper Ossory in Laois and almost the whole of Co Kilkenny).
>
> Ten steeds and ten bondmen and ten women and ten drinking-horns to the king of the Eoghanachta when he is not king of Caiseal (the monarch was invariably chosen from the Eoghanachta, rulers of Deasmhumha or Desmond, as will be seen in the following chapter. This paragraph may have been inserted by pro-Eoghanacht scribes during the ascendancy of the Dál gCais).

Eight bondmen and eight women and eight swords and eight horses and eight shields and ten ships to the king of the Déise Mumhan (including Co Waterford, but also extending north into the Co Tipperary baronies of Middlethird, Iffa and Offa East and Iffa and Offa West).

Five steeds and five matals (cloaks) and five drinking-horns and five swords to the king of Uí Liatháin (the baronies of Barrymore, Kinatalloon and Imokilly in Co Cork, and Coshbride in Co Waterford).

Ten steeds and ten drinking-horns and ten shields and ten swords and ten coats of mail to the king of Raithleann (the baronies of Kinalea, Kinalmeky, East and West Carbery in mid and west Cork).

Seven steeds and seven tunics and seven hounds and seven coats of mail to the king of Muscraighe (there were six areas called Muscraighe, all in Munster. The reference here is to the king of Muscraighe Tíre now the baronies of Upper and Lower Ormond in the north of Co Tipperary).

Seven swords and seven drinking-horns and seven coats of mail and seven ships and seven steeds to the king of Dáirfhine (correctly, Corca Luighe, now the parishes of Myross, Castlehaven, Tullagh, Creagh, Kilcoe, Aghadown and Clear Island in the barony of Carbery).

Seven hounds and seven steeds and seven drinking-horns to the king of Dairbhre of the mountain (according to O'Donovan, editor of the *Book of Rights*, the king mentioned here was ruler of the Corca Dhuibhne, whose seat was at Valentia Island).

Seven steeds and seven drinking-horns and seven swords and seven shields and seven hounds to the king of Loch Léin (the territory around Killarney, and in Duhallow, Co Cork).

Seven women and seven matals trimmed with gold, and seven drinking-horns and seven steeds to the king of the Ciarraighe Luachra (the baronies of Trughanacmy, Clanmaurice and Irachticonnor, north Co Kerry).

Seven steeds and seven shields and seven swords and seven ships and seven coats of mail to the king of Léim na Chon (the peninsula of Schull, Co Cork).

Ten steeds to the king of Uí Chonaill Ghabhra (Upper and Lower Connello in Co Limerick), and ten shields and ten swords and ten drinking horns; and no hostage [is asked] from him except to swear by the hand of the king of Caiseal.

Seven steeds to the king of Uí Cairbre Aodhbha (the barony of Kenry in Co Limerick), and seven drinking-horns and seven swords and seven serving-youths and seven bondmen.

Eight drinking-horns to the king of Cliach (Áine Cliach, of which Knockaney in the Golden Vale of east Limerick was the king's seat), and eight swords and eight steeds, two rings and two chess-boards.

Seven steeds and seven drinking horns and seven shields and seven swords to the king of Gleannamhain (the country around Glanworth, barony of Fermoy, in Co Cork).

Eight steeds and eight swords and eight drinking-horns, with the office

Reconstruction of a crannóg *and a* ráth

> [of chief officer of trust] of a sovereign and monarch, to the king of Uaithne (the baronies of Owney in the counties of Tipperary and Limerick).
>
> Eight steeds to the king of Éile (the baronies of Clonlisk and Ballybrit in Co Offaly; and the baronies of Ikerrin and Eliogarty in Co Tipperary), eight shields and eight swords and eight drinking-horns and eight coats of mail.

The gifts, especially the hounds, swords and shields, reflect the necessary preoccupation of Irish kings with hunting and fighting, but were little more than tokens compared with the tribute paid to the province-king by his vassal kings. For example, the ruler of the Muscraighe was expected to pay ten hundred cows and ten hundred hogs, the ruler of Corca Dhuibhne ten hundred oxen and ten hundred cows, figures which must be regarded with extreme caution as the inhospitable soil of so many of the *tuatha* would have precluded the grazing of an area more than sufficient to provide the milk and meat necessary for a sub-king's *ráth* or seat. Ten hundred oxen and ten hundred cows, even if they existed, could hardly be despatched each year to Cashel without the people of Corca Dhuibhne facing immediate starvation.

Certainly, as an agricultural people, the early Irish regarded cattle, hogs and sheep as the equivalent of our monetary system, but the number of beasts classified in the *Book of Rights*, like the casualty figures so beloved of other annalists, must be viewed with considerable reservations.

Also, because of the fragmentary nature of the Irish policial scene, and the fact that the law of tanistry could one moment place on the province-throne a strong and enlightened ruler, the next a peace-loving, monkish, character without the strength to hold his inheritance, the payment of even basic tributes was frequently unforthcoming. To ensure that some form of authority was maintained over his vassals, the ruler of each province-kingdom and, if strong, the *Ardrí*, took hostages from each royal house, lodging them in his own palace and granting them every convenience but liberty. The consequences, should the families of the hostages prove obstreperous, were clear.

Any form of tribute was unpopular among smaller *tuatha*, where the chieftain and people would resent parting with valuable livestock; and the hint of absolute independence was one form of bait held out in front of many petty rulers by the Norsemen. The invaders were masters of the art of persuasion, both gentle and tortuous, and as they were also traders an alliance could be made with a *tuath* ruler who saw only advantages for his personal kingdom. In return for merchandise and protection, the Norsemen received safe-conduct and hospitality, and the combined forces could wreck havoc upon a neighbour.

Despite inter-state friction, there was no warrior class in ancient Ireland (23), and nothing to compare with the Saxon *fyrd*, or national militia, on the other side of the Irish Sea. Men obeyed the call of their king to take part in a raid, or hosting, against another; the work done, those who survived returned to their families. And seamanship, despite the ships mentioned in the *tuarastal*, practiced so profitably by early pagan kings of Ireland, had for obscure reasons all but died out. The high days of Niall Naoighiallach, when Irish ships brought terror to the coasts of Wales and south-western England — returning with captives such as Patricius, son of Calpurnius, better known as the future St Patrick — were fading memories. A wholesale retaliation against the Land Leapers would have required a national army or a strong navy: Ireland had neither.

Another reason for the invasion being met, at first, with comparatively little resistance, could be the attitude of the Irish people in remote places, where the Norsemen would find little to plunder. Such areas, on wild and desolate south-west coastlands, perhaps, provided refuge from storms. The invaders, driven to an isolated cove by gales, and with hungry, probably wounded, men on board, must sometimes have tried a more subtle approach than usual to those on shore; and certainly the Irish would find much to admire in the northern warriors. Celtic Ireland had never before suffered invasion, but with the inherent passion for fighting that is still characteristic, the natives would be attracted to the tales and legends sung round the alien camp fires. In remote places, tales of the old Irish gods, of the Tuatha dé Danann, were on every man's lips, and

> Caoilte tossing his burning hair,
> And Niamh calling Away, come away,

were still present in the wind that poured down the empty, secret valleys and out across the lonely, pathless bogs.

Christian missionaries, from Patrick onwards, adapted pagan traditions to suit their method of conversion — a far cry from the works of Charlemagne — and the sole reason that conversion was successful in so short a time was due to this recycling of the holy places in the Milesian pantheon. The name of a deity venerated at a holy well may be changed to fit that of an indistinct saint; the goddess of hearth and fire, Brighid, may well acquire respectability — in missionary eyes — as St Brighid, but to the old people the shades remained. Only the names were changed or canonised and, even then, as the Latin speakers were for long in a minority, the Irish tongue knew no difference in many cases.

Thus, to those with whom the Vikings settled in some form of toleration, away from the blood and the burning, the very real regard in which the invaders held their own, dispossessed gods and heroes would command not only respect but a form of kindredship. Irish and Scandinavian mythology was peopled with beings who, with their outbursts of passion and love and superhuman exploits, were much more acceptable to a passionate folk than the scholarly and intense representatives of the newer faith.

Initially, the Viking raids, though persistant and annoying in the extreme, made little headway in overall conquest. For the first quarter of the ninth century no major settlement was made and the fact that Irish civilisation, at its peak, was largely unimpared (24) is evident from the records of 'fleetfuls of foreign students' who came from Europe to the well-equipped religious institutions. At the same time, and for the same period, Ireland had a powerful and intelligent *Ardrí*: Aodh Oirdnidhe, previously king of Aileach, was a bitter opponent of both invaders and internal troublemakers. Unfortunately, he arrived on the scene too late; the invaders had seen their chance in the unsettled state of Irish politics, notably in the kingdom of Munster.

In 820 a new king had ascended the throne of Munster. Feidhlimidh mac Criomhthainn is seen in history as alternately a saint and a tyrant, who began his reign by vigorously enforcing the Brehon laws and who within three years was burning monasteries and slaughtering monks with equal intensity. It has been suggested that he aspired both to the high kingship and to the establishment of his capital, Cashel, as the seat of the Irish primacy, in direct opposition to Armagh; and he was certainly the first king of Munster to press for equality, at least, with the Uí Néill.

He was aided in his pretensions by a long-standing tradition that the island consisted of two equal kingdoms — Leath Mogha, roughly southern Ireland, and Leath Cuinn, the northern half — with a dividing line from Dublin to Galway Bay. According to the tradition, later incorporated into the *Book of Rights* where the scribes emphasised the importance of the king of Munster, often treating him as *Ardrí*, the division had taken place in what is now regarded as a mythological period, the northern half being named after Conn Céadchatach, 'of the Hundred Battles', the southern after his rival Eoghan Mór, also called Mogh Nuadhat, father of Oilill Ólum whom we shall meet in the next chapter. The *Book of Rights* also contains a prophecy (25) that the rulers of Munster would in time become the sole rulers at Tara. Although we must doubt not only the sources but much of the content of the book, it is feasible that such a prophecy was well known in Feidhlimidh mac Criomhthainn's day, particularly as it had been made by a colateral ancestor of his own.

Whether or not the *seanchaithe* of his day declaimed:

> The King of Caiseal, as head over all,
> Is what is here [ordained] until the [day of] judgement,

Feidhlimidh mac Criomhthainn needed little spurring towards his goal of Munster supremacy. That he failed, and that Brian Boru, over a century later, succeeded to a great extent, reflects the futility of trusting to brute force, rather than careful diplomacy, as a means of advancing a cause.

Unsatisfactory as Feidhlimidh's attack on the established order may have been, it paved the way for the arrival in 830 of an army of conquest. It was led by Turges, or Thorgist, said by some chroniclers to be a brother or close kinsman of the reigning Danish king, Hardicanute. Whoever he was — and the chroniclers, both Irish and Scandinavian, loved pedigrees — Turges is the first character we can identify among the Vikings with any certainty. That he actually lived, that he was not the central figure of a conquering Viking myth, is as certain as the fact that his warriors were a seaborne army, organised specifically to subdue Ireland and enable Turges to carve for himself a kingdom. Perhaps even more than Feidhlimidh mac Criomhthainn, Turges was determined to rule Ireland.

Turges was a pure-blooded Dane, a man whose ancestors offered sanctuary to the Saxon refugees whose descendants had preceded him to Ireland. No less than the leaders of the so-called Grand Army which, thirty-five years later, was to land in eastern England and carve out major settlements in East Anglia, Yorkshire and the midlands, he saw the chance of establishing a kingdom of his own.

The Irish themselves distinguished between the first Norse invaders and the more determined companions of Turges by the sobriquets of *Fionnghaill* and *Dubhghaill* — the fair and dark foreigners. The grounds for the distinction are difficult to ascertain (26): certainly it does not refer to known ethnographical characteristics, while the possibility that it was derived from the differing armour of Viking pirates and military Danes is barely plausible. Equally improbable, although suitable from the point of view of Turges and his friends, is that the names referred to their separate methods of conquest — the worse the deed the blacker the character of the perpetrator.

Certainly under Turges the Irish were to suffer as never before. Geoffrey Keating, the seventeenth century historian, summed up Turges when he declared (27), 'the great Tamarlane, called the Scourge of God, could not be compared to him for cruelty', and at first glance the Dane certainly appears to have regarded the extinction of Christianity as his personal objective. In the year of his arrival, the university of Armagh, seat of the faith in Ireland, was sacked thrice in a month, and elsewhere the annalists record the burning of '... Clonvicknois, Clonfert, Tyrdaglasse, Lothra, and withal theire churches and houses of religion ...' The primate, Airtre, episcopal descendant of Patrick, was turned out of Armagh, and at Clonmacnoise — 'Clonvicknois' of the annalists — the important monastic settlement founded in 547, Ota, the formidable wife of Turges, held audience on the desecrated high altar of the cathedral, probably as a priestess of Wodin (28).

And yet, although we may read into this act the especial pleasure of Turges in profaning the highest tangible symbol of a religion he detested; and although the *Four Masters* claimed later that 'the great part of the churches of Erin were destroyed', the destruction of churches in Ireland was not a Viking innovation. Nor was it, under them, part of a crusade against Christianity. The annalists record some thirty cases of the burning of monasteries in a hundred and eighty years (29) before the first Norse invasions. The actions of men like Feidhlimidh mac Criomhthainn were nothing new in the history of inter-state warfare, especially as many of the monasteries had, as their heads, members of the highest families in the land, to whom the taking of vows was no barrier to continuing a dynastic struggle or feud against hereditary foes. Monastery attacked monastery (30), an example being the contest recorded in 763 between Clonmacnoise and Durrow, when two hundred of the Durrow brethren were slain; and although by the early ninth century the clergy appear to have been exempt from anything approaching military service, many hundreds must have died in battle between 695, when recording began, and the year 1162 (31). Long before the Land Leapers came there is no doubt that a religious vocation in Ireland carried with it a good chance of violent death.

Clonmacnoise dates from the sixth century

From the time the monastic system was established, one particular reason for plunder and slaughter had existed. A new community was usually endowed with estates and, in time, became wealthy in a temporal sense. Warring Irishmen and invading Vikings knew that to sack a monastery would bring them not only valuable plate but livestock in the form of cattle and sheep and the results of monastic harvests. In times of war, too, lay inhabitants of the district around a monastery would take their goods there for safe-keeping, the right of sanctuary not being reserved for men and women alone, and the practice continued for centuries after the coming of the Land Leapers (32).

For greater security, the *cloigtheach*, or round tower, became a familiar part of monastic architecture, initially perhaps as a storehouse, then as the last place of retreat for the beleagured monks and laymen (33). Whether or not the round towers were in existence before the Viking era, as a precaution against intermonastic or native raids, is a matter of conjecture, and indeed the real origin of these tall, conical buildings, the only door of which was often as many as thirty feet above ground level, is likely to be a cause of controversy and debate for years to come.

Those taking refuge inside the towers were not always immune from death. For example, *Chronicum Scotorum* records in 949 a Norse attack on the round tower at Slane in Meath, the tower being burned 'with its full of people in it'. The fact that it would be impossible to set fire to the stone building itself, or so we would imagine examining some of the fairly complete specimens remaining, suggests that an entry was forced, the unfortunate inmates being slain and burned where they fell.

From time to time, theories have been put forward which suggest that the towers were built by the Norsemen themselves, or that the etymology of *cloigtheach* can be traced to the German word, *glocke*, a bell, so that the towers were originally belfries. Other theories compare the towers with the *fanaux de cimetiere* of France, beacons erected as memorials of the dead.

There is no evidence whatsoever to connect the towers with Norse builders or with churchyard beacons. And while a bell may have been rung from them to warn a community of impending raids, there is nothing to indicate that the primary function of the towers was anything more than a place of safety.

But if the towers offered protection, Turges knew the weakest points at which to hit Ireland in a wider sense. Sixty ships were sent up the Boyne and Liffey rivers (34), others took sail on the Shannon, and from here the invaders made determined raids on the surrounding countryside. By 833 the monastery of St Kevin at Glendalough, where that mysogynistic holy man had built his seven churches, was wrecked; as was Slane, where Patrick built his Paschal fire on the way to converting Tara. As Turges progressed through the countryside he left behind him an army of occupation; a Danish soldier billeted in every house, and the needs of the unwilling host were totally disregarded in the face of the invader's requirements. In an occupied home the livestock was there for the use of the Dane and, traditionally, a tax or tribute of an ounce of gold a year was to be paid to the Dane by the householder. Failing this, the nose of the luckless host was to be removed in lieu, giving rise to the term *Nosegelt*. But gold was scarce and it seems unlikely that the tax was implemented — otherwise many Irishmen would have lost their noses.

Resistance was certainly offered, at times with success, but Aodh Oirdnidhe was caught in a pincer movement from Turges and Feidhlimidh mac Criomhthainn who, taking advantage of the invasion, was marching northwards to claim the high throne. Maintaining the dubious claims of Cashel as prime see, he burned Armagh — hardly recovered from the visitation of Turges — and for what, to us, must seem an incredibly long period of thirteen years, prevented the *Ardrí* from concentrating his forces against the Danes. In 837 Aodh was killed in battle and Feidhlimidh declared himself high king. That he was effectual ruler of most of southern Ireland is undisputed, and while he had no more, or no less, right to the high throne than the Uí Néill, he was not elected in legitimate fashion. But the 'legitimate' heir to the high throne, Conchobhar, was an extraordinarily poor choice.

Conchobhar 'died of grief, being unable to redress the misfortunes of his country'; and Niall Caille, a son of Aodh, was quickly elected in his place. Like his father, he appears to have been a man of determination, but the Danish-Munster pincer seriously restricted any decisive action. Feidhlimidh mac Criomhthainn may have entered into an alliance with the Danes — he certainly had little to lose, as his attacks on the church were alienating many of the *tuatha* in Munster — but at length a fiery ecclesiastic, Olchobhor, abbot of Emly, Co Tipperary, seized Feidhlimidh's absence in Armagh to revolt in the south. Feidhlimidh was momentarily distracted, and in the time it took him to decide whether or not to return to Cashel, the high king went into action.

Turges had laid waste and subdued most of the easterly kingdom of Leinster, establishing his capital at Dublin — the black pool — which until his coming had been little more than a crossing place of the Liffey, known to the Irish as Áth Cliath, or the ford of the hurdles (35). From a strongly fortified township Turges now had command of the seaward boundaries of the kingdom, as well as a stronghold from which to effectively rule the rich country comprising what is today counties Dublin and Meath. Strengthened thus in his rear, he turned his attention to gaining a similar foothold in the westerly kingdom of Connacht, and it was there that Niall met and defeated him.

Alas for Ireland, the *Ardrí* lost his life in the battle, but not from a Danish broadsword. One of his favourites, attempting to find a suitable place for the king to cross a swollen river, was swept away by the flood, and Niall, approaching too near the bank to save him, fell in and was drowned. The battle certainly halted, for a while, Danish progress in the west, but the Irish army was dispirited by the loss of its leader and Turges himself assumed the title of *Ardrí*.

So two men now usurped the throne but, for both of them, Nemesis was approaching. It caught up with Feidhlimidh mac Criomhthainn, trying to regain control of Munster, in 845. In keeping with traditional superstitition, his death, according to some accounts, was miraculously brought about by Ciarán (St Kieran) of Clonmacnoise who, the *Four Masters* tells us, died in 548. The saint's intervention in Feidhlimidh's career was, according to the legend, in punishment for the king's sack of Clonmacnoise the previous year.

Folk tales and legends often tried to explain national disasters or the sudden death of kings through the vengeance of heaven, but while the presumed interference of St Ciarán makes a good story, the probability is that Feidhlimidh died of some disease contracted during his campaigns.

The end of Turges was more dramatic. The Dane appears to have made a military base at a place now popularly called Ráth an Dúin, near the western shore of Lough Lene, two miles from the present town of Castlepollard in Co Westmeath, where he took over one of the royal residences of Maoil-Seachlainn, king of Meath. And there, in what must have been an unguarded moment of revelry, Turges was captured, probably by a small band of Maoil-Seachlainn's warriors who crossed Lough Lene under cover of darkness. Presumably Turges was carousing with a few favourite warriors who were slain, but the Dane was taken alive, as for him Maoil-Seachlainn had reserved a particularly humiliating fate (36).

Maoil-Seachlainn and his army had gathered nearby present-day

Lough Owel, Co Westmeath

Mullingar and to them the Danish chieftain was taken in chains. In front of his would-be subjects Turges was deliberately drowned in Loch Uair, now Lough Owel — the punishment for sacrilege and the worst fate a Scandinavian warrior could meet. Only death in battle opened the doors of Valhalla, according to tradition — the nine regions of hell awaited those who died without a sword in their hand.

The year was 846 and, for the first time in sixteen years of occupation, the Danes had suffered a major setback. Maoil-Seachlainn of Meath was elected *Ardrí* and, rallying many of the lesser princes, he marched against the enemy. During the next four years the Danes were beaten from Meath to Tipperary and at least one native collaborator, the lord of Breagh, probably a kinsman and potential supplanter of the *Ardrí*, was executed in similar fashion to Turges.

Prisoner's chain and collar

The Danes were not only set back by the death of their leader but by dissension in their own ranks — to be expected on the death of a tyrant. Then, in 853, a new fleet of invasion arrived, commanded by Olaf the White, known by the *Four Masters* as 'king of Lochlann', by the Scandinavian *Eyrbyggia Saga* as 'son of Ingvald, king of Uplands', by other sources as a son of Halfdan III, a powerful Norwegian king whose proven son, Harald Fairhair, was to centralise the scattered Norwegian idea of monarchy. The Scandinavian chroniclers were as prone to exaggeration, or to ennoblement of their particular hero, as their Irish counterparts. At this stage in history it is impossible to formulate accurately the pedigree of any ninth-century Viking chieftain, particularly as many of them claimed an heroic descent from Odin — a descent that may be compared with that of some Irish kings from Fionn mac Cumhaill. It is perhaps sufficient to say that while many of the early Norse rulers of Dublin were undoubtedly connected by blood or marriage, the common use of a name such as Olaf or Ivar and the habit of likening the success of a particular chieftain to the Viking prototype, Ragnar Lodbrok — who may or may not have existed — has resulted in the merging of personalities, and the blurring of any definite identity.

Whatever the origins of Olaf, the Danes were to be disappointed if they looked to him for aid: emulating his putative father in Norway, Olaf was carving himself a kingdom, and falling on the Danes completed that which Maoil-Seachlainn had begun. Dublin was taken over by a new wave of Land Leapers and so was founded the Scandinavian kingdom that was to endure until the coming of Strongbow in 1170.

The new state of Dublin was to be no petty realm or its monarch the occupant of a shadowy throne. It was to become an influential maritime power, the first and strongest link in a chain of Scandinavian domination that extended northwards, *via* the Isle of Man, to the Hebrides and so onwards to Iceland, taking in the Orkneys and Shetlands on the way. It was to extend eastwards into northern Europe and upwards to that part of Dál Riada taken from the heirs of Fearghus mac Earca. At York, English capital of the conquerors, the throne was occupied regularly by a close kinsman, at times a nominee, of the king of Dublin. Olaf's state was to be independent, existing within the Irish shores but no more subservient to the *Ardrí* than was the king of Scottish Dál Riada, the energetic Cionaoth mac Ailpín (37).

Maoil-Seachlainn as *Ardrí* did not create a feeling of unity among the Irish kings, however, nor can that be said to have been his aim. The various kings and their lesser brethren settled down to the old way of life, giving cursory allegiance and hostages to Maoil-Seachlainn; and the *Ardrí*, having achieved his objective as far as Turges was concerned, was content to remain the symbol of temporal power, as his ancestors had been for so many generations, while Armagh, rebuilt, represented power spiritual. The two great European figureheads, Pope and Roman Emperor, were not unique in their respective positions.

For the rest of the ninth century, which saw the death of Maoil-Seachlainn from natural causes in 860 and that of his successor, Aodh Finnliath in 877, and the election of Maoil-Seachlainn's son, Flann Sionna, to the high kingship, Ireland was relatively peaceful. The Norsemen appear to have concentrated their military efforts in subjugating more of England, to meet with serious defeat at the hands of Prince Alfred, shortly to be king of Wessex, at the battle of Ashdown. In times of stress, both in Ireland and England, the 'New and Old Danes' as the inhabitants of Dublin came to be known, incorrectly, could fall back on Dublin or York for reinforcements. And in times of peace, the erstwhile invaders made a genuine attempt to settle down and open commercial channels to their Irish neighbours.

Olaf the White was killed in battle with the Leinstermen — who had long resented the foreign colonisation of part of their patrimony — in 871. His successor, Ivar, lasted little under a year, but it is significant that the annalists awarded him the title 'King of the Norsemen of Ireland and Britain', providing us with a clue towards determining the actual position of 'New and Old Dane' in Ireland. Chroniclers in the centuries to come were not too careful in distinguishing between Norse and Dane, and although it would be simple to classify them all as Norsemen, or even Viking, it would be incorrect, certainly from the time of Olaf the White onwards.

The original invaders of both Ireland and England had been led by men from Norway. Northumbria was strongly Norwegian, while East Anglia was predominantly Danish. Both races had initially a common foe in Christianity, and both were willing to aid each other. As the *Saxon Chronicle* tells us, albeit in confused fashion (38), the Scandinavians, 'black and white foreigners' alike, considered their early conquests as common property, in which all who had contributed to gain had common title. Thus, throughout the conquered areas of these islands, Norwegian and Dane could settle together; and there were also marital ties between the ruling houses of Norway and Denmark. Ivar, successor of Olaf the

Castledermot, where Cormac mac Cuilleannáin was buried

White, had a Norwegian putative father who had extensive interests in Denmark (39), and it may have been a dynastic struggle that sent Ivar to Dublin in the wake of Olaf.

The kingdom he inherited was Norwegian — the successors of the Danish Turges had re-established themselves in the city-state of Limerick. They regarded themselves — and were regarded — as Danes, and the title Norsemen applies specifically to the men of Dublin. The distinction applied far more in Ireland than in England, as will be seen in due course.

Ivar's successor on the Dublin throne, Halfdan, was preoccupied in England, and Dublin was placed in the care of an Irish prince, Cearbhall of Osraighe, who had long been an ally of the invaders. Feeling secure from the wrath of his overlord, the *Ardrí*, in the knowledge that an army could come from England to help him if necessary, Cearbhall allowed his new subjects to raid at will. Affairs in Ireland degenerated rapidly: native kings reverted to their internal bickering, sometimes allying with Cearbhall against a neighbour, and by the time the regent died in 885 the country was again in turmoil.

In 901 a concerted attack by the men of Leinster captured Dublin itself and the owners, weakened by new defeats at the hands of Alfred of

Monastic remains on Inis Cathaigh

Wessex, were not immediately in a position to repossess the town. But the long lapse of time so frequent in Irish history turned the victory of Leinster into a squalid internecine war, and the native inability to present a united front aided yet another arrival from Norway, Reginald, nephew of Olaf the White, to raise his standard over Dublin's walls in 914.

The trouble began in 906, with an attempt by King Cormac mac Cuileannáin of Munster to subdue Leinster and to claim a tribute called Eidirsceol, traditionally imposed on the eastern kingdom in the third century, following the murder of a Munster prince. The tribute, from time to time, had been resisted successfully, and having now captured Dublin the Leinstermen were in no mood to bow their knees to Munster. Eidirsceol they rejected, once and for all, but Cormac mac Cuileannáin, who appears as a good but weak man, lived by the Brehon code of justice, under which the fine had been imposed and under which it could be continued into the second and third generation or beyond. Even so, he might have thought twice about invading Leinster had it not been for the persuasion of Flaithbheartach, the warlike abbot of Inis Cathaigh, or Scattery Island, in the Shannon, and the nobles of south Munster. Whether or not Flaithbheartach was as much the power behind Cormac's throne as some writers would lead us to believe is debatable (40); and while Cormac may, initially, have shown some unwillingness to go to war, by the end of 907 he was plundering from east to west with considerable success.

Cormac's movements were viewed with alarm by the *Ardrí*, Flann Sionna. In 906, according to the *Four Masters*, Flann, 'son of Maoil-Seachlainn, and Cearbhall, son of Muireagán' led an army to plunder Munster from Gowran to Limerick. Cearbhall mac Muireagáin was king of Leinster, which suggests that he had sought the help of Flann Sionna in resisting Cormac's claims to Eidirsceol. Whether Cormac had actually taken an army into Leinster before Flann and Cearbhall joined forces, or whether his preparations for war had spurred the *Ardrí* into what he hoped would be preventative action, is difficult to assess. The variation in dates from one annalist to the next compounds the difficulties that arise as a barrier between us and a clear picture of events in 906 and 907. But whoever made the first move, claims of Munster on Leinster were the root of the trouble and, for a year, Cormac and Flaithbheartach were successful. The Uí Néill of the south and the men of Connacht were soundly defeated and hostages were carried south to Cashel. Flann and the king of Leinster were defeated on the plains of Moylena, in the kingdom of Meath, and for a time it seemed as though the dreams of Feidhlimidh mac Criomthainn for Munster to become the most potent kingdom in the island would be realised by his successor.

But in 908 Flann and Cearbhall were joined by King Cathal of Connacht and at Bealach Mughna, a site north of Carlow town but in south Co Kildare (41), they faced the army of Cormac and Flaithbheartach, to which had been joined a force from the kingdom of Osraighe. The *Ardrí's* forces were victorious: Cormac broke his neck when his horse slipped and threw him on the battlefield and Flaithbheartach was taken prisoner. The man probably regarded as the instigator of the invasion of their kingdom was 'bitterly upraided by the Leinster clergy, and severely used in imprisonment' until the death of Cearbhall mac Muireagáin, when he was released and retired to Inis Cathaigh where, we are told, he 'spent his time in exemplary manner' (42). But he was not yet to pass away from the scene of Irish history.

The war had taken its toll on the land and on the people and when, in 912, Reginald, grandson of Ivar — ancestor of the Norse kings of Dublin — landed at Waterford no-one was capable of resistance. Three years later, Flann Sionna's son-in-law, Niall Glúndubh, was elected *Ardrí* and marched southwards to meet Reginald, now king of Dublin, at Tobar

Gleathrach, a site today unknown. But the battle was indecisive and Niall turned towards Dublin. Alas, fate was against him as much as his more celebrated grandfather, Niall Caille, and he was killed on the north bank of the Liffey at Islandbridge, in a battle sometimes known as the battle of Dublin or Cill Mo Shámhóg — which, it should be stressed, is not modern Kilmasogue in south County Dublin. The *Four Masters* waxed eloquent for the occasion in retrospect:

> Fierce and hard was the Wednesday
> On which the hosts were strewn under the feet of shields:
> It shall be called, till Judgement's day,
> The destructive morning of Áth-cliath,
> On which fell Niall, the noble hero,
> Conchobhar, chief of fierce valour,
> Aodh, son of valiant Eochaidh of Ulidia;
> Malemithidh of the proud, lofty dignity,
> Many of countenance of well-known Gaedhil,
> Many a chief of grey-haired heroes,
> Of the sons of queens and kings,
> Were slain at Áth-cliath of swords.
> The strength of a brave lord was subdued,
> Alas that he was deceived in the strength of an army,
> There would [otherwise] be no moan upon the strand.
> Fierce was the hard Wednesday!

It was a lamentable tragedy. Foreign power was re-established in Dublin, while Waterford had become a second stronghold of the invaders. Had Niall Glúndubh won the battle, or had he not misjudged the power of his adversary which, according to the lament, is what happened, he might have become a power to reckon with. As it was, both Norwegians and Danes met with victory and the last chance of baulking foreign advance was lost. Donnchadh, son of Flann Sionna, became *Ardrí*, but he was a timid monarch whose election seemed pointless, merely a continuance of Uí Néill influence and a rigid observance of tanistric laws.

Donnchadh deputed much of his authority to Muircheartach 'of the leathern cloaks', son of the late *Ardrí* and a brilliant general who not only repulsed Norse incursions into Ulster but retaliated by raiding their settlements in the Hebrides. For two decades he kept them at bay and, in recognition of his efforts, was proclaimed *tánaiste* to Donnchadh. Marching in circuit, he covered the whole of the island, taking from each kingdom a hostage, including a representative of the Dublin royal house. The hostages were sent to Donnchadh because, in a phrase of the time, 'it

Muircheartach's circuit of Ireland

was he that was at Tara, and the sovereignty had come to him' (43), implying that many of the guests were of the highest rank. Among them, as we shall see in due course, was Ceallachán, king of Munster.

Alas, and once more that despairing word echoes down the corridors of Irish history, Muircheartach was never to gain higher rank himself. In 943 he fell at the battle of Áth Fhir-diadh, now Ardee in Co Louth, at

46

which the Danes, led by ferocious Blacar, were victorious. That black day, March 26th, left the country of the Gael an orphan (44). Armagh was plundered by the victors and Donnchadh died shortly afterwards, the throne passing to Conghalach, also of the southern Uí Néill family. By 948 he had avenged Muircheartach and slain Blacar, but the old dismal story of pillage, slaughter and desecration had begun all over again. Alleviated only by the change in *Ardrí* from time to time, the picture is gloomy and repetitive. In 956 the Leinstermen, forgetting their quarrel with Dublin, joined forces with the Norsemen and defeated the *Ardrí*'s army, killing Conghalach in ambush on the Liffey. The Uí Néill blundered once more, placing Domhnall, the peace-loving son of Muircheartach, on the throne.

There was no second Muircheartach to make the decisions and, as internal squabbling increased, so the daring of the Land Leapers grew. In 961 Domhnall roused himself for a moment — even the chroniclers admit that it was an 'unusual thing' — and 'brought vessels over Dabhnall, and across Sliabh Fuaid, to Loch Ainninn, so that the islands of the lake were plundered by him'. In other words, he made a valiant attempt to best the Danes, at least, at their own game and ordered his men to carry over the mountains to Lough Ennell, in present-day Co Westmeath, as many light skiffs or curraghs as possible, so that the waterways long infested by the long-boats could be patrolled by the Irish.

Without real leadership, new tactics were of little use against a stronger enemy. For another decade and two years gentle Domhnall ruled from Meath in everything but reality, while Ireland was lacerated by war.

The tragedy of the century, of course, had been the defeat of Munster at Bealach Mughna. The immediate result of the battle had been, we are told, the 'permanent weakening' (45) of the southern kingdom, and while, as we shall see, the weakness was temporary rather than permanent, it was long-term and of advantage to the Danes who, the power of the ruling family in Munster in abeyance, were able to strengthen their own defences. But Bealach Mughna was also, unintentionally, to bring light to the darkened scene of local and national resistance. With the eclipse of the Eoghanachta, the ruling power in Munster, two brothers from an obscure family in the north-west of the kingdom were able to turn that obscurity into a light that shone more brilliantly than even that of the aristocratic Uí Néill.

Those brothers were Mathghamhain, king of Thomond, and his youthful brother, Brian.

2

The Dalcassians and Munster

OBSCURE beginnings are recorded for many of the figures who have stamped their names, indelibly, on European history. Charlemagne's ancestry could be traced for two generations to the illegitimate son of a Merovingian palace official; Oliver Cromwell came from an unimportant family of Huntingdonshire gentlemen-farmers; and Napoleon was the product of middle-class, if pretentious, Corsicans. To none of them did pedigree mean a great deal, but had they lived in tenth-century Ireland they would have found it expedient to quickly acquire ancestors.

And in a country where, until the advent of Christianity, written records were almost non-existant, it was a relatively simple matter to acquire a pedigree of the highest respectability. Family history was handed down by word of mouth, preserved in each generation by the *seanchaithe* who, doubtless, added a generation here and there, or conjured up a semi-mythical name from the past, to add lustre to those whose praises they sang. The chronicles of later times were written by men vehemently partisan, and the hero of the moment could receive an ancestry to rival even the aristocratic Uí Néill of Ulster.

The family into which Brian was born, probably in 941 (1), was that of the Dál gCais — its members known to us as Dalcassians — at the time of his birth rulers of the kingdom of Tuadhmhumha, otherwise Thomond, which from its name suggests that it constituted the northern area of Munster. But, as we have seen already, the elasticity of Irish states and the vicissitudes of the ruling families make the exact definition of any territory difficult in the extreme.

Todd, in his edition of *Cogadh Gaedhel re Gallaibh*, states simply that 'The district of Thomond . . . is represented nearly by the present county of Clare . . .' and by the time of Brian's birth it seems to have included parts of Tipperary and Limerick. Certainly, with the neighbouring and greater territory of Deasmhumha, South Munster or Desmond, it formed a significant area of the province-kingdom; and according to the *seanchaithe* owed its origins to Oilill Ólum who, in legend, possessed the whole of southern Ireland in the second century. He divided it, we are told, between his sons Eoghan Mór and Cormac Cas; the elder, whose descendants, genuine or adoptive, became known as the Eoghanachta, was left Desmond, Cormac Cas receiving Thomond. The territories of the Eoghanachta included the sub-kingdoms of Cashel or Caiseal; Áine, Loch Léin, Uí Eachach of Raithleann and Magh Glíath, ruled respectively by the kings of the Cinéal Aodha and the Cinéal Laoghaire; Ára, Gleannamhain and Ros Airgid. The triple-fossed royal *rath* of Magh Glíath is near Coppeen in the parish of Enniskean, Co Cork; Gleannamhain is now Glanworth in the barony of Fermoy, Co Cork; Ros Airgid, a name which has been forgotten, was a place near Toomyvara in Co Tipperary. The other kingdoms have already been discussed in chapter one.

In later centuries several historians, and perhaps even some of the descendants of Cormac Cas, were to maintain that Oilill Ólum left a 'will', directing that the throne of Munster itself, with the royal seat of Cashel in present-day Co Tipperary, should be held alternatively by the heirs of the two brothers. The fact that Eoghan died in his father's lifetime and that Oilill Ólum was succeeded by Cormac Cas who, in turn, was succeeded by a nephew of the Eoghanacht line, has been held up as an example of this 'alternate succession'. In fact, it was nothing more than the *táinisteacht* or tanistic system of election, and there is no evidence at all that Oilill Ólum left a will or that the rulers of Thomond pressed their 'right' to the throne of Munster until the tenth century (2) — and then mainly because the Eoghanacht authority had been weakened seriously, first at the battle of Bealach Mughna, in which the Dál gCais had taken no part, and then by internal squabbling.

Whether Oilill Ólum actually lived cannot be proved one way or the other, and the same can be said for so many of the figures from what may be termed the 'shadowy' period of Irish history. But while it would be wrong to dismiss as being a mythological figure anyone who we are told lived before the 'new phase of history', as the fifth century has been designated (3), we must not be as credulous as so many of the old historians, who believed implicitly in dubious records that were, for the most part, in men's minds alone (4). The Eoghanachta do not seem to have known about the legendary will and it may well have been nothing more than Dalcassian propaganda to give a semblance of legality to the

49

mercurial rise and claims of the princes of Thomond.

The first reliable mention of Brian's family in the annals (5) is in the year before his birth, and concerns the execution of Órlaith, daughter of Cinnéide mac Lorcáin and one of the four wives of Donnchadh, *Ardrí* of Ireland, for adultery with her stepson, Aonghus. The tragedy is useful in shedding some light on the position of the Dál gCais at that time. Donnchadh was the timid high king whose reign had seen the Land Leapers kept at bay by the *Tánaiste* Muircheartach, a man who, in 940, was at the height of his career and whose hand can be seen in the execution of the Dalcassian princess.

Adultery was commonly punished by repudiation, or divorce, in which case the guilty wife would have returned to her family in Thomond. But if that family appeared to present a threat to Muircheartach, the need for more drastic action was indicated. Muircheartach's grandfather, the *Ardrí* Flann Sionna, had taught Munster a lesson earlier in the century at Bealach Mughna, and the southern or Midhe Uí Néill were determined that never again would Cashel be a threat to their domination of Leath Cuinn. A strong king of the Eoghanachta could have restricted the power, perhaps even toppled from their pyramid of royalty, the Uí Néill high kings, particularly if he could control the kingdom of Osraighe, the state comprising what is now Co Kilkenny and most of Co Laois.

Osraighe, although nominally a tributary of Leinster, had been growing in power since the middle of the eighth century and, as we have seen in the previous chapter, had provided a regent for the rulers of Dublin in the 880s. It had also supported Cormac mac Cuileannáin at Bealach Mughna and any permanent liaison between a powerful Munster and Osraighe would have little difficulty in subjugating Meath. Although the Uí Néill maintained their authority for the rest of the tenth century, they must have been sufficiently frightened by Cormac mac Cuileannáin to attempt to destroy the threat by dividing it at the roots.

The best method lay in weakening the ruling house in Munster. There is no proof that this is what the Uí Néill tried to do, but I offer it as a plausible theory to explain the rise of the Dál gCais and the marriage of one of their daughters to the mighty Uí Néill clan. It would be simple, with Uí Néill backing, for the Dalcassians to gain stature, with pedigrees rewritten or amended until the Eoghanachta found themselves confronted with rivals for the crown of Munster, a rivalry that should prevent them making larger territorial claims in the fashion of Cormac mac Cuileannáin.

The monastery of Móin na hInse

The Dalcassians were suitably obscure in origin for Uí Néill purposes. Inhabitants anciently of an insignificant territory in eastern Limerick, land lying between the modern Bruff and Thomond Bridge, they had gained the upper hand in the eastern portion of Clare on the collapse of the dynasty in southern Connacht about 400 AD, probably through their own efforts, perhaps as colonists under the Eoghanachta (6). The Dalcassian kingdom was divided into An Déis Tuaiscirt (eastern Clare and part of eastern Limerick) and An Déis Deiscirt (the rest of eastern Limerick), each with its petty king, of whom one was overlord alternately of the entire area known as An Déis Bheag. In other words the alternate succession of northern and southern Uí Néill working on an infinitely smaller scale. The Uí Néill policy of divide and conquer presented a chance of greater power for the Dalcassians (and perhaps the invention of Oilill Ólum's will), and a threat to the Eoghanachta, who would be fully occupied keeping them at bay, particularly as it seems likely that An Déis Bheag was elevated by the Uí Néill into the kingdom of Thomond as a distinct division of Munster (7).

Somewhere between 914 and 920 Flaithbheartach, the abbot of Inis Cathaigh who may have persuaded Cormac mac Cuileannáin to embark on the campaign that ended in Bealach Mughna, was elected king of

Munster. Having been chastised by the 'clergy of Leinster' and, eventually, retiring to his monastery, he must have kept in touch with his Eoghanacht kinsmen who, shattered after Bealach Mughna, were for a time unable to resist Uí Néill interference in Munster affairs but who probably looked upon Flaithbheartach as a figure round whom to rally when the opportunity presented itself. Unfortunately, their new king's 'exemplary retirement' on Inis Cathaigh had weakened his resolve. Despite Fr Gleeson's assertion that he 'ruled for many years with great applause, and gained the affection of his people', a long period of inaction, either confined in Leinster or in virtual exile on Inis Cathaigh, had probably taken its toll on him. Shortly after his election as king, he went on pilgrimage to the monastery of Móin na hInse, near Roscrea, and had the misfortune to be there when it was sacked by a party of Limerick Danes. The king was taken hostage to Limerick and it may have been at this time that Lorcán, king of Thomond, appeared on the scene, either taking advantage of the absence of Flaithbheartach or at the invitation of the leaderless nobility. Whether Lorcán was ever king of Munster is difficult to assess: the regnal lists are unreliable, one maintaining a reign of nine years, another a mere eighteen months, while some chroniclers ignore Lorcán altogether. Greater confusion is caused when we try to discover what happened to Flaithbheartach — the *Four Masters* puts his death at 922, the *Annals of Inisfallen* at 944, and even making allowances for the notoriously inconsistent dating of the annalists, we find a period in which the throne of Munster appears either vacant or, possibly, occupied by the first Dalcassian to break the Eoghanacht succession. It may be that Lorcán called himself king with Uí Néill backing, Flaithbheartach being for the moment in Danish hands, and it may also have been Uí Néill influence that resulted in the marriage of Bé Bhionn, daughter of King Murchadh of west Connacht, to Lorcán's son, Cinnéide. Not only did the marriage reflect the standing of the groom's family, but it was to provide Brian, a son of the marriage, with ancestry of the highest order.

Lorcán vanishes from history, but the Dalcassians were not so easily to disappear. Whatever happened to Flaithbheartach, by 944 the king of Munster was Ceallachán of Desmond, head of the Eoghanachta. His election, if before 940, inspired the Uí Néill in their selection of Órlaith as a wife for the *Ardrí*. Such a move would not only flatter the Dalcassians, but would further Uí Néill influence in Munster. If the Dalcassians could overthrow Ceallachán and plant themselves firmly on the southern throne, the Uí Néill could extend their own power through them.

Cinnéide, delighted with the acquisition of so grand a son-in-law, marched into Desmond to canvass support for his own election to the throne. The result was war between Thomond and Desmond and, as the *Four Masters* records, 'a victory [was] gained by Ceallachán of Caiseal over Ceinnéidigh (Cinnéide), son of Lorcán, at Magh-duine, where many were slain'. Yet, according to one pro-Eoghanacht scribe of later years (8), the contest was decided by no less a person than Ceallachán's mother 'urging her case in tears' and reminding the combatants that as Lorcán had been the last king, it was unjust that the throne should go to anyone but her own son, as representative of the Eoghanacht line.

The tale is unrecorded by annalists such as the *Four Masters* and it is curious that it appears in an Eoghanacht, rather than Dalcassian, chronicle. As we do not really know the date of Ceallachán's succession, it is impossible to say whether or not the 'victory' was final or decisive, but if it was 940, the date of Órlaith's execution, we can surmise that it was due, in part, to a decision of the Uí Néill no longer to support their Dalcassian *protegés*. Cinnéide was probably becoming too independent to suit Uí Néill policy.

Cinnéide did step down, and the princes and nobles of Munster visited Ceallachán at Cashel. There, in accordance with tradition (9), 'each put his hands between those of the prince, the royal diadem was placed on his head; it was announced to the people that Ceallachán, the son of Buadhachán, the son of Lachtna, the son of Ardghal, the son of Snéadhghus, the son of Faolghus, the son of Natfraoich, the son of Colga, the son of Fáilbhe Flann, the son of Aodh Dubh, the son of Criomhthann, the son of Feidhlimidh, the son of Aonghus, the son of Conall Corc, the son of Lughaidh, the son of Oilill Flannbeg, the son of Fiacha Muilleathan, the son of Eoghan Mór, the son of Oilill Ólum, was sovereign prince and ruler of Leath Mogha, and the royal shout proclaimed the public approbation.'

Such was the political scene in Munster when Brian was born to Cinnéide and Bé Bhionn. The birthplace itself is uncertain, but it must have been one of three seats of the Dalcassian princes: perhaps the Grianán of Lachtna, on the western, or Co Clare, shore of Lough Derg and mentioned as a royal fortress as early as 840 AD. It may have been the fortress of Ceann Coradh, anglicised to Kincora, the site of which lies somewhere under the present-day town of Killaloe; or that of Béal Bóramha, northward on the road from Killaloe, from which Brian and other members of his house took the epithet denoting a place to which the

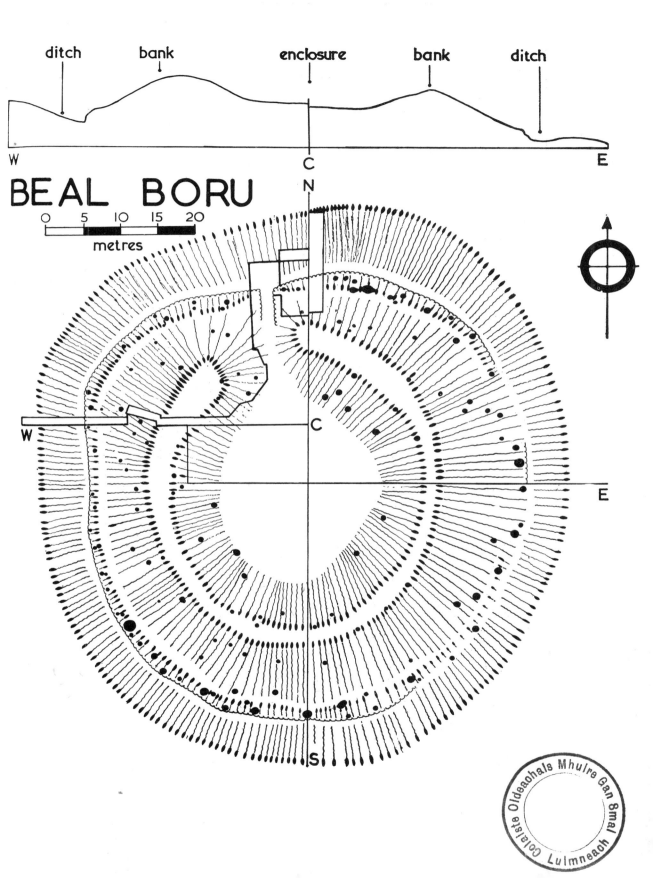

ditch   bank   enclosure   bank   ditch

W   C   E

BEAL BORU

0 5 10 15 20

metres

N

W   C   E

S

royal tribute of cattle — *Bóramha* — was driven by subordinate kings. Kincora, as we shall see in due course, is traditionally associated with Brian (10), perhaps because of his rebuilding or refortification of the palace as a strong base from which to control the Danish Shannon. It might well have been his childhood home, fond memories, as well as defensive potential, making it his citadel at the end of his life.

Whether or not he was born at Kincora, excavations carried out at Béal Bóramha in recent times provide us with some idea of the type of fortress in which Brian's family would have lived. A high ring-fort, with internal stone revetment and external pallisade of wooden stakes, it was surrounded by a defensive ditch and its position on a spur overlooking the Shannon, although relatively small in size — some five hundred feet wide by three hundred and twenty-five feet long — is typical of one from which to command and control traffic crossing or navigating the river.

The excavations in 1961 were somewhat hampered by a thick growth of beech and Scots pine, and a condition imposed by the owner of the fort that no trees should be cut. But the archaeologists uncovered sufficient ground to show that a considerable settlement had existed within the fortress, although it was possible only to identify completely one dwelling-house. Apparently, it had been constructed of posts, paved with large slabs of stone and with a central hearth. Roofing may have been of timber or turf.

Much damage had been caused to the original fortress by an attempt, probably by the Norman adventurers of the twelfth century, to erect a second stronghold on the same site. The Dalcassian fortress was by then in ruins, for the annalists report that in 1116 both Béal Bóramha and Kincora were burned by an invading force from Connacht. That they mention the two distinctly is evidence in refutation of a widely-held theory that Béal Bóramha and Kincora were one and the same place. At the same time it is more than likely that Brian, as a child, lived for a while in both — in troubled times the wife and children of Cinnéide would have found shelter in whichever was the stronger fortress.

Wherever he was born, there was little chance that the new prince would be called to the throne of Thomond. There was already a host of cousins and brothers before him in the line of elective seniority. Perhaps Cinnéide considered entering him for a religious life — no bar to kingship as the accession of holy Flaithbheartach proved — to follow in the footsteps of an elder brother, Marcán, described in 1010, in his obituary in the *Annals of Ulster*, as *comharba* or ecclesiastical heir of Colam mac

Béal Bóramha from the west **top** , *and the base of the excavated house*   57

Criomhthainn, founder of the monastery of Tír dhá Ghlas (Terryglas in Co Tipperary), head of the monasteries of Killaloe and Inis Cealtra and, from 990, abbot or bishop of Emly. It would appear that the abbacy of Emly, at least, was assumed, rather than earned, by Marcán, with family backing, the leadership of important monasteries being often treated as political, rather than spiritual, posts. Marcán, being the priest in the family, was the obvious candidate to fill such posts from which previous, probably anti-Dalcassian, dignitaries had been expelled.

In common with other Irish royal houses, the Dalcassians regularly provided nominees for ecclesiastical offices in monasteries which, after all, had probably been founded by an ancestor. Because of the tribal conditions of Irish life, the episcopal and unified church planned by St Patrick in the fifth century had degenerated in most areas into a monastic church, in which the powerful *tuath*-appointed abbots, such as Marcán, were the equivalent of bishops; and to be abbot of Emly was a plumb worth picking, for until Cashel was erected into an archbishopric at the Synod of Kells in 1152, Emly was the most important diocese in Munster (11).

But if thoughts of a religious career were entertained for Brian, they were probably dismissed by the boy himself, at an early age attracted by the songs and legends of his forebears, putative though many of them undoubtedly were. In the wooden hall of his father's seat at Kincora, or in Béal Bóramha, he would hear the tales of two of the greatest Celtic heroes, Conn Céadchathach, 'of the Hundred Battles', and Fionn mac Cumhaill, leader of the Fianna of Erin, both of whom had been attached to his pedigree. His young blood would stir to the sound of their exploits:

> Oh, delight to Fionn and the heroes,
> Was the cry of his hounds afar on the mountains,
> The wolves starting from their dens,
> The exultation of his hosts, was his delight.

> Fionn never suffered in his day
> Any one to be in pain or difficulty;
> Without redeeming him, by silver or gold,
> By battle or fight, till he got the victory!

Such verses, taken here at random from the *Agallamh na Seanorach* of Fionn's bardic son, Oisín, would resound through the smoke-stained halls and around the camps of the Dalcassians. Brian would linger by the fireside to hear first-hand accounts from battle-scarred ancients who had fought alongside the great Cormac mac Cuilleannáin earlier in the century; men whose fathers may have fought with Maoil-Seachlainn of Meath and who had witnessed the end of Turges and who continued a tradition of bravery founded centuries before among the ranks of the Clanna Deaghaidh, a legendary band of champions in Munster long before the coming of the Land Leapers. As soon as he could walk, Brian, in common with other boys, would, as he grew, become proficient with the Irish missile, then the casting spear, javelin or dart, and he may have practiced with the deadly *crann-tábhaill*, or wooden sling.

But while the shouts of war were foremost in his mind, Brian was not allowed to neglect his other studies. He was probably sent to the monks of Inisfallen in the lakeland of Killarney, where a monastery and college had been founded by Saint Finnian (12) at the end of the sixth century. Inisfallen had received students from throughout Christian Europe, and with other Irish seats of learning had continued the tradition of Christian teaching almost extinguished on the continent after the collapse of Roman civilisation. By the time of Brian's birth, however, long years of plunder and destruction — by native and foreigner alike — had greatly

Inisfallen, in the lakeland of Killarney

Early monastic remains on Inisfallen

reduced the number of such establishments, and manuscripts of Greek and Latin text, brought to the monasteries by missionaries and students, had been lost or destroyed to an extent we shall never know. It was to be Brian himself, in his last years, who supervised the provision of fresh literature and an attempt to rewrite the decaying manuscripts long concealed from the hands of the vandal.

Innisfallen had endeavoured to preserve much of Ireland's literary heritage, as had Cashel, which from the time of St Patrick had been the most influential religious centre in the south of Ireland. The patron saint had arrived there about 455 to baptise King Aonghus and, unintentionally, to try the royal courage by piercing his foot with a ceremonial crozier. 'It seemed to me', said Aonghus, when asked why he did not cry out, 'that it was a rite of the faith'. The story could be adapted easily to portray the stoicism of the surviving monasteries in the face of ravages by Norseman and Irishman.

And so, to Inisfallen and Cashel came the sons of the kings and sub-kings of Munster; and the sons of the privileged, although not royal, classes of *airigh* — the *flatha*, owners of landed property and counterparts of the eorls or eorlcundmen of later Anglo-Saxon times; and the *bó-airigh*, or cow aires, a higher grade of freemen whose rank depended on the possession of cows or who grazed their herds on the common land (13).

Brian and his fellows would be instructed not only in religious matters but in scientific (14) and astrological doctrine, and in the *Seanchas Mór*, embodying the Brehon laws. What could be termed extramural education was provided at home by Cinnéide's *ollamhain*, men who attained the highest degree in any art or profession. As today there are doctors of law, literature or medicine, so did the Irish of Brian's day and before, and for centuries after, gain distinction as *ollamh* poets, minstrels, lawyers, divines and so forth, and to these men the greatest respect was paid. In times of war, Brian would be taught by them at Kincora or Grianán Lachtna, with journeys to Inisfallen too perilous to undertake; and they would report to Cinnéide, not only on his son's work but on his general character: whether he was 'upright, free from unjust dealings and pure in conduct and word' (15).

As a boy, Brian must have longed for the day on which he could take arms against the Danes in particular and against the enemies of the Dál gCais in general. Two of his brothers, Echthighearn and the older Donn Cuan, *Tánaiste* of Thomond, at least twenty years his senior, had served in the army of Ceallachán of Munster who, after his accession, had begun to rebuild Eoghanacht supremacy in the kingdom, taking the Danish strongholds in Cork and Waterford. Following usual procedure, the towns had been evacuated, but not reduced, after their capitulation; and while Ceallachán concentrated on his scores with the Uí Néill, he allowed the Danes slowly to return and restore.

The involvement of the Dalcassians in Ceallachán's advance suggests that the execution of Órlaith might not have had the effect on Cinnéide that the Uí Néill expected. The *Ardrí*, Donnchadh, viewed developments in silent fury for, as the annalists recount (16), he 'displayed no great talents or patriotism, and envied the exploits of Ceallachán, which he ought to have imitated . . .'

Twice Muircheartach marched south to re-establish Uí Néill power in Munster and, at length, as the *Four Masters* records, he went

> '. . . to the beautiful chalk-white Caiseal,
> And he brought with him Ceallachán of troops;
> He did not accept of any other hostage for him . . .'

Ceallachán was sent to Donnchadh as a hostage for the good behaviour of Munster. One account (17) would have us believe that he was captured, not by Muircheartach, but by treachery of the Danes of Waterford. The story goes that Sitric of Waterford, whose wife came from an Ulster family, connived with Muircheartach at Ceallachán's capture. Requesting peace with Munster, he offered Ceallachán the hand of his sister, who had the Irish name of Bé Bhionn, in marriage — and Ceallachán is supposed to have fallen for the trick, which is unlikely, knowing what we do of him. But the legend maintains that Ceallachán, accompanied by Donn Cuan of Thomond, was captured by the Danes and taken to Dundalk, where both men were tied to the mastheads of Danish ships. That the tale is almost certainly Dalcassian propaganda is suggested by the message supposedly sent by Ceallachán to Cinnéide, commanding him to destroy the Danish fleet but, if attempts to rescue him proved impossible, to 'assume the throne of Munster, which your virtues so fully entitle you to ...'

The legend would have us believe that a fleet was sent to Dundalk, that Sitric was killed and the prisoners restored to the bosom of Munster. Whatever did take place, Ceallachán returned to Munster and, within three years, Muircheartach and Donnchadh died, the high throne passing to Conghalach who, faced with the ravages of the Danish Blacar, had no time to reassert his predecessor's claims on the southern kingdom. Donn Cuan and Echthighearn eventually died fighting against the Ardrí, probably in a border war, while Ceallachán, free from Uí Néill interference, decided to regain the whole of Munster for the Eoghanacht inheritance.

Allying himself with the Danes of Waterford, he ravaged the province for the next seven years and in 951 defeated the Dalcassians in battle, slaying Cinnéide. Some consolation was at hand the following year, however, when Ceallachán's abuse of power was ended during a thunderstorm. Having survived attempts on his life by Dalcassians and Danes, he was struck by lightning.

The electors of Munster, ignoring any Dalcassian pretensions, elected a kinsman of Ceallachán in his place; and the Dalcassians, stricken by their recent defeat, were in no position to oppose the election. Lachtna, eldest surviving son of Cinnéide, became king of Thomond, and the Dalcassians licked their wounds — and waited.

Lachtna's reign was brief and uneventful. The annalists, usually so preoccupied with morbid accounts of the death of kings, make no mention of his end, which came about 954.

He was succeeded by his next brother, Mathghamhain, and Brian, at the age of fourteen, found himself a hair's breadth from a throne, perhaps only the son or sons of his dead elder brother, Donn Cuan, standing

Inisfallen, from the lake

between him and Mathghamhain. The likelihood of his sudden accession was increased by the arrival in Ireland of Olaf Cuarán, king of Dublin, who had crossed the sea after losing his throne in Northumbria. Had he been in Ireland at the time Sitric was plotting the overthrow of Ceallachán there might well have been a different outcome, for Olaf was a determined and competant general who for four years 'held Northumbria by the strong hand'. He would also establish for himself an enviable position in Ireland through marriage: by his first wife he was step-father of Maoil-Seachlainn II of Meath, and to increase his influence he became Maoil-Seachlainn's father-in-law. And when Olaf married for a second time, his wife was Gormfhlaith, a kinswoman of the neighbouring king of Leinster and someone who, in time, was to become the wife both of Maoil-Seachlainn and of Brian himself.

In 956, two years after Mathghamhain's accession, pious Domhnall became *Ardrí* and the dogs of war broke lose once more. In Munster, the Danes, inspired by the new state of affairs in Dublin and aided by the disturbed condition of the southern kingdom, rebuilt their old strength. *Tuath* after *tuath*, weakened during the internal wars, submitted to Danish rule rather than suffer more bloodshed. But in Thomond, Mathghamhain and the Dalcassians, refusing to surrender, were slowly pushed back among the impenetrable wastes of Clare, from where a campaign of harassment was directed against the Danes of Limerick.

Brian, nearing the age of seventeen, would have been among that guerilla band, for Mathghamhain would have need of every virile young warrior. And as seventeen was the age of mating in ancient Ireland, perhaps it was at the beginning of this first, long struggle of Brian's life that he married. His bride was Mór, daughter of Éidigeán of Uí Fhiachrach Aidhne, a *tuath* prince whose territory is represented by the present-day diocese of Kilmacduagh in south-western Co Galway, the land of the original rulers of much of Thomond. She was to bear him three sons at least, of whom Murchadh was to be his father's right-hand man in the years to come; and Conchobhar and Flann, of whom nothing is known.

The last years of the sixth decade of the ninth century can hardly have been a propitious time for contemplating marriage, especially in Thomond. Limerick was a Danish stronghold and the enemy had established a second base on the Clare side of the Shannon at Tradree. The river was completely under their control and, as in the days of the first raiders, long-boats were sent inland to pillage. Eastwards to Osraighe the Danes infiltrated the kingdom — the 'arrow of fire' which, says the *Annals of Ulster*, 'came along Leinster from the south-west' and 'killed a hundred thousand of men and flocks' was doubtless a Viking raid, if exaggerated — and Mathghamhain's announcement, in 959, that he was king of Munster seems pointless. If he hoped to rally despairing Munster around him he was to be disappointed, and by 962 it seemed a matter of time before his little band was driven back into the ocean by the advancing Danes.

Then, in that year of despair, an unforeseen event occurred. The men of Osraighe, an area the Danes considered they had effectively subdued, rose against their oppressors, perhaps given courage by the resistance carried on across the Shannon. Despite the assistance of an army led by Olaf of Dublin himself, the Danes were soundly beaten.

The victory provided a much-needed respite for the Dalcassians. The Danes had been taken unaware and were ready to sue for peace. Mathghamhain, worn with fatigue and by the gradual erosion of his own troops, would have accepted a truce. It could not be expected to last, but it would provide a breathing space in which to reorganise Thomond, even Munster, before Danish reinforcements arrived.

Mathghamhain found opposition within his own camp from Brian, at twenty-one a tried warrior. To him, any thought of peace must have been a betrayal of the Dalcassian cause. Hot-headed and impetuous Mathghamhain may have thought him, but Brian had seen and heard of the ascent of the tribe of the Dál gCais. He knew how weakness at Cashel, weakness at Tara, was of advantage to the Land Leapers, and he knew that there could be no benefit to Thomond in fresh weakness. Perhaps he had already set his sights on a throne greater than that of Thomond, on a title greater than that claimed by Mathghamhain in Munster.

3

Hibernicis ipsis Hiberniores

UPON this stage of Irish history we have now seen, and finally recognised, the principal actors. It may seem a perpetual crowd scene, but even so we may differentiate between the crowds; while, if there is a chorus, as in classical Greek productions, it is the compelling voice of Ireland herself, bemoaning her sorrows but at the same time calling upon us to be wary of the open trap — of looking at the play strictly through glasses of black and white.

Brian, son of Cinnéide, has organised his guerilla bands in the mountains and forests of Clare. He is determined to avenge the rape of his homeland and, like Alfred of Wessex nearly a century before, to keep at least his own corner of the island free from Scandinavian domination. But before we pursue his course it is fair, both to Brian and to his adversaries, to stand objectively in the wings of the stage and to examine more closely the offering made to us by one particular band of players — the Norsemen themselves.

We have seen how the original Land Leapers came, adding greater confusion to an island already torn by internal warrings. Turges, the greatest and worst of the invaders, has met his end at the hands of the king of Meath. Since his death new waves of invasion have come and gone, fresh atrocities have been committed; but still we must examine both sides of the invaders' coin.

By the time Brian made his stand in Clare, Norse traditions had been established in Ireland for well over a century and a half. The Scandinavian kingdom of Dublin, as historians have termed the city-state that developed from the early invaders' *longphurt*, was used as an important base in conjunction with the colonies in England, much as two English kings, William of Orange and luckless James II, seven centuries later used Ireland generally as a means by which to gain, or regain, the English throne. William of Orange has his partisans to this day, vociferous in their

Excavations at Wood Quay, Dublin

protestations of loyalty, but the true motives of those kings in raising their standards on Irish soil are forgotten or ignored.

The Norsemen of Dublin have a far stronger claim to supporters if we are talking of loyalty. Although they owed a technical allegiance to the kings of Norway or Northumbria, it was a technicality that did not prevent them gaining a greater independence and security than many of the native Irish kingdoms. After the invasion of Olaf the White in 853, and that king's consolidation of the position of Dublin, the Norsemen no longer regarded Dublin as a colony in a foreign country (1), but as their own territory. The position in the Orkneys, ceded to Scotland by the Norse only in 1469, was similar to Dublin, perhaps more so, for the Norse in the Orkneys took possession of a land virtually depopulated of its original inhabitants.

The Norse rulers of Dublin conferred considerable lasting benefits on Ireland as a whole. Those benefits are worthy of examination, weighing the outcome of investigation against the knowledge that the benefactors were also guilty of oppression.

The early Land Leapers were driven by two primary desires: one, an inherent love of piracy and adventure; the other, the colonisation of fresh territories to relieve population pressures in Norway. It is unfortunate that throughout history, and certainly in their own day, the tendency was

Detail of a post-and-wattle house at Wood Quay

to regard the Norse simply as pirates, obscuring more important facets of their character. Piracy was doubtless an element in their impact on people outside Scandinavia (2), but their basic economy was largely founded on agriculture, and it was this, together with their mercantile traditions, that aided the steady development of Dublin and the other territories.

A modern historian (3) has shown how quickly the Saxon invaders of the former Roman colony that became England embarked on the task of clearing the forests and cultivating the stubborn clay soils. Like the Norsemen, whose kinsmen they were, the Saxons 'loved the symbols of death and carnage ... the raven who followed the host with his beak dripping blood ... the funeral pyre hung with shields and helmets ... Though to the defeated Britons, to whose homes they had brought fire and sword, they seemed only cruel, boorish savages, they were great farmers ... by far the best the island had known ...'

The Norsemen were no worse farmers for being pirates. When Charlemagne's subjugation of Frisia had driven men and women in their hundreds to seek shelter in Norway, and when that land began to suffer from too great a population, the plough might have been abandoned for the battle-axe; but the inborn skills of husbandry did not forsake those who took sail across the North Sea.

Dublin quickly became a flourishing city-state, not simply a harbour

Gold armlets and a trial piece found at Wood Quay

for Viking long-boats sheltering after the latest raid. Examples of bone-
and metal-working, leather processing and weaving discovered in
excavations in the city are proof that the inhabitants were no mean
craftsmen. Not only did Dublin become an important administrative
centre, with its *thingmote*, or public assembly on a grass mound recalled in
tradition as late as the seventeenth century (4), but also a commercial
centre for related Norse territories and for much of independent Europe.
Trade was an essential part of the Norse economy, important enough for
guilds or merchant fraternities to be set up to protect their members in
foreign markets.

Ireland had neglected maritime affairs long before the first Land
Leaper set foot on Lambay Island. As the base of the European church,
particularly after the collapse of the Roman empire, education and
learning, the compilation of histories and hagiographies and the
promulgation of literature and art, had been the Irish contribution to
national prosperity for generations. Students from Europe had crossed to
Ireland in their hundreds, but the world of commerce had been largely
ignored. The Norseman brought Ireland into financial contact not simply
with sister states in England and Scandinavia, but with Russia and even
with the East. From Dublin and Waterford, both ports on the eastern

coast of Ireland, a continuous intercourse with foreign merchants and shipping was established, and Dublin became one of the wealthiest towns in the western world.

The profits did not fail to inspire, or arouse envy in, native Irishmen, and Brian was soon to realise that an increasing national prosperity was due to Norse influences. After his later successes he allowed the enemy to retain their coastal fortresses for the purpose of attracting commerce from abroad.

Those among the Norsemen who preferred agriculture to commerce came to regard Ireland as their home through the practice of their skills. Many of the early invaders settled on land far from the *longphuirt* and became naturalised more rapidly than their kinfolk of the towns. Marriage was essential if the objective of creating a new home was to be achieved; Norse and Dane married Celt, and in *tuatha* in remote places men whose fathers had fought with Turges became accepted as brothers. The battle-axe was laid aside for the tools of cultivation, and doubtless many of the families who fled for refuge to the round tower of the district in times of raids were of Norse blood themselves.

A parallel may be found in the settling of what became known as the English Danelaw — that part of the country north of a line from the Thames to modern Liverpool recognised as a distinct political entity by Alfred the Great in his truce with Guthrum in 886. The society of the Danelaw, which survived in diminishing form until the Saxon victory at Brunanburgh in 937, had as its backbone a peasant aristocracy: not warriors but smallholders with twenty-five acres of land and ten or twelve cows.

Language may have presented initial difficulties in Ireland, but the influence of Norse on the native tongue is significant. Examples may be found in *garrdha*, Middle Irish for garden, and *garthr*, the Old Norse equivalent; *trosc* and *thorskr*, denoting codfish, or *cnap* and *knappr* for button. An intermixture, long continued, of the two peoples can be seen in many Irish words today, and it is obvious that any races with similar words for such leisurely activities as gardening, or for such domestic articles as buttons, must have had relationships other than combats to the death on bloody battlefields. Closer human ties are needed, ties found through commerce and marriage, and John of Wallingford, a ninth-century English chronicler, shows that the Danes at least were not unattractive to native girls. The invaders were 'frequently combing their hair . . . and bathed regularly on Saturdays', a change apparently from the local Anglo-Saxon youths who, one imagines, had provided smelly, unkempt *beaux* for generations.

Another tie was made through the custom of child-fosterage, common to the Irish and Norse (5) and still practised in Ireland as late as the middle of the nineteenth century (6). Such ties were as strong as those of blood in all classes. Kings might send their sons to be brought up at foreign courts or with more lowly families of their *tuatha*; and a runic inscription found upon a Norse cross on the Isle of Man (7) shows how close a relationship of this sort might be. Erected in memory of a foster-son, it ends: 'It is better to leave a good foster-son than a bad son'.

What is almost certainly a case of Norse fostering Irish is found on several occasions in the annals of the late 850s (8). It is the mention of the *Gall-Ghaedhil* — 'foreign Irish' — who, we are told, were 'men who had deserted their faith ... they had the habits of life of the Norse and had been brought up by them'. It may have been a case of the Norse fostering, rather than slaughtering, boys found in a raided settlement or monastery, and was still of sufficient interest fifty years later, when the Saxon chroniclers reported how a Norse army led against Chester by Ingemund of Dublin included 'many an Irish foster-son'. In Dublin, in the country, the Norse were becoming assimilated into the population and looked upon the island as their home. Olaf of Dublin, first husband of Gormfhlaith of Leinster, lost his Northumbrian throne and settled in his Irish citadel about the time of Brian's accession in Thomond. By the time of his departure to the peace of Iona he was as much an Irish monarch as the rulers in Leinster, Munster and elsewhere.

Apart from marital and commercial ties, there was another influence at work upon the heirs of the Land Leapers. Although, even by Brian's day, not all traces of paganism had vanished from the native Irish (9), Christianity had made a considerable advance, in a way Charlemagne himself would have envied.

During the late ninth and tenth centuries there had arisen a practice known as prime-signing, which was simply marking commercial produce with the Sign of the Cross. The practice had become common among European merchants for, having prime-signed, they could with clear conscience associate with Christian and pagan alike, while retaining their own faith. The system worked both ways, and the men of Dublin, expanding their trade routes, found it expedient and profitable to follow a custom established originally for use by Christian merchants trading abroad. Christianity thus made inroads into what had been founded as a pagan state and, even as the early Irish missionaries converted local deities and temples to their own use, so were the Norse gods and goddesses baptised in most unwarlike manner (10).

Even in the time of Turges, Christianity had made some progress in the land of his birth, although it seems, for long, two faiths existed side by side. Helgi the Lame, Norse grandson of that Cearbhall of Osraighe who was regent in Dublin, was typical of the period, for he was 'very mixed' in his faith. He believed in Christ, but invoked Thor for seafaring and brave deeds. When he built himself a house, having asked of Thor where he should settle, 'he made a large fire near every lake and river, thus sanctifying all the land between . . . Helgi believed in Christ and therefore named his house after Him . . .'

Thus says *Landnamabok*, a contemporary Icelandic saga, and other examples are numerous. When Danes and Norwegians fought at Carlingford Lough in 853, following the invasion of Olaf the White, the Danish leaders advised their forces to pray fervently to St Patrick, 'archbishop and head of the saints of Erin'. Under his protection they placed themselves, and after the battle a trencher full of gold and silver 'to give to Patrick' was put by in the victorious camp by 'a people with a kind of piety; they could for a while refrain from meat and women'.

At the same time Norsemen were erecting memorials to their dead in the form of crosses, and although at first the carvings and inscriptions were in keeping with Scandinavian paganism, Christian engraving was soon adopted, the names of saints such as Patrick and Adhamhnán appearing as Bathrik and Athanman. When marriages took place, such as that in the family of Cearbhall of Osraighe, the issue were frequently given names not merely Irish but Christian; and the *Four Masters* records, among other significant names, those of Giolla Ciaráin — the servant of St Ciarán — and Maol Muire — servant of Mary. One of the sons of Olaf the White was named Carlus, indicating his presence in France at the court of Charles the Bald, whom he took as godfather. This may have been a political move, following a treaty between his father and the Frankish king, similar to that made in 925 between Sitric Gale, king of Northumbria, and Athelstan of Wessex. The Norseman was converted to Christianity as a condition of an alliance with Athelstan — an alliance which also gave him the hand in marriage of a great-granddaughter of Alfred the Great.

The Isle of Man, a Norse colony from the time of Olaf the White, is rich in stone monuments engraved with Christian symbols — monuments

Wheel-headed cross and memorial stone on the Isle of Man

deliberately erected by Norsemen who had come under the influence of Christianity in Ireland; and while conversion to the new faith might not end the assaults on monasteries, we have seen that such assaults were not carried out solely by erstwhile followers of Thor or Wodin. Indeed, Gothfrith, a king of Dublin described by the *Annals of Ulster* as 'the most cruel of the Norsemen', specifically spared the church and 'houses of prayer' when he plundered Armagh on St Martin's Day, 921.

The gradual conversion of the Norse in particular, Scandinavia in general, to Christianity, was achieved not by the merciless efforts of men like Charlemagne, but through far more natural channels. To the Norse, as to the Saxons hearing the gentle teachings of Augustine and his band of thirty monks on the thyme-scented Kentish downs, there came a realisation that while Christian virtues might be different from their own — gentleness instead of force, mercy instead of revenge — the basic message was worthy of acceptance. The concept of the Trinity was not new to the Norsemen, for their own supreme beings were the Mysterious Three — Har, the Mighty; the Like Mighty and the Third Person — who sat on thrones above the rainbow and to whom even Wodin and the Aesir, feasting in Valhalla among the heavenly hills between the rainbow and earth, were subject. But there the comparison ended: the Scandinavian faith was one of confusion, in which no feasting god was safe from the dreaded hags, Weird and Hel, and it brought their worshippers little comfort. The promise of life after death, and the sensible way in which the great Pope Gregory warned his missionaries against offending the traditions of the people they were to convert were methods more effective than that of the Frankish sword.

The conversion of a pagan king was even more effective. In pagan Norse society the king's position was one not merely of military leader but of high priest (11), and his acceptance of Christianity was bound to have a far-reaching effect on the whole community. The entire concept of kingship benefitted from a royal conversion, the claim of the church that royal authority was derived from God alone — the divine right of kings — aiding the rise of dynasties throughout Europe, and, in time, bringing stability and unity to countries in which anointed sovereigns commanded greater loyalty and affection than those who usurped the throne by force. That it also produced periods of civil war was due to inevitable human frailty, and the continuing existence of the royal houses in England and Denmark, albeit in constitutional form, provides an interesting study in the moulding of a semi-divine principle to suit an ever-changing and far from divine world. England and Denmark, two of the smallest and earliest states to accept Christianity, have, almost alone among the European network, preserved an appearance of national unity that is far from superficial.

In 995 the old gods were attacked more vigorously in their own country when Olaf Trygvaeson seized the throne of Norway, a policy continued in the reign of his son and eventual successor, Olaf II. Olaf's death in battle in 1030 was followed shortly by his canonisation as the Norwegian patron saint and by, what is more important, the establishment of a church dedicated to his memory in Dublin. The benefactor of the church, Sitric Silkenbeard, was the son-in-law and adversary of Brian Boru.

Thus it is that to the Norsemen Ireland became indebted for commercial development and a reopening of links with the rest of Christendom, links the Norse had severed when their long-boats first appeared on the horizon. That Christianity was to an extent responsible for that debt is ironic as far as the Norse are concerned; although it must be emphasised that except, perhaps, in the time of Turges and his pagan-priestess wife, Christianity was in no great danger of becoming extinguished by paganism in Ireland. The Norse were never missionaries for their own faith.

But they were missionaries, in unlikely guise, for the development of a side of life common in Scandinavia and Ireland. Norse influence in Irish literature has for long caused controversy among historians, a certain sign that there is something to be said in favour of the argument.

The Irish were excessively fond of hearing tales and poetry recited, and in every royal court, in every *tuath*, were the *seanchaithe* whose duty it was to recount the exploits of their patron's house in love and war. At every festivity, from the making of the *Ardrí* to local merrymaking, the *seanchaithe* would recite into the early hours, a programme interspersed with contributions from the guests, for everyone was expected to know by heart a reasonable number of Irish sagas, and to be ready to take part in the entertainment of the hour.

The sagas, though embellished by any good story-teller, filled a vital place in Irish life. They conveyed a sense of history and geography and, by the heroic deeds enshrined in them, were designed to inculcate a sense of chivalry and honour among the listeners. As a result of this tradition the Irish have retained to the present day an aptitude for story-telling virtually unparalleled in Europe. Yet, it was unavoidable that the principal stories to survive were those taken in hand by the missionaries.

After the time of Patrick the monasteries and palaces of Ireland were rich in manuscripts, the direct progeny of Patrician inspiration. But they were, in most cases, an unindexed miscellanea of genealogies, histories, annals and poems mixed up with little attempt at orderly classification. In this way many of the tales became confused and far removed from their original purpose of encouraging nobility of character among young Irishmen. Much, too, was lost as a result of monkish modesty or through an attempt at literary conversion of basically pagan heroes and heroines. When men like Brian tried after years of Norse and native depredation to restore the great collections, they had to work on scattered fragments of Christian writings. Although something of the ancient romance was recaptured, much more was lost for ever.

The most valuable works of Irish literature remaining, in part or whole, today are almost entirely the work of a new wave of monastic scribes. The *Leabhar na hUidhri*, or *Book of the Dun Cow*, was written by Maol Muire mac Céileachair, who died in 1106 and who gathered much of his material from surviving fragments of earlier manuscripts. The more famous *Book of Leinster*, now in Trinity College, Dublin, was written by Fionn mac Gormáin, bishop of Kildare from 1148 to 1160, about 1130; while the *Book of Ballymote* and the *Yellow Book of Lecan* are both products of the

Page 55 from Leabhar na hUidhri

Cṁṅ comláṅ ṁ lóiḡeṁ móṅ
la ṁnúcṁ .ı. la ṁulıll ṁ lameṁb
ṁ ṁ eṁṁ ṁ ṁṁ ṁṁṁ ...

[The main body consists of two columns of Old Irish text written in a heavily abbreviated medieval Gaelic minuscule hand, with large decorated initial capitals beginning several paragraphs. The text is not legibly transcribable with confidence.]

[2]

[3]

alenni

last decade of the fourteenth century. The great *Book of Lecan*, in the library of the Royal Irish Academy, dates from an even later period, probably about 1416.

All, particularly the *Book of Leinster*, contain historical and romantic tales of early Irish kings, the existence of many of whom is doubtful; while the *Book of Ballymote* goes a step further and offers a narrative of the most remarkable women of Ireland up to the Cambro-Norman invasion of 1169. They owe their existence partly to dog-eared and decaying manuscripts rescued in Brian's day or before, manuscripts perhaps already doctored by priestly hands; and while the essence of the old Irish art of story-telling is not completely absent — exaggeration is certainly present — they are valuable mainly as examples of Irish literature in what might be termed the Early Middle Period — between Brian's death and final English colonisation.

History, however, is full of irony, and while the learned men of St Patrick's day onwards might dilute the character of these fireside legends, that character was maintained to a great degree by the Norsemen. The *seanchaí* method of story-telling was in the form of a life-cycle of a given hero, or group of heroes, and concerned itself with such important events in the subject's life as his battles, hostings, tragedies, courtships and feastings. Slaughter and destruction stood side by side with love and victory in the ranks of these tales, while mythology played an important but not — at least in the original mouth-transmitted sagas — vital part. The Norse, pagan and piratical as they were at their entry into Irish history, were no different from those they ravaged in the manner of preserving the adventures of their heroes, gods and ancestors. In Norse literature there are two distinctive types of saga: the *Fornaldur Sogur*, or stories about early times, and the *Konunga Sogur*, or stories about kings, notably those in Norway. Most of them have their origin in Iceland, colonised by Norsemen under Ingolfur Arnarson in 874 — a comparatively peaceful time for Ireland — and which, for four centuries until subjugation by a centralising Norwegian government, flourished as a Norse republic and trading partner of Dublin.

At the time of the Icelandic colonisation, Norsemen had been in Ireland long enough to forge links through marriage and even religion; so that although the bulk of Icelandic settlers were drawn from Scandinavia, many of them must have been Dublin born. *Landnamabok* mentions several settlers by name, among them Aud the Deepminded, widow of Olaf the White, king of Dublin. In the train of so exalted a personage

The knoll on Papataettur in Iceland

would have gone many native Irishmen and women, foster-children, allies or slaves; following, perhaps unconsciously, in the footsteps of Irish monks who had settled briefly in Iceland at the end of the eighth century (12). The monks may have gone by the time the Norseman founded Reykjavik, although their tradition lingers on in place-names such as Papey, Papafjordur and Papafjall, so called by the Norse after the *Papar*, or 'fathers', whose stone ruins remain on the knoll of Papataettur. So, whether Irish by ancestry or adoption, or influenced by what they found in Iceland, the founders of the little republic were imbibed with Irish tradition. In Ireland they had found a custom of story-telling that was essentially no different from their own; in due course the sagas of the two peoples became intertwined and were carried across the sea.

A far-fetched theory? An exaggeration worthy of the *seanchaithe*? Scholars may say so, but they have enveloped themselves in controversy on this very point for generations, and the evidence remains the same. In the cold, barren Icelandic landscape, around the camp fires of the long, sunless days of the northern winter, the *seanchaithe* or their counterparts would come into their own. The 'foreign Irish', the slaves or mercenaries, away from native soil, would recount the unadulterated cycles of the Red Branch Knights, of Fionn mac Cumhaill and his companions; and as they had been heard and early recognised by the Norse invader in Ireland, so would they be welcomed by that same conqueror in Iceland. The earliest,

The drystone ruins of the Irish settlement

and most basic, tradition of each man reciting his own contribution to the assembly was reborn:

> Full they were of fighters
> and flashing bucklers,
> western war-lances
> and wound-blades Frankish;
> cried then the bear-pelted,
> carnage they had thoughts of,
> wailed then the wolf-coated
> and weapons brandished (13)

It was language appreciated by all fighting men, but the most significant point is in the gradual transition in the style of the Norse sagas. Until the colonisation of Iceland they are frequently narratives of fiction (14), while those of pre-Patrician Ireland are largely the exploits of people who, at least in the minds of the *seanchaithe*, were more tangible than figures in the Norwegian *Volsunga Saga* or *Hervarer Saga*. In short, the later sagas of Iceland bear the unmistakable stamp of Ireland.

This is supported further by the development of story-telling in the genuine *seanchaí* vein; with history and geography as main ingredients, and with the occasional myth as colouring, it has occurred nowhere in Europe as much as in Iceland. No other European people have a tradition of story-telling in the style of oral prose as have the Icelandic and the

Irish; and although it might be suggested that as the prose saga was a spontaneous feature of early Irish life, there was no reason for it not to have occurred independently in Iceland, the similarities are too many to ignore.

The great Norse sagas date mainly from the thirteenth century (15), but that the Icelandic form of story-telling owes much to what Norsemen heard in Ireland cannot really be disputed. And, strangely, the Norsemen, who 'burned and drowned' priceless manuscripts in monasteries from Armagh to Kerry, helped to keep alive one of the most Irish of traditions. To credit them, as Dr Nora Chadwick has done (16), with the development of Ireland from several small states into a nation with, in theory, a single monarchy, is to ignore both the work of Brian Boru and the fragmented condition in which Ireland was discovered by the Norman mercenaries of the twelfth century. But the Norse ability in commerce and in maintaining at least one native tradition caught the imagination of the young Dalcassian prince who was to become their greatest adversary.

Miniature wooden ship, and incised plank

4

'The Wild Huts of the Desert'

CLARE, in Thomond, is a country well suited for guerilla warfare. Even today there is a wildness in the landscape, which alternates between remnants of the vast, antedeluvian forest into which the pre-Celtic tribes had retreated between 800 and 500 BC (1), and those fifty square miles of bare limestone upland known as the Burren. On the western boundary it is safe from attack; the coastline of sheer cliffs from Black Head in the north, towering over Galway Bay, to Loop Head on the southernmost extremity, acting as a buffer to the Atlantic Ocean, which stretches out illimitable and awe-inspiring. The cliffs of Moher rise sheer and straight for miles above the sea, the red sandstone of which they are formed having the peculiarity of being without foothold or loose scree.

On the eastern border with Limerick is the bold mass of the Slieve Bernagh mountains, rising south of Scariff to 1,748 feet above sea level. On one side the mountains drop down to Lough Derg and the Shannon, on the other to a wasteland. To the north, an imaginary boundary with modern Co Galway has a backcloth of the Connemara mountains, a panorama of nature at her wildest, dominating the skyline.

Despite the untamed appearance, the high degree of exposure and the westerly gales or winds prevalent in winter, the climate, as an early nineteenth-century topographer (2) wrote, is often 'cool, humid, and occasionally subject to boisterous winds, but remarkably conducive to health'. The high winter temperatures and the humidity in summer which prevail in west Munster generally have been appreciated by man for two thousand years at least; and more recently it was on the rich blue-black soil in the Tradree district (3) that the merchants of Limerick and Cork grazed the cattle that brought them fortunes on the markets of the continent. And while the soil of the mountainous areas, and much of the level districts, was long composed of moorland and bog, lime from the Shannon has always been at hand for use in improvement and cultivation.

The cliffs of Moher, Co Clare

The Burren, Co Clare

Just as the men of the Fir Bholg turned westwards in the face of the advancing Celts, so did the early Land Leapers look towards that countryside as a base not only from which to raid and plunder but to settle and cultivate their peace-time occupations of commerce and agriculture. Limerick and their settlement in Tradree became strongholds, and although it took another nine centuries for the Shannon to become completely navigable (4), the Norse and Danish experience of the waterways of Scandinavia and the Baltic enabled them to penetrate much of the land that the Celts had been content to leave to their predecessors.

Into this mixture of moorland, mountain and potential wealth, Brian led his guerilla band in 962. Gathering in the fastnesses, hunting across the plains and fishing in the innumerable mountain streams that feed the Shannon, they emulated the heroes of the old Irish sagas; those warriors who fought with Conchobhar and the Red Branch Knights, or with the Fianna and Brian's putative ancestors. Caves and mountain lairs formed a vital part of the geography of those sagas, and Brian's followers precisely imitated the adventures of which they were composed. From lairs in the foothills of the Slieve Bernagh, they could sweep down under cover of dark to bring destruction to Danish outposts on the Shannon edge; retreating like goats along a labrynthine system of trackways across the

Lough Derg and the Slieve Bernagh mountains

bogs, or through the thick forests of fir, oak and yew, in which the Danes, less familiar with the secret ways, could be lured to destruction.

The little army travelled as lightly as possible; indeed heavy packs or superfluous weapons would have been out of the question. Each man would have been armed with the deadly *tuagh chatha*, or battle-axe, with a head of iron, copper or stone, an implement with which the Irish had long been accomplished and which the descendants of Brian's warriors used with such success against the Norman invaders of two centuries later, as the official Norman historian of that conquest, Giraldus Cambrensis, recorded:

> They make use of but one hand to the axe when they strike, and extend the thumb along the handle to guide the blow: from which neither the crested helmet can defend the head, nor the iron folds of the armour the rest of the body. From whence it has happened, even in our times, that the whole thigh of a soldier, though cased in well-tempered armour, hath been lopped off by a single blow of the axe ...

To the Danes, cut off from their ships or strongholds, the devastation would be no less complete.

At their waists the Irish wore, loose or in a highly decorated scabbard, the short *cloidheamh* from which the Scottish claymore developed.

Usually no longer than two feet, the sword was used for close, hand-to-hand fighting, and Brian's men had taught themselves to use it with the left hand, as well as the right, so as to be able to alternate or fight with one in each hand as occasion demanded. When the warrior was travelling, in the hand not used to carry the battle-axe would probably have lain the equally effective javelin, recorded in the tales of Fionn mac Cumhail, and as deadly to a Land Leaper as to a deer.

A bag of hide, slung around the neck, would contain provisions for a day, the guerillas relying on daily hunting or the culinary results of a raid. Hide was also used to fashion and repair the corslet that covered the body, the legs being protected by leather greaves and the head by a form of tanned helmet, possibly chequered with bands of iron or bronze. Any form of armour elsewhere on the body was little used by the Irish, even as late as the sixteenth century, and accounts of the Danes wearing the *lúireach*, or coat of mail, cannot be substantiated (5). Both sides had to rely on swiftness of reflex, or fleetness of foot, to avoid losing their limbs.

Speed was essential, and, even if the terrain had made it possible, the use of cavalry was not yet a feature of Irish warfare. In major battles the king and his staff may have fought on horseback — Cormac mac Cuileannáin of Munster had lost his life at Bealach Mughna earlier in the century, when his horse slipped on the battlefield — but it was not until the coming of the Normans that cavalry came into general use. In Brian's day, and for centuries afterwards, with half the island covered by scrubby forest and undrained bog, a fate like that of Absalom would have awaited many Irish warriors. It was still fleetness of foot that counted with a group such as Brian's, as the Danes soon discovered.

Brian's chief strategy, now and throughout most of his life, was surprise. He avoided pitched battles with the enemy and concentrated on harassing small parties, waylaying them and cutting off stragglers. His aim was to make the whole district west of the Shannon unsafe for any Dane, and in this he appears to have succeeded, but not without suffering casualties himself. The guerillas must have changed encampments almost daily, and even if they cheered themselves with the thought of liberating their homeland, or gave themselves new courage through the songs of the Fianna, they soon found that a human frame can stand only so much hardship. Hunting expeditions were not always profitable: the Danes had probably been ahead of them and killed or frightened away the game. The hunters would often fall victim to the enemy, and the hungry fighters, waiting in some sheltered estuary or isolated cave, would find little comfort in song alone. The Irish winter, too, could prove a bitter adversary, although the climate of the area could produce strong, chilling winds, much rain, sea mist and fogs, rather than long periods of frost or snow (6). At least pursuit was made no easier, as the limestone plains dry out rapidly, and there were no freezing footprints for the Danes to follow.

The Danes, more accustomed to the storms of the Scandinavian seaboard, but also with the knowledge that at the end of the day the comfort and shelter of Limerick or Tradree were their own, became bolder. One by one, the guerilla army was cut down, and at the end of a year Brian had but fifteen men around him, survivors of a band that, at the start, had probably numbered one hundred (7). The dispersal of the Fianna after the death of their leader was not more tragic.

We do not know whether Mór, Brian's wife, accompanied him on the campaign. The annalists tended to ignore women unless they were of significance in their own right, and in 962 the wife of a Dalcassian prince, herself the daughter of a relatively obscure sub-king of Connacht, would hardly be a person of significance. Mór is completely faceless, unlike one of her successors, although it appears she died young — she could have been little more than sixteen at the time of her marriage.

Brian, sheltering over a fire in some draughty cave, must often have thought of her, and his infant sons. Those sons would seem far away, and although Grianán Lachtna, or whichever fortress sheltered them, might be regarded as impregnable, their father's mind was filled with fears of treachery, both on the part of the Danes with whom Mathghamhain had made an uneasy peace, and on that which could arise within the palace walls. Not all, from nobleman to servant, could be properly trusted; no one knew when, prompted by Danish reward or family greed, a man might steal or murder the children of the Dalcassian prince to whom peace was impossible.

As the guerilla band diminished, Mathghamhain decided to call an end to his brother's self-imposed task. To the handful of worn, hungry and battle-scarred Dalcassians the sight of their king entering their poor encampment, his well-fed troops around him, would have struck a discordant note, and perhaps to some the futility of the guerilla struggle would be bitterly obvious. And yet, it was for the privilege of comfort, for the knowledge that they could, one day, live in safety with their families, as those who had stayed with Mathghamhain appeared to do, that the little band had waged this seemingly endless struggle. The sigh for home, for the sound of their sons' voices and for the warm companionship of their wives, which must have escaped those weary lips, would have been fixed with one of anger at the sight of their fellows, apparently remote from danger while part of their homeland was held in bondage.

Mathghamhain, more a politician than a warrior, again urged Brian not to turn his back on a hope of peace. Why did he not return home and rebuild his physical strength, as Mathghamhain had done, while peace lasted? Brian, embittered and exhausted, answered his brother with a reproach (8): he would never abandon to 'dark, grim foreigners' the inheritance of his father and grandfather, an inheritance his ancestors had known how to defend. It is unfortuante that we have no genuine account of that meeting between brothers, but we can visualise the haggard countenance of Brian, eyes flashing below the long forehead and above the prominent nose — features said to have been inherited by his descendants — as he railed against Mathghamhain and those who, he thought, had taken an easy route. And while the 'inheritance of his ancestors' was perhaps not all that ancient a patrimony, and his father, Cinnéide, and brothers Donn Cuan and Echthighearn, had died in wars against the Eoghanachta and Uí Néill, rather than the Land Leapers, there was no doubt that the princes of the Dál gCais had defended it bravely. Mathghamhain might well have said:

> Alone art thou, Brian of Banba,
> Thy warfare was not without valour,
> But where hast thou left thy followers?

but Brian could answer:

> I have left them with the foreigners,
> After being cut down, O Mathghamhain:
> In hardship they followed me over every plain,
> Not like as thy people. (9)

Whatever he said, Brian won the day. Either his taunts, or his reasoning, at first impressed, then convinced, Mathghamhain. Brian's eighteen months of living 'in the wild huts of the desert, on the hard, knotty wet roots' paid off, and the king decided to call a meeting of the Dalcassian chieftains, agreeing to leave the ultimate decision to them. The call for war came with 'the voice of hundreds, as the voice of one man' from those chieftains and the spark of vengeance was fanned into a mighty fire throughout Munster. At least, so we are led to believe by pro-Dalcassian scribes and chroniclers. Those who, down the centuries, have taken the Eoghanacht point of view, and have disregarded the rise to power of the

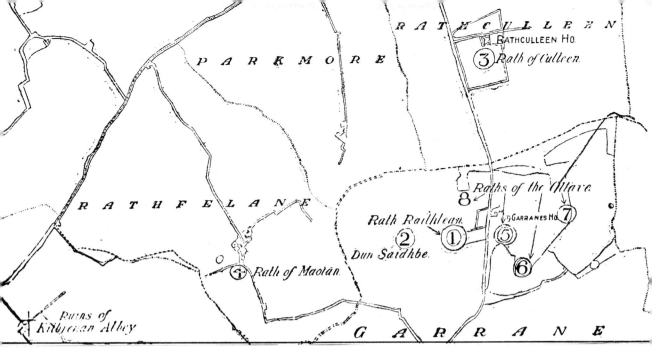

Plan of Ráth Raithleann

Dál gCais, would have us believe that Mathghamhain, far from gathering an army to liberate Thomond from the Danes, was more concerned with gaining the throne of Munster. *Cogadh Gaedhel re Gallaibh* records 'great plunders and ravages were made by Mathghamhain throughout Munster' in what appears to have been a campaign to weaken, stage by stage, individual septs of the Eoghanachta so that, when the time came for him to take the throne, Mathghamhain would face no united opposition from them.

Yet, would there have been united opposition? One writer, of Eoghanacht stock and no great admirer of Mathghamhain (10), tells us that in 959, on the death of King Fear Gráidh of Munster, the vacant throne was claimed by Maolmhuadh, 'lord of Desmond', and head of the Cinéal Aodha branch of the Eoghanacht Uí Eachach of West Cork — the late king having belonged to the Cinéal Laoghaire branch. Maolmhuadh's historic capital was Ráth Raithleann in the present barony of Kinelmeky, Co Cork, and about seven miles north of Bandon. The *Four Masters* has been used as proof, by certain writers, that he gained the throne without opposition; this, because of an entry that suggests 'the hostages of Munster' were in his possession, and housed in his residential fort of Sciath an Eigis which was probably adjacent to Ráth Rathlainn. This would imply, under the Brehon laws, that he was king of Munster,

having been acknowledged as such by the other chieftains of the kingdom, who sent hostages to him as proof of their loyalty.

But nowhere do the *Four Masters* actually term him 'king of Munster', and if there was no opposition from the Eoghanachta, this was probably due less to hostages than to the fact that they were still not only suffering from the long-term effects of the battle of Bealach Mughna half a century before, but from a marked inability to elect a strong central leader. Like the Uí Néill, internal jealousies prevented the rise of a notable king in the Eoghanachta. And while Mathghamhain may have been ambitious for personal glory, it is also reasonable to assume that he and Brian saw that the only way to present a united front against the Danes was for the Dál gCais to rule Munster, the Eoghanachta, the *ancien regime*, being unable to do so because of this internal dissension.

Maolmhuadh, one imagines, was the strong man of the Eoghanacht Uí Eachach, and the 'hostages of Munster' may have been nothing more than a grandiose term for hostages of his immediate vassals. Indeed, a glance at the actual *Four Masters* entry shows that it is capable of a double meaning. It refers to a sorté into Maolmhuadh's territory by Math-ghamhain in 967 — doubtless during his campaign to weaken chieftains whose animosity to the Dál gCais was well-known. It reads: 'An army was led by Mathghamhain to Sciath an Eigis; and he carried off the hostages of Munster with him to his house . . .' Whatever this passage suggests to other writers, it does not seem sufficient proof to me that the hostages were actually at Sciath an Eigis, or that they were held by Maolmhuadh as 'king of Munster'.

Whether Maolmhuadh was really proclaimed king by the Eoghan-achta, or whether he assumed the title himself is unimportant. What does matter is that he saw the successes of the Dál gCais not as heralding the end of Danish power, but as a threat to his own unstable position and to the ancient prescriptive rights of the Eoghanachta in the southern kingdom. Had he joined forces with Mathghamhain, Danish power could have been ended as far as Munster was concerned; the southern Irish kingdom could have been another Wessex, a bastion of native interests against the foreigners. There was no such union. The melancholy lament of a nameless annalist, made a century earlier, still rang true:

> Alas indeed, as we say often, it is a pity for the Irish that they have the bad habit of fighting among themselves, and that they do not rise altogether against the Norwegians . . . (11)

Entrance to Ráth Raithleann top
and during the 1937 excavations

And yet not every Irish chieftain was a petty despot whose self-interest and personal ambition were placed above the good of his particular area of the country. The driving force behind Brian and, despite what the pro-Eoghanacht writers say, I think behind Mathghamhain too, was a desire to end Danish power in Munster. That success would mean a rise to power by the Dalcassians was inevitable and, under the circumstances, can hardly be abhorred. The Dalcassians managed to achieve a greater unity than the Eoghanachta — and in a short space of time.

As we know already, Irish leaders were not averse to canvassing for help among the Danes. In due course, Brian himself was to use a Danish contingent, probably mercenaries, among his army, so that we can believe that Maolmhuadh and Donnabhán, king of Uí Fhidhghinte, entered into negotiations with the Danes of Limerick in an attempt to reduce Dalcassian influence. It may have been news of such negotiations that caused Mathghamhain and Brian to attack Limerick itself. That it took them four years to raise a sufficiently powerful force to do so, indicates how lacking they were in men of suitable age; but at least the Danes were faced with the same problem. Ivar, king of Limerick, summoned help from other Danish communities in Ireland, and Limerick was restocked to withstand a seige under the command of Bearnard Muiris, called a 'military governor' by some sources, but more likely a well-tried veteran.

The attack came in 968, Brian and Mathghamhain sending their troops in detached parties to worry the Danes and joining forces again at Solchóid, present-day Solohead, four miles north of what today is Tipperary town, where the sallow, or shrubby, low-growing willow trees which gave the place its name, provided cover for the Irish. The Danes, lacking restraint — inevitably, perhaps, after four years behind the walls of Limerick — attacked first, charging the hill on which Mathghamhain had stationed his men. The battle lasted from sunrise to mid-day, the Danes throwing rank after rank into the wood of shrubby willows, wherein the Irish *thuagh chatha* made short work of unarmoured limbs and the natural growth served to hamper Danish retreat.

At noon the Danish army turned and fled in disorder, pursued by Brian who slaughtered without mercy — and indeed, what mercy could the Danes expect? Feelings fired during eighteen months of hunger and frustration in Clare had not been dampened during the intervening years, and while the 'two thousand Danes' who died during the retreat were more likely two hundred, victory for the Dalcassians was complete. Pursuit continued all afternoon, the vanquished fleeing 'to the ditches and the valleys and to the solitude of the great sweet flowery plain' (12) beyond Solohead. Brian and Mathghamhain chased them until dark and then slowed down to a night-time march, bringing themselves, at daybreak, to Limerick. The city, in confusion, had not expected an attack so soon, and no resistance was offered.

The Irish cut down every Dane they met and sacked the town, burning every building from Ivar's palace to the lowest hovel. The spoil that fell to them was considerable, for Limerick was a wealthy commercial centre. 'Beautiful and foreign saddles; jewels, silver and gold and silks . . . soft, youthful girls, blooming well-clad women and active, well-formed boys' fell into Dalcassian hands. Ivar himself escaped, but anyone else who was fit for war was put to death on the hill on Saingel — present-day Singland in the city — above the smoking ruins. Those suitable for enslavement were carried away.

Silver coins found at Mungret, Co Limerick

Whether Maolmhuadh and Donnabhán were present at Solchóid remains a point of debate. Eoghanacht eulogists, notably Canon O'Mahony, maintain that the absence of their names in the Dalcassian chronicles celebrating the rout is evidence that they stood aloof from the encounter — and that their subsequent involvement in the death of Mathghamhain was caused by a desire 'for revenge for unprovoked injuries' — in other words, Mathghamhain's rise to power, not because they had been chastised for supporting Ivar. Yet we cannot believe that they were the innocent victims of Dalcassian oppression, as O'Mahony suggests. As we shall see, there is evidence to show, or at least to suggest in the strongest terms, that jealousy of Mathghamhain's defeat of the Danes (which, in earlier days, the Eoghanachta might have accomplished) motivated subsequent events.

For the moment, however, Maolmhuadh was unable to oppose Mathghamhain's claims to the throne of Munster. Mathghamhain was inaugurated at Cashel about 970 (13) and, to secure his position, he followed the tradition of taking hostages from vassals, even Maolmhuadh and Donnabhán giving up members of their families. For the next six years Munster enjoyed relative peace and prosperity and, at Grianán Lachtna or Kincora, Brian had time to devote himself to his family: Mór, if she lived, and the sons, Murchadh, now aged about five, Conchobhar and Flann. The home fires would blaze as they never blazed before, and the old *seanchaithe* would seem young again as they spoke the praises of Mathghamhain and Brian, sons of Cinnéide; as they recounted the adventures of the prince in the wilderness and the tale of how the place of sallows ran red with Danish blood.

There would be hunting expeditions into the forests of Munster and Brian would ride with Mathghamhain as the king made his customary ceremonial visits to tributaries in the multitude of *tuatha*. Brian, now twenty-seven or twenty-eight, was in the bloom of manhood, well-built — else how could he have withstood the rigours of the guerilla campaign in Clare? — with the brown, silky hair of the Munsterman flowing down to his shoulders or tied back with a chaplet of gold or bronze. The years of anxiety would probably have brought grey prematurely to those locks, but it doubtless added a distinguishing feature to the aspect of a man who was shortly to become the most powerful figure in Ireland. To those around him, Brian symbolised all that was noble and worthy of emulation in Celtic history, and his appearance at camp fire or in the council hall of his brother would mean an instant pause in the debate as the assembly turned their eyes appreciatively upon him.

The position occupied in Dalcassian society by Brian is uncertain. There is no record of his election as *tánaiste*, or heir-designate to Mathghamhain, and while the priestly brother, Marcán, may have been passed over, there were, doubtless, cousins with rights of seniority. The dead *tánaiste*, Donn Cuan, had left one son at least, as we shall see later; and while he was certainly junior to Brian in age, there must have been older members of the family, descendants of Lorcán, entitled to the throne after Mathghamhain.

Any thoughts of succession were interrupted, however. Ivar, ex-king of Limerick, had fled after the sack of his city to the island retreat of Inis Cathaigh, years before the home of King Flaithbheartach, where he sought the sanctuary established generations earlier by St Seanán. Mathghamhain had respected this immunity on condition the Dane restricted his activities to commerce, but the position of a petty merchant soon began to rankle with the old warrior. Maolmhuadh and Donnabhán, who had as much to lose from the rise of the Dalcassians as he had, retained their own subordinate thrones while Limerick was lost; yet they were vassals of a Dalcassian, and it was probably on this point that Ivar exerted cunning and pressure, taunting Maolmhuadh with his subjugation to a man whose family had only recently risen from obscurity.

O'Mahony, and other supporters of the Eoghanachta, would have us understand otherwise, of course. Any linking of Ivar's name to Maolmhuadh was, in his view, a perversion of the truth; and yet it would be perfectly natural: a cunning old Viking taunting the representative of the Eoghanacht kings of Munster, working on his battered pride and sense of family. Ivar may, of course, have simply sown the seed: it appears to have been cultivated by Donnabhán of Uí Fhidhghinte.

On a day in 976, Donnabhán, apparently on pretext of sorrow for his former ways and of friendship for the future, invited Mathghamhain to a conference or banquet at his palace of Bruree, in what is now Co Limerick. O'Mahony maintains that Mathghamhain, alarmed at a conspiracy formed against him by the Eoghanachta, agreed to negotiate with Donnabhán, stipulating only on the safe conduct of Colam mac Ciaragáin, Bishop of Cork. In addition, he carried in his clothing a relic of St Fionnbharra, apostle of Christianity in Cork and patron of Munster and, confident of immunity from any new misdeed, set off to meet Donnabhán. At once the story breaks down: Mathghamhain would hardly have negotiated, except on neutral ground, and even then accompanied by a strong bodyguard, if he was hoping to persuade Donnabhán to join him against Maolmhuadh and Ivar. But if Donnabhán had pleaded sorrow for his lack of support in the past, and offered the hand of friendship, Mathghamhain, seeing an opportunity for a more lasting peace in Munster, might well have set forth with little more than holy relics as protection.

Whatever the reason, Mathghamhain fell into Donnabhán's clutches. The king of Uí Fhidhghinte made him prisoner and despatched him southwards to Maolmhuadh. O'Mahony refuses to accept that Maolmhuadh, Donnabhán and Ivar had pre-arranged Mathghamhain's assassination, yet why was Mathghamhain, once captured by Donnabhán, allowed to leave Bruree alive? Maolmhuadh is too conveniently close for comfort, a plot is all too obvious. It was Maolmhuadh's pride that had been injured by the Dalcassian ascendancy, it was he who must have the satisfaction of dealing with his supplanter.

Certainly, O'Mahony admits that Donnabhán behaved treacherously in delivering up Mathghamhain to Maolmhuadh; but can we really believe that the sudden appearance of Mathghamhain as a prisoner came as a surprise to the king of Desmond? The pro-Dalcassian *Cogadh Gaedhel re Gallaibh* (14) says that as the party journeyed south it met with an escort sent north by the king of Desmond, probably at Red Gap — Bearna Dhearg — sometimes called Redchair on the mountains of Feara Mhaighe Féine, through which the main Kilmallock to Fermoy road now runs. As dusk fell, Bishop mac Ciaragáin, who according to this version was still with Mathghamhain, had fallen to the rear of the group, where he was joined suddenly by Maolmhuadh himself. Within minutes all was over: Mathghamhain was cut down, and whether or not he tried to prevent desecration of the holy relic by tossing it to a priest, is immaterial. A sword was plunged into his heart, and he fell dead on the road.

Other annalists agree that Maolmhuadh was the man who killed Mathghamhain, and any argument for or against 'treachery' on his part is no more than an attempt at splitting hairs. The king was dead and, for the moment, the Dál gCais must have been so horrified that Maolmhuadh was able to declare himself, once more, king of Munster. Perhaps he hoped that the murder would plunge Munster, Thomond particularly, into sufficient chaos for him to overcome the Dál gCais once and for all. But he underestimated Brian.

As an unidentified chronicler was to write in later years (15), Brian was 'not a stone in the place of an egg, and he was not a wisp in the place of a club; but he was a hero in place of a hero, and he was valour after valour'.

'My heart shall burst within my breast, unless I avenge this great king,' Brian is supposed to have cried when the news reached him. 'They shall forfeit life for this deed, or I shall perish by a violent death'.

Eulogy and melodramatic rhetoric apart, Brian was to be a great leader of the Dál gCais, indeed, had already proved himself a leader during his campaign in Clare. A modern writer has suggested that the guerilla campaign was nothing more than a romantic myth (16), yet admits that Brian had 'established himself as one of the leading dynasts of the Dál gCais' at an early age. Had that sojourn 'in the wild huts of the desert' been mythical, would Brian have achieved so great a following among his people, in an era when leaders were chosen for seniority in age rather than by popular acclaim?

5

Brian, King of Munster

Got revenge for his brothers death.

After the murder of his brother, Brian, now thirty-five years of age,
became king of Thomond, presumably unopposed by any member of his
family who might claim seniority under the tanistric code. With the Dalcassians firmly behind him, his first regal task was to deal with Maolmhuadh, an event only accelerated by Mathghamhain's death, for a
conflict between the Dál gCais and the Eoghanachta was inevitable. The
Dál gCais had become the strongest force in Munster after a chain of
events that had started with the Eoghanacht defeat at Bealach Mughna,
and one could hardly expect them to retire subserviently to Thomond
after Mathghamhain's death when there was an opportunity not only for
revenge but for finally overthrowing the Eoghanacht ascendancy.

The murder brought to a climax the feud between Thomond and
Desmond and paved the way for Brian, now well advanced on the road of
ambition, to increase Dalcassian power. And as much as Canon
O'Mahony and the Eoghanacht eulogists might protest otherwise, it
seems certain that Ivar, the ex-king of Limerick, had some hand in the
events that led to Mathghamhain's death. For Brian's first attack was on
Ivar, still sheltering behind the holy associations of St Seanán on Inis
Cathaigh; and if the Viking had been nothing but an innocent trader, why
did the attack take place? Brian was in no mood to respect a sudden piety
among the Danes. With his kinsmen, the Uí Dhomhnaill of Corca Bhaiscinn (1), he collected a small fleet, doubtless comprising long-boats taken
from the Danes, as well as large corracles, attacked Inis Cathaigh and
annihilated the enemy.

Ivar and two of his sons were among the slain, a third son, Harald,
escaping to Donnabhán who proclaimed him king of Limerick as a figurehead round whom to rally the Danes. Harald's reign was to be brief: by
the end of 977 Brian had entered Donnabhán's territory of Uí
Fhidhghinte, captured his capital at Cathair Chuain and killed both

Harald and Donnabhán, a deed acclaimed by the annalists as 'most praiseworthy'. And with their leaders dead, the Danes offered little resistance. Limerick, which Mathghamhain had allowed them to rebuild as a trading centre, was again plundered, but Brian recognised, even in the midst of vengeance, the need for commercial strongholds, and permitted the Danes to remain in the town on payment of an annual tribute of wine. In later years Danes and Norsemen were to play a prominent role in financing Brian's enlarged kingdom.

Next, Brian turned his attention to Maolmhuadh. Despite pro-Eoghanacht writings, there is no evidence that Maolmhuadh ever occupied the hill of Cashel; indeed, it is likely that the occurence at Red Gap, a violation of sacred safe-conduct, excited a feeling of horror among many chieftains in Munster, much as centuries later in England the supposed murder of the 'princes in the tower' by Richard III, who had been their protector, caused righteous indignation among many of the English nobility of the day. And while few Irishmen would have baulked at raiding a monastery and slaughtering monks in a neighbour's territory, they would surely have regarded what amounted to the desecration of a Munster relic as nothing short of sacrilege.

We are told by the pro-Dalcassian *Coghadh Gaedhel re Gallaibh* that Brian tried to avoid a full-scale war by claiming compensation in the shape of Maolmhuadh himself and offering his son, Murchadh, as Dalcassian champion to meet Maolmhuadh in single combat to decide the issue. It is a romantic story, but can hardly be taken seriously. Brian could not afford, despite the legend, to risk a gathering of the Eoghanachta — he must act at once if Mathghamhain was to be avenged and if the Dalcassians were to take power in Munster. And, as in later years, he did not win his victories by warning his foes in advance of what action he was to take. Time was essential, and a chivalrous pause while the Eoghanachta decided whether or not to risk their future in single combat was a risk Brian could not take. The two armies met at Bealach Leachta, identified today as low meadow land near the junction of the Sullane and Lany rivers, a mile east of Macroom, Co Cork. The *leacht*, or memorial, which gave the battlefield its name, consisted originally of three large stones set on edgewise to one another, the middle one being five feet broad, seven in height and two thick; the other two much smaller. A fourth stone stood about sixty yards south-east of the middle stone — this was larger than the two small stones, but not as large as the seven footer. The largest stone, and one other, still remain.

The leacht or memorial stones at Bealach Leachta

Leachtanna, it should be noted, were numerous in ancient Ireland and were intended to commemorate prehistoric combats — Brian was to meet his adversary on a site probably steeped in legend. The battle may have lasted the whole day (2), and 'large quantities' of human and animal bones excavated on the site in the last century suggest the ferocity of the encounter. Whether Murchadh, a youth of seventeen, was given the honour of tracking down his uncle's killer, as some annalists suggest, need not concern us; Maolmhuadh was slain, either in the battle or in the retreat, and for the immediate future Eoghanacht power in Munster was destroyed (3).

The battle of Bealach Leachta was a turning point not only in Brian's career but in Irish history. No longer would there be the need for Dalcassian warriors to lurk in the wilds of Clare; the Danes, had they contemplated renewed incursions into Munster, would have had second thoughts. Not only was Limerick sacked, but the Eoghanacht king, with whom they might have made a pact against the Dalcassians, was dead. Brian at once declared himself king of Munster and, to secure a more personal hold on the house of Maolmhuadh, arranged a marriage between his late enemy's son, Cian, and his own daughter, Sadhbh. In such a union we may begin to understand how a king in ancient Ireland, be he *Ardrí* or ruler of a kingdom such as Munster, attempted to hold his king-

97

ship without a standing army. It was not simply by taking hostages, a tradition we have already examined, but by diplomacy such as the marriage of sons and daughters. A successful king must be a successful diplomat — the Uí Néill were not always so, but Brian achieved as much by negotiation and alliance as by war.

Certainly the marriage of Cian to Sadhbh was a success, at least in Brian's lifetime. Cian was the antithesis of his father, being commemorated by Dalcassians and Eoghanachta as:

Cian of the golden cups,
Whose store outlasted his life;
Who never drove anyone from his house,
And who was not driven from God's house.

In other words, Cian, whom Brian recognised as Maolmhuadh's successor as king of Desmond, was politician enough to avoid risking the enmity of his new father-in-law, and was to prove a useful ally until the end of Brian's life.

As king of Munster, by acclaim and military success, Brian turned in triumph to Cashel for his coronation. It is not difficult to visualise the procession to that venerable seat of monarchy, or the passage of Brian through the jubilant ranks of the Dalcassians. In silence would be heard the Brehonic recital of the laws of the kingdom, and Brian responded, swearing faithfully to observe both laws and customs and to rule with justice. An official of the court approached him and handed him a white wand, signifying his authority as king and the purity and justice of his future decisions; and putting aside his sword and taking the wand in his hand, Brian turned thrice round to view his dominion and, in the manner of the king supposedly baptised by St Patrick, to pay tribute to the Holy Trinity (4).

Ceannfhada, who seems to have been the Dalcassian replacement of the Eoghanacht abbot or bishop of Emly, placed the royal diadem on Brian's head, and the nobles of Munster each placed their hands between those of their new sovereign to signify obedience. Then was it announced that Brian, son of Cinnéide, son of Lorcán, son of all those other ancestors, mythical or otherwise, was king of Munster.

No annalist, contemporary or in the future, mentioned the presence of a queen at Cashel, although by the time of his coronation Brian had probably married for a second time, his bride being Eachraidh, daughter of Cearbhall, son of Oilill Fionn, ruler of Uí Aodha Odhbha, a Meathain *tuath*. She, in course of time, was to bear her husband at least two sons, Tadhg, who was to be a king after Brian, and Domhnall, who was to die before him; and a daughter. But, like Mór, she is completely faceless.

It has been suggested (5) that the marriage with Eachraidh did not take place until the last decade of the century, and then as a political manoeuvre aimed at Brian's greatest adversary, Maoil-Seachlainn II, the *Ardrí* in whose home territory Eachraidh's father had been a subordinate king. It is a feasible suggestion, but the same source argues that Brian's second wife, taken about the time of his coronation at Cashel, was the notorious Gormfhlaith. As I will attempt to show in due course, the Gormfhlaith affair has been exaggerated in the fashion of the most shamelessly inventive *seanchaithe*, while it seems certain that only in 984 did she become wife of Maoil-Seachlainn, whose repudiation made her available to Brian.

It is more likely that Eachraidh was the means by which Brian, looking for allies outside Munster, formed a bond with vassals of the mighty Uí Néill as an early, and subtle, infiltration of their territories.

Brian hardly regarded his coronation as security for the future. He had seen where a certain level of self-assurance had led his brother, Mathghamhain, and he was now determined to turn the throne of Munster into an unbreakable force. He was not long in gaining an opportunity to show his strength, for in 979, within months of his elevation at Cashel, the first and most deadly threat to his hold on the kingdom materialised.

The Danes of Waterford, having assisted Ivar in his early struggles with Mathghamhain and Brian, had for almost a decade remained entrenched in their eastern stronghold, viewing Brian's climb to power with alarm, but resisting any move that might end in a repetition, for them, of the Limerick disaster. At length, however, they discovered an ally among the native Irish in the person of Ua Faoláin, king of Déise Mumhan (the Decies), a tributary of Munster, who resented the ascendancy of the Dalcassians no less virulently than his late neighbour, Maolmhuadh. And when Domhnall, king of Leinster, who regarded any strong king in Munster as a threat to his own independence, sided with Ua Faoláin and the Danes, the odds against Brian were formidable. Through Leinster, too, was a safe passage for the Norsemen of Dublin, if they decided to make inroads upon Munster; and while Dublin did not enter into the struggle, the ravages of Ua Faoláin (6) as he began his march were more than reminiscent of the days of the Land Leapers.

By a series of forced marches, Brian brought his army, augmented by the troops of Cian of Desmond, to the rear of Ua Faoláin's forces, routing them. The vanquished fell back on Waterford, where a final and hopeless stand was made. Brian entered the town, put to the sword any who were capable of resistance, and after sacking the fortress marched northwards to deal with Domhnall of Leinster.

It will be remembered* that in the third century a tribute known as Eidirsceol had been imposed on Leinster as punishment for the murder of a prince of Munster. Whether it had as little basis in fact as the will of Oilill Ólum or not, it had been used by several of the more powerful kings of Munster in an attempt to subdue the eastern kingdom, not least by Cormac mac Cuileannáin in 906. His attempt, of course, had been forestalled by the then *Ardrí*.

But Brian now decided that the time was ripe to revive the tribute, and demanded from Domhnall three hundred gold-handled swords, three hundred cows with brass yokes, three hundred steeds and three hundred cloaks, as well as the allegiance of Leinster to himself as king of Leath Mogha. If we are to believe the account of his demand, Brian had doubled the number of cows awarded under the original Eidirsceol (7), but significantly omitted to claim another part of it — the hand of the king of Leinster's daughter. That this omission was probably deliberate, and that it was later to be rectified, we shall see presently.

The resurrection of Leath Mogha as a territorial claim reflects Brian's mounting ambition. Traditionally, it was a sovereignty first claimed by Eoghan Mór, son of Oilill Ólum; historically, it was claimed by a succession of kings of Munster and was strongly resisted by the kings of Leinster, who had no desire to become tributaries to Munster. To the *flatha* and *airigh* of Leinster the renewal of Eidirsceol alone would have been sufficient to spur them into arms — for even under Brehonic law, whereby murder was punished by the imposition of a fine of cattle, the number varying according to the rank of the victim, it would have seemed that they had long ago paid for their errors. In Brian's revival — a successful revival — of Eidirsceol, it is easy to suggest that personal ambition triumphed over good sense, and that the new king of Munster, having vanquished internal rivals, must now enlarge his possessions on the pretext of ancient and dubious legend. For generations his policy over Leath Mogha had given his critics the opportunity to decry him as a usurper and petty war-lord. Why did he not simply take the usual hostages from Domhnall, as guarantee of good behaviour in the future, and return to Cashel?.

Vide Chapter One, page 43.

Brian was ambitious. At times he was capable of cruelty that savoured more of Maolmhuadh or the Danes than of the avenger of Thomond. But cruelty, seen, as all acts in history should be seen, in the context of its time, becomes tempered with the customs of that time; while ambition must be examined in both a personal and a national context. If Brian was ambitious only to secure peace in Munster and safeguard against Danish resurgence, it would seem more politic to seek the friendship of Leinster, a Lagenian princess for one of his sons, rather than claim hegemony over a fiercely independent people. He had forged a bond with the hereditary enemies of his family in Desmond by marrying his daughter to their king; and in Cian's sons the blood of the Dál gCais would run as swiftly as that of the Eoghanachta, the throne in time being occupied by Brian's descendants. Through similar unions family influence could be extended, and there seemed no reason why the throne of Munster could not be controlled indefinitely by the Dalcassians, with either a king of their own stock at Cashel, or an Eoghanacht prince, closely related to them, under their supervision. Thus family ambition might be achieved, but national ambition was a different matter. Did Brian think that, as king of Leath Mogha in more than name, he could rule Ireland? Did he, at this stage, begin to think of Tara? If he was formulating a plan to increase the Dalcassian ascendancy he could do no worse than the Uí Néill, who had claimed to rule Leath Cuinn for six centuries.

Brian could hardly fail to notice, and to be impressed by, recent events in England. Nearly half a century before his birth, the Saxons had mourned Alfred the Great, whose reign had seen the first real steps towards a consolidation of the monarchy, at least in the southern half of the country. By the time when Brian had persuaded Mathghamhain that guerilla warfare was preferable to uneasy peace, Edmund of Wessex had conquered Mercia and the five boroughs of the northern Danelaw, and under Edgar an unparalleled era of peace and prosperity had been brought to England as a whole.

The accession, in 978, of the twelve-year-old Ethelred Unraed, or the Redeless, was to herald a new wave of Viking invasion under Olaf Trygvaeson, later king of Norway, and the humiliating payment of Danegeld levied on Ethelred's unhappy subjects. Subsequent events, inspired by Ethelred's cowardly and spiritless nature (8), were to lead, in Brian's lifetime, to Danish control of England and its eventual erection, under Cnut, into the centre of a powerful Danish empire.

But Ethelred's predecessors had shown Brian that a strong, central

Dún na Sciath, seat of the southern Uí Néill

monarchy, not merely a collection of jealous states beneath a figurehead king, was possible. Ethelred had shown him the effects of weakness. And while Brian never made any attempt to abolish the sovereignty of the other thrones in Ireland, in the way that Sussex, Kent, Mercia and the rest of the heptarchy was dissolved and moulded into the English nation by Wessex, his intelligence told him that a tighter federation than had existed under the Uí Néill was both desirable and attainable. This was national ambition, and because Brian was a Dalcassian it became synonymous with family ambition.

In 979 Domhnall, son of Muircheartach, was still *Ardrí*, and Brian was surely tempted with the idea of camping before Domhnall's gates at Armagh or at Dún na Sciath, the southern Uí Néill seat near present-day Mullingar, or even on the ceremonial hill of Tara, and demanding his abdication by a show of force. Yet, such a violent step, virtually unprecedented in Irish history, could not have been made without confronting the Uí Néill *en bloc* (or so it would appear), and Munster would have been left vulnerable. Perhaps, at this stage, Brian was content to wait until Domhnall's death or retirement behind monastic walls provided an opportunity to place himself forward as a contender for high kingship. As ruler of a substantial kingdom he had the right to do so, and he had the power of Munster with which to back his claim. So far everything he had achieved had been won legally. He had succeeded Mathghamhain either under Brehon law or through overwhelming popularity with the Dál gCais; his succession in Munster could be seen as a natural sequel to the claims of his forebears; and it is unlikely that he would jeopardise his greater ambitions at a crucial hour by unseating the *Ardrí* with force.

As it happened, he had no choice. At the end of 979 Domhnall died after a reign of twenty-four years 'in the victory of penance', within the hallowed walls of Armagh that he had been denied for most of his life. The grandson of Niall Glúndubh, who as *Ardrí* had died fighting the invaders at Islandbridge in 915, poor Domhnall occupies a shadowy place in history. He had come to the throne because he was of the Uí Néill, and had maintained a pretence of monarchy he was far from enjoying. The annalists at least were kind to him (9), recalling him for posterity as the 'Monarch of Ireland who bestowed horses ... a worthier man on the surface of earth was never born ...'

The Uí Néill, who had no wish to see their own tradition or prestige ended, immediately elected as *Ardrí* Maoil-Seachlainn, to be known as Maoil-Seachlainn Mór, 'the Great', a member of the ruling house of Aileach, or the northern Uí Néill, which alternated with Meath in furnishing *Ardrí* material. As if to double his claim on Tara, Maoil-Seachlainn had some years earlier inherited the southern throne and was, therefore, representative of both lines of the Uí Néill, a not insignificant position. He was but a few years junior to Brian — the *Annals of Ulster* tells us he was born in 948 — and he was certainly the one man in contemporary Ireland to equal the recently obscure Dalcassian.

Brian's activities in Leinster were not, in themselves, viewed by Maoil-Seachlainn with any great misgivings. He may even have welcomed the efforts of another king in subduing rebellious elements and uniting boundaries against Norse advance from Dublin. He may hardly have heard of Brian until the invasion of Leinster, for Scandinavian ravages of Meath had been too frequent for its king to pay undue attention to guerilla tactics in Clare or to Dalcassian and Eoghanacht squabbling. The sack of Limerick and, later, that of Waterford was cheering news, particularly as Maoil-Seachlainn, the festivities for his coronation hardly finished, had to contend with long-awaited movements from within the walls of Dublin.

Sixty-five years earlier, Reginald, successor of Olaf the White and grandson of Ivar, the first Norse king of Dublin, had recaptured the city from the Irish and had reigned there until his death in 921. He was succeeded by his son, Godfrey, who (10) immediately commenced hostilities against the Irish before crossing to England in an attempt to recover Northumbria, annexed by Athelstan of Wessex in 926. Within six months he had returned to Dublin and, for the rest of his life — which ended, according to the annalists, with a 'filthy and ill-favoured death' in 932 — engaged in perpetual warfare with both Irish and Danes, whose mercantile growth he saw as a threat to his own city-state.

By 980 Dublin was ruled by the elderly Olaf Cuarán, 'of the sandals', who had been in the throne for nearly forty years and who was no less a threat to his neighbours than Godfrey, although he made the most determined efforts of any of his family to form marital alliances with native dynasties. One of his daughters, Radnalt, had married Conghal-ach, *Ardrí* before Domhnall. In his old age, as already mentioned, Olaf himself took as a final wife Gormfhlaith, daughter of Murchadh, Lord of Nás (Naas), a member of the ruling dynasty in Leinster, by whom he had a son, Sitric. Mother and son were to become leading, and sinister, figures in Brian's career.

After a lifetime made interesting by plundering and parleying Olaf made a fatal mistake. Summoning auxiliaries from the Norse-ruled Scottish isles and from the Isle of Man in 980, he prepared to attack Meath, but reckoned without the strength of the new high king. Domhnall would have been easy prey — indeed in 977 Olaf had slain two of the late *Ardrí*'s sons, presumably in a skirmish — but Maoil-Seach-lainn met the invaders at Tara and vanquished them. Another Reginald, Olaf's heir, was killed and the old king took himself on pilgrimage to Iona, the first Scandinavian prince to do so (11), dying there in the same year 'after penance and a good life', as the *Four Masters*, sometimes gracious to a foe, records.

Despite the tribute, Olaf had been far from lenient to those beneath him, and although the annalists decided that his conversion was worthy of praise, Dublin had acquired a name synonymous in history with Babylon as a place of captives. Maoil-Seachlainn followed up his victory with a seige of Dublin, which surrendered after three days and nights. As he entered the gates, the *Ardrí* decreed that 'as many of the Irish nation as lived in servitude and bondage in the territory of the foreigners should presently pass over without ransom and live freely in their wonted manner in peace and happiness'. Peace and happiness were relative qualities in Ireland inside or outside Dublin, but among those 'in servitude' was Olaf's neighbour, Domhnall of Leinster, who had either

Maigh Adhair, inauguration place of the kings of Thomond

fled to Dublin after Brian's invasion of his kingdom — his kinswoman was Olaf's wife — or had been taken hostage by Olaf to ensure his obedience.

No sooner was Domhnall peacefully and happily restored to his patrimony than he showed his colours, allying himself with the new ruler of Dublin, Sitric, whom Maoil-Seachlainn had allowed to retain the throne on payment of the usual high tribute. The two kings took arms against the *Ardrí*, who marched into Leinster in 983.

Although the march was intended primarily to put down the new confederacy, Maoil-Seachlainn was to use it as an opportunity of reminding southern Ireland in general that there was but one senior monarch in the island. Brian might have contained the Danes of Limerick and Waterford, but to the *Ardrí* a threat was posed by his increasing power, a threat now seen to be as great as that presented to earlier high kings by Feidhlimidh mac Criomhthainn and Cormac mac Cuileannáin.

Brian, watching the movements of the king of Leinster, incredulous that Maoil-Seachlainn would attack him, was for the first time in his life caught off guard. Maoil-Seachlainn wheeled suddenly across Munster into Thomond and uprooted the royal tree of Maigh Adhair (12). The tree, which stood in what became the demesne of Moyare, about half way between Tulla and Quin, Co Clare, was to the Dál gCais what the Stone of

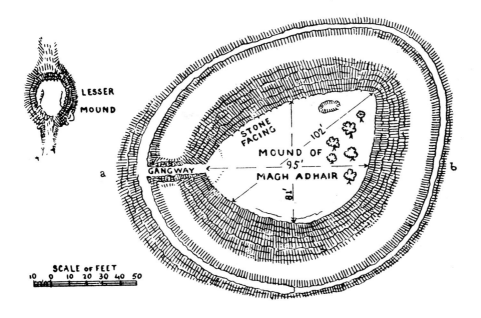

Plan of the mounds at Maigh Adhair

Scone became to their Scottish kinsmen and, afterwards, to the English. Under its venerable branches the kings of Thomond had been inaugurated and Maoil-Seachlainn's act was the greatest insult he could offer to Brian and his people. Perhaps into it we can read a reminder — Maoil-Seachlainn may have hoped it to be a timely one — that Brian's ancestors owed the throne of Thomond to Uí Néill patronage.

Like Maolmhuadh of Desmond before him, Maoil-Seachlainn underestimated Brian, for as quickly as he had entered Thomond he left it, marching back into Leinster with his half-brother, Glúiniarainn of the Iron Knee — so called, presumably, from his protective mail, then a novelty — and soundly trounced Domhnall of Leinster and his allies. 'All Lynster was preyed and destroyed' by the army, and in 984 Domhnall was killed in a squabble with the Uí Chinsealaigh, the rival, southern, dynasty of the province. The throne passed to his son, Donnchadh, who, like the *Ardrí* Domhnall, was an extraordinarily poor choice for king in so unsettled a time. He was already facing problems within his own family, notably from Maol Mórdha, Lord of Naas, whose father, Murchadh, had been killed by Donnchadh's father. It is likely that Maol Mórdha whose sister, Gormfhlaith, was now queen mother of Dublin, was scheming to win the throne of Leinster for himself.

Before long he was to gain it, but in the meantime found himself brother-in-law to Maoil-Seachlainn, for the *Ardrí* consolidated his position by taking Gormfhlaith as his wife, thus becoming step-father of the, potentially, most influential foreigner in Ireland and connecting himself to a kingdom whose vassalage was claimed by Brian.

Brian saw how quickly the situation could develop into a severe obstacle for his own plans, and how equally quickly he must act to reverse the scales of balance. Following Danish tactics, he collected a fleet of long-boats and sailed up the Shannon, placing the country on either side under contribution. He next marched boldly into Meath and, according to the chroniclers, laid it waste. The insult at Maigh Adhair, at least, might be avenged.

As Alexander the Great remarked, the world cannot be ruled by two suns, nor can it contain two empires of the greatest magnitude without disturbing the peace of other nations; and the peace of Ireland was certainly threatened, not only by the usual causes but by these two rising suns, the king of Munster and the *Ardrí*. Now that a strong high king had emerged from the Uí Néill ranks, and now that Munster had produced a champion to break Danish power, was fate to be so cruel as to return the island to the conditions in which the Land Leapers, to their advantage, had first discovered it?.

One of the curiosities of Irish history is the length of time that invariably elapsed between events of magnitude. We have already found evidence of this in, for example, the inordinately long time it took for the Dalcassians to challenge the monopoly of the Eoghanachta; also, on a smaller scale, in the four-year space between Brian's return from his guerilla campaigns in Clare and the sack of Limerick. Now, with Brian and Maoil-Seachlainn facing each other, as it were, across the chess-board of Leinster, no less than fifteen years were to elapse before they joined forces in an offensive against those whom they both regarded as the common foe.

Why did it take so long, and does it not suggest that neither king was willing to put Ireland, or his own concept of Ireland, before purely personal ambition? The first part of the question can certainly be answered as being partly due to geographical conditions and partly to population, or lack of it. Ireland, in the tenth century, was a land of vast uncharted forests, bisected by bog-filled valleys; a topography that was to cause problems for Elizabethan generals six centuries later. When battles were fought, they took place, as a rule, upon open ground, where opposing forces had purposely marched. So far as Brian was concerned, the most suitable battleground, the plains of Maoil-Seachlainn's homeland of Meath, was convenient only for an occasional surprise attack or hosting when its owner was occupied elsewhere. If continual warfare had taken place, with pitched battles fought until one king was the undoubted victor, there would have been few subjects left for him to rule. As late as 1641, the estimated population of Ireland was about a million and a half — in Brian's day it would have been very much smaller, despite the annalists' enthusiastically long casualty lists. If the slaughtered thousands in the *Four Masters*, for instance, were added up over two generations of battles, the population would have nearly been extinguished.

Genuine casualties in any great number would mean that one or both sides must return home, the survivors to heal their wounds and to produce a new generation of warriors. Since Brian's campaign in Clare had ended and since the accession of Maoil-Seachlainn this new generation had been growing up. Of age at seventeen, their deaths would be a serious setback to any army.

Continuous warfare would have also proved difficult and expensive because of the weather. In the wars of the sixteenth and seventeenth centuries, the 'eternal damp' was a problem for the English troops in Ireland, and during the seige of Kinsale in the winter of 1601, the English lord deputy, Mountjoy, constantly wore three sets of clothes and sat before a turf fire in a hut made of peat, with a hole in the roof to let out the smoke. The English, of course, were not used to such conditions in their own country, and while it was largely the Irish soldiers in Mountjoy's army who survived and actually won the battle, they would have had better protection against the climate than their ancestors of Brian's day. Even the Norse and Danes, accustomed to severe winters in Scandinavia, retreated into their strongholds for the winter (13), and war was in most years a seasonal occupation.

Also, as much as either king might desire supremacy over the other, their kingdoms were providing urgent domestic and civil problems. Both men knew that before the final confrontation Ireland, north and south, must be prosperous enough to withstand it — England had taught them this lesson since the accession of Ethelred the Unready. Ambition, if it was to be successful, must be tempered carefully until one side was strong enough to press its claim, or until a flaw in the opposing ranks appeared. That the two did not rush at each other's throats, regardless of lack of troops or of the consequences to the country, shows that burning ambition of the purely personal type was not involved.

One potential flaw, which provided common ground for the fears of Brian and Maoil-Seachlainn, was the kingdom of Leinster. It was an eternal problem for any man hoping to rule the whole of Ireland, actually or officially; and invade and lay waste to it as they might, they were unable to quench the spirit of the Leinstermen. In later years Leinster was to gain a wholly undeserved reputation for treachery, and a future king, Diarmaid mac Murchadha, was to be vilified for generations as the man who invited the ultimate in Land Leapers to Irish shores. But, as a modern writer (14) has shown, Diarmaid was not the monster history has portrayed him to be, nor did Leinster of 1169 regard itself any more a part of an Irish 'nation' than it did in Brian's time.

Unlike the rulers of the other major kingdoms, the king of Leinster who, since 738, had come from the northern dynasty of Uí Dhúnlaing (15), was satisfied with provincial authority. Like the Uí Néill, the Uí Dhúnlaing regarded the Dál gCais as upstarts, interlopers in the serious business of monarchy; and with ancestral claims on Tara, they also regarded the Uí Néill as usurpers of part of their kingdom. If Maoil-Seachlainn's claims upon them were gall, Brian's were wormwood.

Leinster, the Danes and the shortage of manpower consorted to ensure that the two most able leaders in Ireland were at loggerheads for fifteen years. It was indeed like a game of chess, both sides moving backwards, forwards and sideways across the countryside, the problems already listed providing an occasional situation of stalemate. In an attempt to gain the upper hand both kings ravaged Connacht, hitherto a relatively peaceful and remote kingdom; and at Lough Ree, in 988, Brian, having sailed up the Shannon with his growing fleet, met the Conatians who, not unnaturally, had taken to arms to preserve their dignity and their territory. There is also evidence to suppose that Brian did not merely adopt the methods of fighting of his Danish foes. The *Four Masters* records, almost ominously for them, that 'the men of Munster came in hosts upon Lough Ree and the foreigners of Port Lairge. The Connacht men assembled to oppose them, and a battle was fought between them ...' The 'foreigners' may, of course, have been a detrimental term employed by a pro-Connacht scribe. But Port Lairge was — is — Waterford, and a foreigner from that part of the country could mean only one thing. As we shall see, Brian was to make two dynastic alliances with that other eastern city-state, Dublin, and he knew well the importance of all the Viking settlements as trading centres. Waterford, having seen their kinsmen beaten in Limerick fifteen years before, had themselves fallen to Brian after allying themselves with the kings of Leinster and the Decies; and they cannot have been oblivious to the benefits of now supporting a king whose star was, it seemed, in the ascendant. Brian himself saw the considerable benefits to his economy and, it seems, to his army, in fostering relations with the Danish states.

The battle at Lough Ree was a resounding victory for Brian in more sense than one. Muirgheas, *tánaiste* of Connacht, was killed, as was Dúnlaing, tánaiste of Desmond — this last a particularly fortuitous occurrence for the Dalcassians, as it brought Cian's sons, Brian's grandsons, nearer the throne.

It would be tempting to suggest that it was at this time that Gormfhlaith, queen mother of Dublin and wife of the *Ardrí*, saw a chance of advancing her own career and perhaps that of her son, Sitric, king of Dublin. There is no evidence that the 'foreigners' included a contingent from Dublin, but a hint of danger reached Maoil-Seachlainn from that quarter, and in 989 he marched on the city, laying it seige 'for the space of twenty nights, so that they drank no water during this time but the brine', which says little for the provision of wells in Dublin. Sitric capitulated, recognised his stepfather as overlord, and promised to pay an ounce of gold for 'every garden' in the city, payment to be made annually on Christmas night. If Gormfhlaith had left Dublin before the seige we know not, for she was yet of little interest to the annalists (16).

Twice within the next five years — somewhere in Meath in 992 and at Aonach Téide in 994 — today, Nenagh in Co Tipperary — Maoil-Seachlainn encountered Brian's forces and trounced them; although whether Brian himself was present on either occasion is questionable. Delegation to a lesser general may have been the cause of those setbacks. But it was after the second meeting that Maoil-Seachlainn again visited Dublin — had Gormfhlaith plotted anew in his absence? — and to make humiliation complete carried off the ring of Tomar and the sword of Carlus (17), two heirlooms of the ninth century much valued by the Norsemen.

The position was, generally, stalemate, and in Dublin revolt was impossible for two or three years. But when Sitric did rise, he marched straight into Leinster and plundered the prosperous little town of Kildare. The raid has an air of pre-arrangement, for Maol Mórdha, Lord of Naas, brother of Gormfhlaith, was declared king of Leinster (18) and at once offered Sitric the resources of his new kingdom. Poor Donnchadh, the previous monarch, was presumably deposed — the *Annals of Ulster* shows him a prisoner of Sitric that same year — and taken to Dublin. It cannot be doubted that Gormfhlaith had been at work this time, and her repudiation by the *Ardrí* must have followed swiftly on the events in Kildare.

Unfortunately for Leinster, their new ruler's move served only to bring Brian and Maoil-Seachlainn to their senses. Brian mustered his forces and marched northwards, being joined by the *Ardrí* on the way. In 999 the combined armies met the enemy at Gleann Máma, a site today unidentified with any certainty, but lying probably between the hills of Oughterard, Lyons and Newcastle in Co Kildare on one side, those of Saggart, Co Dublin, on the other; and on, or near, the road from Kill, Co Kildare, to Rathcoole, Co Dublin (19). It seemed that in the penultimate year of the old century, a century filled with turmoil and misery, Ireland was to unite to deliver herself from the heirs of the Land Leapers and any who might succour them.

Site of the battle of Bealach Leachta

6

Emperor of the Gael

THE news of the hosting of the troops of Brian and Maoil-Seachlainn at
Gleann Máma gave heart to those tired of internecine strife. It also
provided the bards with material for a splendid prophecy which,
although it has all the appearance of being made after the event, is worth
repeating:

> They shall come to Gleann Máma
> It will not be water over hands,
> Persons shall drink a deadly draught
> Around the stone at Claen Conghair (1).
> From the victorious overthrow they shall retreat,
> Till they reach past the woods northwards,
> And Áth-cliath the fair shall be burned,
> After the ravaging of the Leinster plain.

However genuine the 'prediction', Gleann Máma was to prove a major
engagement in this period of Irish history. From Brian's point of view it
was to be significant as the penultimate move in his progress towards a
throne higher than that of Munster. It was also a battle that might lead a
disorganised confederation of states nearer a union hitherto thought
impossible, and one in which the supremacy of the Dál gCais would be
undoubted.

Did Brian dream of a united Ireland? In as much as the power of his
own family was concerned I believe that he did, although it is unlikely
that in his most optimistic moments he ever hoped for suzerainty over the
Uí Néill strongholds of the north. Even the Land Leapers had failed to
subdue any great part of the kingdoms of Ulster; but for Brian three-
quarters of the island and the high kingship was a goal worthwhile.
Traditionally (2), the Uí Néill had to hold authority not only in Leath
Cuinn but in one kingdom of Leath Mogha before their representative
was 'coumpted to be of sufficient power' to be high king; but if the high

king came from the south, he must command all Leath Mogha 'and Taragh with the Lordshipp thereunto belonging, and the province of Ulster or Connaught (if not both) . . .'

It is a tradition based on a particular, and partisan, translation of the annals, and whether or not it might have been believed in eleventh-century Ireland is immaterial. The high kingship was, as we have seen, little more than an office created by early Uí Néill in a futile attempt to gain hegemony over an area greater than their hereditary territories. Occasionally, as in the time of the *Tánaiste* Muircheartach, the Uí Néill may have seen their goal in sight, but their domination of Irish regality, more often in name than in reality, was due to their powers of durability — and the fact that few seriously contended the issue with them.

That Brian did, in time, command all Leath Mogha, and forge links with Connacht, and at least gain grudging respect among some of the northern clans, is a tribute to his ability, rather than the observance of a doubtful tradition. It is also a reflection on the disunity, or jealousy, that prevailed among the princes of the north. Even as the threat of outside invasion had failed to unite Irishmen in the widest sense, so the threat from Munster did little or nothing to create a feeling more potent than outraged pride among the Uí Néill.

The threat to the Uí Néill was certainly unique in as much as it was presented by a hitherto obscure clan. That Brian achieved a position in which he could challenge the pretences of Leath Cuinn made him the more determined to create a stronger central monarchy. To his hubcap of government the other kings and their tributaries would be spokes in an Irish wheel. In place of a vacillating association could be a closely-knit federation, benefitting as Munster benefitted from the Dalcassian rule. Charlemagne had achieved as much in Europe, although the new Roman empire had hardly outlived him; and the Wessex kings, when strong, had accomplished much in England. As Brian reviewed his troops on the morning of Gleann Máma, he knew that a victory would be a victory for his ambition.

Maol Mórdha of Leinster and the 'foreigners of Áth-cliath' came out from Dublin to meet their enemy. Possibly they believed that the prolonged conflict between Brian and Maoil-Seachlainn had weakened the strength of their foes, or the resolution of any lesser kings and chieftains who might have supported Brian; perhaps they thought that the combined forces of the eastern side of the island would be more than a match for men who must have been weary of war. The Norsemen also counted on their superiority by the use of cavalry, and they might have been successful if they had reached the plains of Kildare, where they hoped to face Brian and Maoil-Seachlainn. But they had not foreseen the speed with which the opposition marched and, if the probable site of the battle, between the hills of Oughterard, Lyons and Newcastle in Co Kildare on one side, and those of Saggart in Co Dublin on the other, is genuine, cavalary was of little use against those who had the advantage of higher ground (3).

'The foreigners were routed and slaughtered' recorded the *Four Masters* in, for them, an unusually matter-of-fact manner. The slaughtered included Harald, brother of Sitric and next in line to the Dublin throne, 'Cuileán, son of Eeidigeán, and other chiefs of Áth-cliath; and many of the foreigners were cut off in this conflict'. Maol Mórdha of Leinster, dreading the results of capture, hid in a yew tree, whence he was dragged by Murchadh, Brian's eldest son. But his life was spared — a mistake Murchadh lived to regret.

The victors next turned down the slopes to Dublin, which was taken and sacked. The spoils must have been considerable, for before the battle we are told that the women of Leinster had been lodged inside the city for safety, and the cattle also taken inside the walls. Sitric escaped north to Ulster, looking for refuge among the Uí Néill, while Brian and Maoil-Seachlainn remained for a week in Dublin, collecting the 'gold, silver, hangings and other precious things' left behind.

It is hard to decide whether it was through strategy alone or by the union of the armies of Maoil-Seachlainn and Brian that the battle was

Handle of a double-edged iron sword, found at the Viking cemetery outside Dublin

won. Partisan accounts, written in later years, either exclude Maoil-Seachlainn altogether from the conflict, or award him alone the honours of the day (4). That he was present, and that he took part in the sack of Dublin is indisputable; while as far as the battle was concerned, surely it is fairer to grant both kings equal honours? Could they have defeated the Norse-Leinster union and taken the city without each other? The fact that the women of Leinster, as well as the cattle, had been sheltered in Dublin would suggest that every available fighting man had followed Maol Mórdha to Gleann Máma — with the Norse, forming a considerable force. Was it a force that Brian or Maoil-Seachlainn could have tackled alone?

But if Maoil-Seachlainn had entertained any doubts before joining his army with Brian's before Gleann Máma, he surely saw his misgivings about the ascendancy of Munster doubled after the sack of Dublin. Brian, not the *Ardrí*, sent messengers after Sitric, demanding surrender but promising the restoration of his kingdom; and Brian, not Maoil-Seachlainn, was to be recognised as overlord of the city-state. And I believe that, to make his position, and his ambition, perfectly clear to Dublin, Leinster and Meath, it was now that he took Gormfhlaith, mother of Sitric and repudiated wife of Maoil-Seachlainn, as his wife. It would have been, as we shall see, a politically astute move.

Professor Macalister, for whom Maoil-Seachlainn occupies a more honourable position in Irish kingship than Brian (5), regards Brian's dealings with Dublin as part of 'his machinations to secure the High-Kingship'. 'Machinations' is a word suggestive of treachery or double-dealing — 'ambition' is, I think, a fairer noun, and in any case as self-styled king of Leath Mogha Brian had no reason to profess loyalty to Maoil-Seachlainn as *Ardrí*. Both men doubtless recognised the other's abilities, but both regarded themselves as equals and, as we have already remarked, there cannot be two co-existant supreme powers in one island.

Brian had also seen that Maoil-Seachlainn's earlier victories over Dublin had been short-lived, and he was not now willing to observe useless rituals and allow Maoil-Seachlainn, as *Ardrí*, sovereignty over the Norse when it was obvious that, before long, the Norse would be in rebellion against it. As he had subdued the great western fortress of Limerick, and then used its non-violent qualities of trade and commerce to the benefit of his kingdom, so would he rule and develop Dublin on similar lines.

Marriage to Gormfhlaith would have appeared, at the time, a sensible move. Whether they ever went through a marriage ceremony has long been the cause of controversy among historians, notably those who were also clerics. For instance, Canon E. A. Dalton (6) looked at the event through the censorious eyes of a clergyman when he wrote: 'She can not have been his [Brian's] wife if she was also Malachy's (Maoil-Seachlainn's) wife, for they were all Christians, and the bond of Christian marriage is the same for a king as for a subject'. He suggests, instead, that 'as kings have rarely been slow to break through moral restraints, it seems likely that Gormfhlaith's connection with Brian was one of those irregular and illicit connections that have often disgraced a throne ...'

But Dalton and others overlooked, either through ignorance or, perhaps, through choice, that in Brian's day and much later in Irish history the Brehon and Christian codes existed side by side, both working for the benefit of those for whom they had been formulated. Almost a century after Gleann Máma, Archbishop Lanfranc of Canterbury wrote to Brian's descendant, the *Ardrí* Toirdhealbhach (7):

> We hear that marriages in your kingdom are dissolved without any cause, and wives exchanged; and that blood relations under colour of marriage or otherwise do not fear to unite openly and without blame, contrary to canonical prohibition ...

and even in the seventeenth century it was possible for a couple to marry for a 'year and a day of probation, and at the year's end [for the gentlewoman] to return home upon any light quarrel ...' (8).

The Brehon laws catered for every conceivable type of union, whereas the church admits but one, and that indissoluble. It was presumably with the indissoluble union in mind that Fr Ryan wrote when he presented Gormfhlaith as Brian's second wife, the marriage taking place about 985. This I doubt for two reasons: the first based on the movements of Maoil-Seachlainn in 983 and 984, the second on the lines in the *Four Masters* that record Gormfhlaith taking 'three leaps which a woman shall never take': a leap at Dublin, when she married Olaf; a leap at Tara, when she married Maoil-Seachlainn; and a leap at 'Cashel of the goblets', when she became the wife of Brian.

While, once more, we must be wary of the face-value of certain statements in the *Four Masters*, there seems no reason to doubt the 'three leaps' story, particularly as it presents a logical sequence of events. Maoil-Seachlainn had become *Ardrí* in 979, and in 983 was marching against the forces of Sitric of Dublin and the king of Leinster. His marriage to

Gormfhlaith, by then the widow — one source says repudiated wife (9) — of Olaf Cuarán, and mother and kinswoman of those whom he had defeated, would have been a sound move politically, especially as her brother, Maol Mórdha, had aspirations to the throne of Leinster. Also it is logical to suppose that Maoil-Seachlainn repudiated Gormfhlaith under Brehonic law when, in 999, Maol Mórdha and Sitric joined forces. She must have been deep in intrigue.

Although, politically, Brian had reason to seek a wife from Leinster as early as 979, when he marched into that kingdom, Olaf Cuarán was still living — the story that he repudiated Gormfhlaith is probably groundless — and Maol Mórdha was not yet king. As for Maoil-Seachlainn taking Gormfhlaith as his bride after repudiation by Brian, as Ryan infers, there was nothing to gain from such a union, and Maoil-Seachlainn, an astute king, would hardly marry a woman whose duplicity and cunning nature were by then well-known.

But after Gleann Máma Brian had more reason to seek marital ties with Leinster and Dublin, just as he had reason to find a wife from Connacht after his victory at Lough Ree. And it seems probable that his third wife was Dubhchobhlaigh, daughter of the king whom he had defeated with the help of the 'foreigners of Port Lairge' in 988. It was a dynastic alliance with the powerful royal house of the west, a considerable fillip for Brian's destiny and dynasty, providing him with the foothold in Connacht traditionally required for a king of Leath Mogha who aspired towards greater power. If we ignore the tradition, as perhaps we should, the marriage alone formed a fresh and influential family connection.

Dubhchobhlaigh, according to the *Four Masters*, died, Brian's queen, in 1008. As we know, the annalists were inaccurate over many dates, but Ryan says 1009, and a few months is scarcely worth worrying about. What does matter is that Dubhchobhlaigh was queen and that Gormfhlaith was very much alive at the same time. Even Ryan admits that she 'co-existed for some years' with Dubhchobhlaigh, and possible Eachraidh as well, a reason for his doubts about the 'canonical validity' of the marriage. I have already given my reasons for placing Brian's four wives in a particular sequence, so it would appear that he was married to two women at once.

This, of course, has caused previous writers to offer a different sequence of marriage; and yet, under Brehon law, it was permissible for a man to have more than one wife, although 'mate' would probably be a more appropriate term. Dubhchobhlaigh would have been Brian's *ceadmhuintear dhlightheach,* or 'lawful' wife, to whom any other wives, or concubines, made obeisance. Any other women involved, whose union might only be regarded as temporary, were fully recognised by law and the offspring suffered no disability or stigma, as children were to suffer when marriage was regulated entirely by Christian doctrine (10). Gormfhlaith would have appeared perfectly acceptable as a secondary, perhaps a temporary, wife, to everyone at the time, but not to ecclesiastical historians of a later date.

How long Gormfhlaith remained with Brian is open to question, and will be examined further in chapter eight. It is interesting, however, that in the *Annals of Inisfallen* her obituary refers to her as 'queen of Mumu', otherwise Munster. She outlived Brian by sixteen years, so that for at least one body of annalists to have named her queen at the time of her death would suggest she held the title during her life, presumably after the death of Dubhchobhlaigh.

Gormfhlaith was probably fifteen years younger than Brian, say about forty-three, as her first marriage, to Olaf Cuarán, must have taken place about 970, when she was aged about fifteen (11), so that all physical charms might not have passed away when Brian met her.

Brian, nearing sixty, was still an active man, but by claiming her as his wife, as I suggest he did, he was implementing the section of Eidirsceol left in abeyance when he marched into Leinster in 979, rather than seeking the production of a son by a Lagenian princess. This is an important point to remember, and one apparently overlooked in the past. In his role as king of Leath Mogha, Brian already considered himself overlord of Gormfhlaith's homeland.

According to Ryan, Gormfhlaith was mother of Donnchadh, Brian's eventual successor, but he is relying on the account in *Cogadh Gaedhel re Gallaibh*, a work which, although originating from the pen of a contemporary of Brian, seems to have suffered much from interpolation and modernisation in later centuries (12). There is no evidence to prove that Donnchadh was Gormfhlaith's son; but if, as I maintain, he was Brian's son by Dubhchobhlaigh, he would have been in his late twenties by the time of Clontarf — an age which fits in well with subsequent events. Had he been the son of Gormfhlaith, and presuming that my contention that she married Brian in 999 is correct, he would have been no more than fifteen; and while this might not have prevented him from taking part in the battle, it is unlikely that a boy of fifteen would have been entrusted with leading a *sorté* into Leinster, as Donnchadh was to be.

Another point in favour of my argument lies in the behaviour of Gormfhlaith towards the end of Brian's life. Had she been the mother of any of his sons, would she have conspired and intrigued against Brian as she did? There is no evidence that she did so to place Donnchadh on the throne of Munster (which might have been an excuse for intrigue), or that she felt maternal affection for him.

To cement ties with Dublin, Brian gave his daughter in marriage to Sitric, who returned from Ulster in submission. That submission was made not, as it should have been made, to the *Ardrí*, but to Brian. From that time Maoil-Seachlainn's throne was doomed. It may be argued that Brian violated his pact with Maoil-Seachlainn by his next move. But that pact, or union of arms, had been one only through which to crush the Norse-Leinster alliance. Maoil-Seachlainn realised as much, and after the sack of Dublin, returned to Meath, there to put his troops into new order. The inevitable confrontation between the two kings, postponed by Gleann Máma, was again imminent.

Initially, Brian made a foolish move. Away from Munster and doubtless concerned that Maoil-Seachlainn, who had less distance to travel from to reach his own base, could strike the unprotected south, he turned his forces towards Meath. According to the *Four Masters*, he led 'a great hosting, with the chiefs and forces of south Connacht, with the men of Osraighe and Leinster, and with the foreigners of Áth-cliath' towards Tara — a Tara long deserted of life and habitation but still a significant military position. It commanded the plains of Meath and, if they still existed in any form of repair, the ancient high roads from the various corners of the island.

Did he intend to follow up his victory at Gleann Máma by claiming the high throne? If the annalists' account is to be believed, even in part, it would seem that Brian recognised an opportunity of realising his ambition before Maoil-Seachlainn had rested and rearmed his men; and the forces comprised in that 'great hosting' appeared sufficiently powerful to gain Brian another success. The men of south Connacht were doubtless allies gained with his marriage to Dubhchobhlaigh, or even kinsmen, for we must remember that Brian's mother had been a princess from western Connacht. Those from Leinster and Dublin were conscripted into his army or given by Sitric, while the presence of the men of Osraighe reflected how powerful Brian had become. Osraighe was a vital kingdom in the bid for supremacy by northern and southern kings. Any past attempts by the Uí Néill to weaken Munster — attempts that I have already suggested resulted in the setting up of the Dál gCais as rulers of Thomond — may have been caused by Uí Néill fears that a united Munster would gravitate towards Osraighe (13), the strength of the two kingdoms enabling their rulers, or ruler, to dominate the southern half of the island.

But if Brian had been underestimated by others, he certainly underestimated Maoil-Seachlainn, if he thought that this powerful hosting would be sufficient to warn the *Ardrí* against standing in the way of Dalcassian ambition. Maoil-Seachlainn was prepared for the invasion, and the Norse cavalry, pushed forward by Brian ahead of his other troops, was cut to pieces. Brian, disconcerted, withdrew without meeting Maoil-Seachlainn in battle and, after a *sorté* into what is now Co Fermanagh, returned to Kincora. Maoil-Seachlainn, meanwhile, formed an alliance with Brian's late enemy, and relation by marriage, King Cathal of Connacht, making a causeway across the Shannon at modern-day Lanesborough so that, in the event of attack, either side could help the other more quickly.

There followed a year's grace, during which Brian and Maoil-Seachlainn built up their resources. The Dublin cavalry was reorganised, so that for virtually the first time in history horse formed an integral part of an Irish army. Brian not only gained cavalry by his triumph over Dublin: in 1001 we read of a 'predatory expedition' made by his son-in-law, Sitric, into Ulster 'in his ships', doubtless at Brian's command and in order to weaken or distract the more uncertain of the Uí Néill who had so far stood aloof from their kinsman Maoil-Seachlainn.

The climax of the clash between the old and new orders in Ireland was approaching. Brian, for the moment, appeared to be testing the strength, not so much of Maoil-Seachlainn, but of the other Uí Néill chieftains; to ascertain the degree of family unity and, doubtless, to form new liaisons with *tuatha* traditionally subject to the Uí Néill but who might be prepared to change their allegiance.

Shortly after Sitric's raid on the coast of Ulster, Brian marched to Dundalk, but to provide the country with a display of arms, rather than meet the Uí Néill in pitched battle. 'Aodh, son of Domhnall Ua Néill, heir apparent to the sovereignty of Ireland' and a gathering of the Uí Néill confronted him — the *Four Masters* records that they 'did not permit him to advance further, so that they separated in peace, without hostages or booty, spoils or pledges', and in view of imminent events one wonders what to make of this meeting. On one side was Brian, king of Munster and

Aerial view of Tara

now most certainly an aspirant to the high throne; on the other an aristocratic gathering of northern princes led by the man to whom the high throne would descend on Maoil-Seachlainn's death. Did they separate in peace because both armies were of equal strength, or did Brian and Aodh come to some arrangement, or agreement, over the future of Maoil-Seachlainn? It is difficult to imagine Aodh, king of Aileach, supporting Brian's claims on Tara, or even recognising his indisputable overlordship of Leath Mogha, particularly as Aodh's own interests were in serious jeopardy. The meeting was of greater significance than one between Brian and Maoil-Seachlainn, for it was soon to become obvious that with the exception of his Meathian subjects, the *Ardrí* had been deserted by his kinsmen. Did Aodh, whose brief appearance on the stage of Irish history shows him in a light altogether less favourable than Maoil-Seachlainn, see an opportunity to gain the high throne before Maoil-Seachlainn's death — and to use Brian in the process? If Aodh was weary of waiting for the crown, yet sufficiently afraid of Maoil-Seachlainn, his nephew, to attempt a *coup*, did he decide to let Brian supplant the *Ardrí* and then step in himself? Both men were playing a political game, and one can only suppose that Brian agreed to recognise Aodh's independence in the north if no attempt was made to aid Maoil-Seachlainn from that quarter. Both, perhaps, thought it would be a simple matter to deal with the other when the time came.

In 1002 Brian again marched into Meath, heading towards Tara, having made short work of his wife's kinsman, Cathal of Connacht, on the way. The climax had come, so far without bloodshed, and to Maoil-Seachlainn, encamped on the ceremonial hill of Tara, a messenger was sent, asking for his abdication in the name of the king of Leath Mogha.

What was Maoil-Seachlainn to do? He had long recognised Brian's abilities and known that in time he would need to defend his throne. The meeting between Brian and Aodh at Dundalk, although it might only have been bloodless because of the size of the two armies and although no agreement might have been made between the two kings, must have alarmed Maoil-Seachlainn seriously. The Uí Néill of the north had met Brian Boru and turned away: Brian had an army drawn not only from Munster but from Dublin, Leinster and part of Connacht, and Maoil-Seachlainn's one ally, Cathal, had been trounced. Could the *Ardrí* really defend his throne with what must have been little more than the men of Meath?

Although Aodh and the other Uí Néill princes might demur from meeting Brian in battle, Maoil-Seachlainn decided to make a final effort to maintain Uí Néill authority. Traditionally, he asked Brian for a month's truce in which to ascertain the opinion of his family and allies, emphasising that he would give Brian battle or hostages — in other words, submission — according to their replies. Brian, again according to tradition enshrined in *Cogadh Gaedhel re Gallaibh*, chivalrously agreed. But while Brian, taught by *ollamhain* well-versed in Brehonic law, doubtless possessed a high degree of chivalry, the story is probably nothing more than Dalcassian propaganda. It does not deflect from Brian's reputation, for propaganda has been used in all ages. But we cannot believe that Brian agreed to a truce now that his ambition was so near fruition.

More probably, Maoil-Seachlainn had attempted to raise support during the last month before Brian's messenger arrived at Tara. With the passionate eloquence of his calling, the *Ardrí*'s bard, Sléibhín, had visited in turn the princes of the Uí Néill and the *tuatha* of Connacht, appealing for aid. It was not forthcoming.

There was little love lost between the Uí Néill princes and while it might be imagined that Aodh of Aileach, Maoil-Seachlainn's uncle and *tánaiste*, would hasten to defend the throne that would one day be his, he did nothing to oppose the Dalcassian menace. That meeting of Aodh and Brian at Dundalk should not be forgotten: whatever had passed between them, Aodh had decided to bide his time.

Maoil-Seachlainn's next move must have been a surprise; for the *Ardrí* offered to abdicate the high throne immediately in his uncle's favour. The chieftains of Aileach were probably as surprised as their king, but demanded that half of Meath be annexed as 'punishment' for Maoil-Seachlainn's inability to hold the throne. It was the final insult to the *Ardrí* and typical of the mistrust that characterised Irish royal houses and prevented the development of a nation or dynastic superiority on anything more than a casual basis. Had the Uí Néill thrown down the barriers of their petty kingdoms and united behind one strong king of their realms, they might have held the throne of Ireland as the house of Edgar came to hold the throne of England.

Maoil-Seachlainn, tired and deserted, could do nothing but abdicate in Brian's favour. On a day appointed, he rode out to the Dalcassian camp beyond Tara, the crown of Ireland upon his head and dressed in the full regalia of a king. What happened next was recorded by the mac Bruaideadha, hereditary *ollamhain* of Thomond, and is possibly the most

Allegory of living and dead kings at Abbey Knockmoy, Co Galway

exceptional piece of Dalcassian propaganda invented.

Maoil-Seachlainn, we are told (14), dignified as befitted a prince of the Uí Néill, walked to where Brian stood surrounded by the chieftains and priests of Munster, and delivered what would be, if true, the most poignant abdication speech in history:

> Through the defection of my troops, and the unreliability of my friends, I find myself unable to oppose your pretensions to the monarchy. I surrender you this sceptre and this crown which my ancestors for so many generations bore, and which I have now worn for above twenty years. They are the rewards of your virtue, and I submit.

The mac Bruaidheadha tell us that Maoil-Seachlainn stopped, visibly moved, and Brian approaching, embraced him — and to the amazement of the gathering handed back to the *Ardrí* the trappings of sovereignty. For twelve months more Maoil-Seachlainn was to retain the throne, and only then, if still unable to oppose Brian's claims, should he surrender peacefully.

125

It is a good story — and nothing more. Even the *Four Masters* ignores it, merely replacing Maoil-Seachlainn with Brian 'in sovereignty over Ireland', and if the story of the month's truce is doubtful, that of the year is a myth, and a positive example of Dalcassian propaganda. Todd, in his invaluable editing of *Cogadh Gaedhel re Gallaibh*, sees the legend of the first truce as invented 'to give some colour of generosity to Brian's conduct', which seems unnecessary as even Professor Byrne, no great admirer of Brian, has pointed out (15) that no one had a 'strict legal right' to the high kingship.

Brian doubtless received the formal abdication and submission of Maoil-Seachlainn as soon as he reached Tara, but the truce legend — or legends — raises the question as to whether or not Brian's eulogists, in his lifetime and afterwards, secretly feared that he would be regarded as an usurper. In the last century, Todd was adamant that Brian's accession to the throne was usurpation, although in this century Byrne prefers the word 'succession'. The Uí Néill, having held the crown if not always the authority, and scarcely ever universal recognition, were of course of the opinion that Brian had usurped their hereditary rights; pro-Uí Néill writers, then and now, are of the same belief. Dalcassian scribes, and pro-Dalcassian historians, go to extremes to show Brian's chivalry and generosity to Maoil-Seachlainn and, thereby, involuntarily suggest that their hero was indeed a usurper.

Of course, he was not one. He had as much right to the high throne as any Uí Néill and during his all-too-brief reign displayed an ability sadly lacking among most of the Uí Néill who had preceded him. As ruler of Leath Mogha and overlord of Dublin he was the strongest king in Ireland at the time, and if the strongest can prove themselves able, and rule well, as Brian did, accusations of usurpation fade into insignificance, as do claims — as I have shown in chapter one — that Brian's success brought chaos to the Irish political scene. That scene was in chaos before he arrived upon it.

Another question that must be asked concerns Maoil-Seachlainn. Why did a man who, without doubt, was worthy of the best of his ancestors, suddenly lose the support of his family? Aodh of Aileach may have been intriguing against him for some time, but was it likely that he could so disparage Maoil-Seachlainn in the eyes of the Uí Néill as to turn the majority of their kinsmen against him? Had Maoil-Seachlainn, like Conn, deposed in the mists of the second century from his priestly office at Tara, become neglectful of his duties and 'failed to protect his

126

subjects'? According to several chroniclers, Maoil-Seachlainn had 'sunk into a state of indolence and apathy' after the first five years of his reign. This is not borne out by what we really know of the man, and in any case, had the accusation been true, surely proud Aodh, or another Uí Néill potentate, would have preceded Brian with a demand for his removal, and retained the throne within family influence?

Perhaps the answer may be found in the inability of the Uí Néill of the north to put aside personal jealousy and join in a united front against the Norse incursions both from Dublin and Scotland. In Maoil-Seachlainn they found a convenient scapegoat for their failures.

And so Brian mac Cinnéide was *Ardrí* of Ireland. The youthful years leading resistance against the Danes in Clare, the subjugation of the hereditary enemies of his house in Desmond, the campaigns of the last twenty years, had helped him to acquire a near-legendary status in his lifetime, and now he had achieved the ultimate ambition of placing Ireland, or some three-quarters of the island, under homage to the Dalcassians. It had been a lifetime in every sense of the word, a long and arduous climb to power and success; but by a determined and intelligent campaign, unprecedented in Irish history for patience and caution (16), old powers had been eroded, old obstacles overthrown; and while the 'new nation' with which Brian is so often accredited with creating was only to be new in the sense that a fresh dynasty was in power, a new era had certainly dawned over the island.

Had Brian been a revolutionary, in the sense that Ireland, under him, was to become a distinct nation with historical differences between the various kingdoms remoulded until the heptarchy and even Dublin ceased to exist as separate entities, it is unlikely that he would have allowed those kings he had defeated to retain their thrones. Maoil-Seachlainn, for instance, received from Brian undisputed possession of his own kingdom of Meath and could look forward to a quiet old age at his ancestral home at Dún na Sciath on the western shores of Lough Ennell, although he was not yet to vanish from the pages of history.

Brian's aim was to *rule* Ireland as high king in fact, not only in name, and through the allegiance of lesser kings to build up the united front that foreign — and internal — aggressors had found lacking under the Uí Néill. He was to be a great king, and his accomplishments before Maoil-Seachlainn's abdication are proof of this. Like other great kings, his rule once accepted, he was to endow liberally the scholastic and monastic world; but unlike the Uí Néill he was not to be the father of a dynasty of endurance, at least as far as holding the 'throne of Ireland' was concerned. Had the tragedy that was to befall the Dál gCais, and Ireland, twelve years later, been in any way avoidable, Brian may have been remembered by future generations as the father of his nation.

Nevertheless, as the royal diadem was placed on his brow, most probably by his brother Marcán; and as the royal shout of acclamation sounded about the hill of Cashel — for Brian was a Munsterman, and had no need of ritualistic Tara — the new *Ardrí* was entitled unreservedly to an inscription that was to fill a blank page of vellum in the *Book of Armagh*: 'Briain Imperatoris Scotorum' — Brian, Emperor of the Irish — Scots being the name given to the Irish until the following century.

That it was written in his presence, by an intimate friend and counsellor (17), in no way detracts from Brian's achievements and character. And while we know that Irish chroniclers were not averse to rewriting Irish history to bring it into line with international events, the suggestion that Brian regarded himself as the equal of the Byzantine or Holy Roman emperors (18) has been made unnecessarily. Brian was an individual (as, indeed, had been the great Niall Naoighiallach), which is more than can be said for many of the squabbling successors of Charlemagne or Constantine the Great.

Viking-type axe with portion of the original handle

7

A Notable Reformation

'THE most famous king for his time that ever was before or after him of the Irish nation for manhood, fortune, manners, laws, liberties, religion and many other good partes ... [he] in fine brought all to a notable reformation'. So eulogised Conall mac Eochagáin (1), six centuries after Brian's death, and certainly the ages have coated Brian's life and reign with an almost stifling gloss. Of all Irish kings he has proved the easiest over whom to wax eloquent — as Diarmaid mac Murchadha of Leinster has provided a target for vitriol — and to some extent the eloquence is justified. No Irish leader of men, at least no leader whose existence can be taken as fact, in the centuries before Brian's rise to power achieved so great a sense of unity. And while it is unfair to make modern, or more recent comparisons, it should be remembered that Brian did not have the advantages of better communication, easier travel and the 'printed word' enjoyed by patriots of later date.

That over-used word, 'patriot', is undoubtedly justified in connection with Brian, although whether he was patriotic only as far as the ascendency and influence of the Dalcassians were concerned is a matter for the reader of these pages to assess. Maol-Seachlainn, even Sitric of Dublin, can be termed patriotic if the dictionary definition of 'desire to serve one's country' is applied in the context of Meath or the city-state of Dublin. At some stage of his life, Maol Mórdha of Leinster must have shown feeling for his nation: certainly the fierce expressions of independence that had characterised his predecessors for so many generations, and had brought them into conflict with successive high kings were as patriotic as, say, the resistance of any small nation to external advances in our own time.

But it is dangerous to make modern comparisons — particularly as Brian and the Dalcassians were no 'super power' attempting to obliterate the traditions and individuality of a smaller state. Brian hoped to achieve a better federation of Irish kingdoms, without abolishing boundaries or thrones; and had he never lived it is feasible to suppose that another powerful monarch, Maoil-Seachlainn perhaps, would have made similar attempts. Brian, as I have said before, happened to be the strongest king at that particular time in Irish history.

The fortunes, manners, law and other attributes of mac Eochagáin's posthumous tribute — attributes in the flowery language of the sixteenth century and from the pen of a man to whom Brian was a hero — are unnecessary appendages to that final, significant statement: 'he brought all to a notable reformation'. Had Brian been nothing better than a petty chieftain who seized the high throne and ruled despotically until a well-deserved and violent end, he could not have achieved more. The Celtic world, in the few short years following the events of 1002, received the most considerable fillip to potential since the coming of Patrick and the first intensive Christian crusade which, starting in Ireland, had swept across the European continent.

The wealth, culture and position of the Irish monasteries, although

The Cooley mountains in Co Louth

constantly under threat by kings and chieftains whose fathers had been instrumental in creating them, had suffered little major erosion until the coming of the Land Leapers. By the end of the tenth century, *Pro Christo peregrinari volens enavigavit*, the motto of early saints and scholars, was a distant memory; and the affairs of the church had too often reached the squalid level of jostling for supremacy between Armagh and Cashel. As in temporal matters, external aggression refuelled the old native jealousies and suspicions, and aided the schemes of men such as Feidhlimidh mac Criomhthainn of Munster.

After his coronation, Brian's first move was in the direction of the church, a move seen by some as evidence that his relationship with Gormfhlaith was the cause of raised eyebrows even then, at least among the clergy. But this is ignoring the Brehonic code explored in the last chapter, and also underestimating Brian's strategy.

In 1004 he marched into Ulster to receive the formal homage of the Uí Néill — that the northern princes had acquiesced in his assumption of the high kingship was probably nothing more than a delaying tactic, inspired by confidence that Brian's power was but transitory. While there, he confirmed the See of Armagh in its primacy over Ireland, and his friend Maolsuthain Ua Cearbhaill made the necessary entry in the *Book of Armagh*:

> St Patrick, when going to heaven, ordained that all the fruit of his labour, as well of baptisms, as of causes and other alms, should be carried to the apostolic city, which in Irish is called Ard Mhacha (2).

So reads the translation. If it was an act of pacification to any of the clergy who questioned the Gormfhlaith affair, it was certainly unique in Irish history. More likely, it was a sound political move, showing that the new king was serious in his attempt to rule the island, and was not simply another Munsterman who wanted the power and the glory confined to his own province-kingdom. That he was crowned at Cashel, rather than Tara, was more symbolic of the passing away of Uí Néill power — had a king from another part of Ireland gained the throne, he would probably have been crowned in his own capital.

Brian's treatment of Armagh compares favourably with that meted out by Feidhlimidh mac Criomhthainn, two and a half centuries earlier. On the high altar of the cathedral, Brian laid an offering of twenty ounces of gold, an immense sum in those days, and one which, inevitably, has attracted the attention of latter-day historians as an attempt to buy support, or buy off criticism. More prosaically, the cathedral of Armagh was doubtless in need of finance — apart from successive raids, it had suffered serious damage in 996 from lightning, as the *Annals of Ulster* records — and the Uí Néill do not seem to have been over-generous subscribers to the sustenance fund of nine centuries ago. Brian, on the other hand, had at his disposal the treasures of Dublin, and could afford to distribute largesse.

It would have been simple for Brian to announce that the supremacy of Armagh had been supplanted by that of Cashel, at the same time keeping religious influence within the family, for his brother Marcán, abbot of Emly, was 'head of the clergy' in Munster until his death in 1010. But in his climb to power he was quick to use two traditional institutions: one of the high throne, as ultimate temporal authority; the other, the position of Armagh, as ultimate spiritual authority. To have done otherwise Brian would indeed have been a revolutionary, but his concept of ultimate power was no less conservative than that of his greatest Uí Néill predecessors (3), and once his authority was established, he ruled much as they had done. Modern writers who have termed him 'radical' have no real basis for their claim, and there is no reason to seek explanations, as they search, for the rise of the Dalcassians. The old dynasty had shown itself generally incapable of achieving unity, within itself or within Ireland, even against the Land Leapers. The time for removal was ripe, and Brian happened to be the man to arrange that removal.

Brian was no revolutionary, but his rise to power was viewed by certain sections of Irish society as the triumph of a particularly brilliant man. And while the accolade 'Imperatoris', unprecedented in Irish annals, was written in his presence by an old friend and supporter, Brian could no longer be dismissed as an adventurer from the wilds of Thomond.

One reason for the aura of radicalism that many historians have chosen to see reflected from Brian's reign, concerns the use of surnames in tenth- and eleventh-century Ireland. Traditionally, the use of a family name, rather than the custom of calling a man by an additional name in recognition of some physical attribute or mode of dress, dates from Brian's day. The only basis for this tradition seems to lie in a manuscript supposed to have been written by mac Liag, Brian's bard or poet — 'Arch-Poet of Ireland, a very good man', according to the *Annals of Clonmacnoise* — who died in 1016. Mac Liag is also supposed to have written a *Life* of Brian (4) and a book of the battles of Munster which Todd, editor of *Cogadh Gaedhel re Gallaibh*, thinks may have been the same as the copy of *Leabhar Oiris* — now in the library of the Royal Irish Academy. Unfortunately, Todd says that the dialect in which *Leabhar Oiris* is written 'cannot be older than the seventeenth century', so that here (as with *Cogadh*) its real origins are lost.

The story that, by Brian, '. . . surnames were first given and territories allotted to the surnames . . .' is without foundation. As one of the greatest authorities on Irish surnames has written (5), the system developed in Ireland as elsewhere — spontaneously and in accordance with the growth of population. The clan system of selecting either an eponymous or a recently distinguished ancestor from whom to take a surname was known in the ninth and tenth centuries — the Uí Néill were so called from the great Niall Naoighiallach — but does not appear to have been in common usage. And in this context it is interesting to note that one of the many suggestions made by Edmund Spenser (6) for the 'reformation' of Ireland was the renewal of '. . . that old Statute that was made in the raigne of Edwarde the iiijth in England, By which yt was comaunded, that whereas all men then used to be called by the name of theire septes according to their seuerall nations and hadd noe surnames at all, that from thenceforth each one should take unto him self a seuerall surname eyther of his trade or facultie or of some qualitie of his bodye or minde, or of the place where he dwelte, so as everie one should bee distinguished from other or from the most parte whereby they shall not onelye not depend upon the head of theire sept as now they doe, but also shall in shorte tyme learne quite to forgette his Irishe nation . . .'

Had the statute been successful in the time of Edward IV, or even in the sixteenth century of Spenser, it would have merely eliminated one custom in favour of another. In the end, the custom of selecting a surname in honour of a distinguished ancestor became more popular than taking a name denoting some personal characteristic — although the latter has caused difficulties enough in the field of Irish genealogy (7). Brian, had he used the more popular system, would have been Brian Ó Lorcáin, grandson of Lorcán, the first distinguished member of his family. Or he could have insisted that all his descendants continued his own appendage of mac Cinnéide. Future generations could have been Larkins or Kennedys, although the direct line became known as Ó Briain, anglicised O'Brien, through pride in descent from Brian himself. According to William Hennessy, in his translation and edition of the *Annals of Ulster*, published in Dublin in 1887, the first Ó Briain to adopt the surname was Brian's grandson, Toirdhealbhach, who became king of

Thomond in 1058. Even so, not all Brian's descendants perpetuated his name (8).

From what we are told (9), those twenty ounces of gold comprised no empty gesture; for in the years that followed '... in the churches the priests could offer Mass and the people worship in security, the monks in the convents chanted the psalms as of old, the hermit fasted and prayed without his devotions being interrupted by a pagan foe, and in the schools and colleges erected and liberaly endowed, the *ollamh* was paid to teach and the children encouraged to learn ...' An idealistic picture, perhaps, and Westropp, in *Brian Boru, The Hero of Clontarf*, published nine centuries after Brian's death, has suggested that it was a false one. As evidence for his claim that Brian's reign as *Ardrí* was not as peaceful as we might be led to believe, he cites a catalogue of internecine strife from Ulster to Leinster, flavoured with occasional raids by Brian and Murchadh, including one by Brian in 1010 into the land of Cinéal gConaill, in Ulster, at the end of which the local king was taken as a hostage to Kincora. Certainly Ireland was not suddenly transformed into a pleasant pastoral land under Brian — and it would have been too much to hope that the days of bitterness and faction would suddenly end because of a change in the high kingship. Yet, the breaking of the Bachall Íosa — the 'crozier of Jesus', traditionally believed to have belonged to St Patrick — by members of the Conaille Muirtheimhne in 1013 (10) was probably the most serious act of vandalism recorded. A dispute between Connacht and Bréifne, friction in Meath and Ulster and the blinding of the abbot of Downpatrick in 1009, again after a local dispute, are the most the annalists can show between 1002 and 1014. In Munster itself peace seems to have reigned.

Of course, Brian himself would have had few qualms about invading religious ground or putting monks to the sword if they were serious threats to his ambition. His invasion of the sanctuary on Inis Cathaigh in 977 is example of this, but mac Eochagáin shows him otherwise occupied:

> K. Bryan, seeing into what rudeness the kingdome was fallen, after setting himselfe into the quiet Governmt. thereof, restored each one to his auncient Patrimony, repayred theire Churches and houses of religion, caused open schoole to be kept in the seuerall parishes to Instruct theire youth, which by the sd Long warres were growne rude and altogether illiterate, he assembled together all the nobility of the K.dome as well spirituall and temporall to Cashell in Mounster, & caused them to compose

a booke contayning all the Inhabitants, euents and scepts that lived in this island from the first peopleing, Inhabitacon and Discouvery thereof after the creation of the world untill that present. Which booke they caused to be called by the name of the psalter of Cashell, signed it wth his owen hands together wth the hands of the K^s of the five provinces, & alsoe wth the hands of all the Bushops and prelates of the K.dome ...

This weighty tome, a mixture of Patrician and Brehonic legacy and *Domesday Book* precursory, was to be the official history of Ireland, 'any other Chronicle thence forth [should be] held as false, Disannulled and quite forbiden for ever', and it was to be copied and distributed among the lesser kings for public instruction.

How far can we trust mac Eochagáin's eulogy, and how far can we trust the *Saltair Chaisil* as being the work of Brian? It is claimed (11) that most, if not all, the content of the celebrated *Leabhar na gCeart*, setting forth the rights and stipends of the principal Irish kings, was compiled in the eleventh century, perhaps by Brian himself. For many years it was accepted that the passages devoted to Munster had come from the hand of Cormac mac Cuileannáin, the king-bishop who fell at the battle of Bealach Mughna in 908; and while doubt is now cast upon so early a date for any part of the work, it is evident that Munster aggrandisement is its principal theme.

And yet even if we dismiss early claims that the *Leabhar na gCeart* formed part of the *Saltair Chaisil*, and that it was compiled at a comparatively late period in history, it seems certain that the author, whoever he might have been, had an older model from which to work. The innate conservatism of Irish society, exemplified in the Brehonic code, would have precluded the sudden introduction of revolutionary legislation, although it would have been possible for what was already in existence to be altered, enlarged or vetoed.

Obviously a high percentage of the *Saltair* is pseudo-history — those events and septs that lived in the land from the first 'peopleing, Inhabitacon and Discovery', for instance — and much is obviously the work of Brian in bringing up to date what had existed for many generations — the inclusion of kings from the mythical Éireamhón to himself is an example. At the same time the compilation, or extension, of such a volume was certainly necessary from the dynastic angle. Old manuscripts were largely irreparable, having suffered from damp and Danes, and while there was no point in destroying harmless legends — the tale of Oilill Ólum's will for instance — there was much sense in amending the law to suit the conditions of a new age. There was nothing outrageous in the concept, for scribes of all ages are notoriously partisan, and at least Brian was willing to include in history his defeats as well as his victories. With misplaced confidence in the ability of his dynasty to retain that which he had gained, he had no fear of dissection and analysis by historians of future centuries. He faces them, as he faced enemies in his lifetime, unflinchingly.

From childhood, Brian had seen the work of past generations destroyed by invading and internal vandals. Now, in old age, he would rebuild what had been lost in education and architecture. As Ireland settled down under what, to a great extent, was the most peaceful era for six centuries, the old king laid aside his sword and looked for time in which to expend his zeal for learning. Just as Alfred of Wessex had set men to work on the great *Anglo-Saxon Chronicle*, over a century before, so Brian set scribes to work on his *Saltair*. Like Alfred, too, whose origins and career so closely resemble those of Brian — a younger son, the guerrilla war against the Danes, the great years of peace and prosperity — he organised scholarships, sending students to study at the great continental universities and encouraging young men to visit Ireland from the courts of the saintly Robert II of France and the German emperor, Henry II. Armagh filled up again and its renewed influence can be seen in the Latin renaissance that was to be conceived during the eleventh century and blossom forth during the twelfth.

Close intercourse between Ireland and Europe was encouraged by Brian (as Alfred imported foreign monks to fill up his new community of learning and piety at Athelney) not merely for scholastic reasons. At the time he was meeting Connacht in battle on Lough Ree in 988, dynastic changes were taking place on the continent, with the death of the last of Charlemagne's line and the rise, in France, of the Capets. Knowledge of such events was brought to Ireland by merchants sailing into Waterford, Dublin, Cork or Limerick, and men could hardly have failed to compare the rise of Hugh Capet, the new ruler of France, with that of Brian. In many respects they came from similar backgrounds, and though by the time Maoil-Seachlainn handed over the diadem and sceptre Hugh was six years dead, and Robert II was mentally the opposite of his forceful parent, the French throne seemed secure in the grasp of its infant dynasty.

At the time of Hugh's succession — and it should be stressed that he had as little right to the French crown as Brian had to that of Ireland —

the kingdom had degenerated into an enlarged version of Ireland. Primogeniture was as yet an unknown quantity in Europe, and while Hugh Capet's father, Hugh the Great, had been crowned Duke of France by his fellow nobles and was effectively a rival to the king, the heirs of Charlemagne were elected from within the family circle with monotonous regularity. But they were mere baubles with whom the nobility played until they shattered. Unruly feudal tributaries of the king, reminiscent of the multiplicity of Irish principalities, abjured central authority, and the same picture of internecine strife, long known in Ireland, was painted in France in all its gory and violent colours. Scandinavian invaders under Rollo had been ceded what became known as the duchy of Normanday — of the Norsemen or Northmen — by the treaty of St Clair-sur-Epte in 912, and while invasion may have ceased, the attitude of the barons more than compensated for outside aggression.

Capet, like Brian, came from a family which from time to time had produced a contender for monarchy, but before his day they had never attempted to seize the throne. The Carolingian kings, obese, obstinate and frightened, were insulted or ignored by their subjects but, like the Uí Néill, remained with an apparently irreplaceable sense of tradition. It was a tradition of less standing, for they had evicted the Merovingian monarchs only two centuries earlier; and while in Germany imperial power had been taken from them in 899, there seemed no one capable of replacing them in France.

Then came Hugh Capet, Count of Paris, whose accession has episodes that might be carbon copies of Brian's rise to power. Both men waited until they held sufficient prestige — willingly given or not — and both took the throne without spilling the blood of the previous occupant. But it was Hugh who set the precedent, and one cannot doubt that Brian was inspired. His initial act of wooing the church was a replica of the policies of the first Capetians: the church in Europe awarded Hugh and his morbid, venerable son the title of 'eldest sons of the church'; Armagh was to give Brian the most splendid funeral of the age.

Brian's emissaries travelled throughout Europe, encouraging learned men to come to Ireland to take part in his reformation. Works of art, manuscripts of the gospels — many of them Irish in origin — were returned to Armagh or to the new, or re-established, monastic settlements liberally endowed by Brian. Often, a holy relic or treasured article of plate lost for generations, must have been rediscovered among Scandinavian spoil and returned to its original custodians.

Church at Killaloe left, *and inscribed tomb on Inis Cealtra*

His native Thomond benefitted particularly, the churches at Inis Cealtra, Tuamgraney and Killaloe being earmarked for restoration and embellishment. At Inis Cealtra, the round tower, eighty feet high and forty-six feet in circumference, was probably built, or rebuilt, by Brian (12); and the great church, destroyed by Land Leapers, was replaced with what is today known as St Caimín's Church, the fine, semi-circular chancel arch, formed of cut stone, becoming a favourite example of eleventh-century craftsmanship with Victorian antiquaries. At Tuamgraney the now-vanished round tower was also restored, while the existing thirteenth-century cathedral at Killaloe stands on the site of a church built by Brian (13) on an ancient site.

Brian gave Ireland, or at least Leath Mogha, a decade of relative peace. By 1012 the most dramatic event the annalists could find to record was 'a great malady, namely lumps and griping, at Armagh, from Allhallowtide till May ... so that a great number of the seniors and students died, together with Ceannfaoladh of Sabhall, bishop, anchorite and pilgrim' (14). And that was a natural disorder, unconnected with Land Leapers or dissident Irish princes. Apart from the regular catalogue of quarrels

Inis Cealtra in Lough Derg

among the Uí Néill, in the course of which Aodh, king of Aileach — the prince who refused aid to Maoil-Seachlainn — was slain, little of dramatic interest occurred.

Of course, we have already examined the causes of long truces between warring princes, and during that decade of peace — at least for Munster — another generation of fighting men was being groomed. Yet the fact that the universities attracted a heavy influx of students from abroad is some indication that the peace was deeper, or at any rate the fighting more confined, than usual. 'Briain Imperatoris' looked forward to spending the rest of his life in peace, for although he ruled vigorously he was, at more than sixty, an old man by eleventh-century standards. As no Uí Néill arose to recontest the throne, as the Danes of Waterford and Limerick enriched the seaport towns and fostered trade with Europe, Brian can have wanted nothing more than to relax and direct operations of a nature less trying and consuming than war. Three-quarters of Ireland, literally or officially, paid him homage, but much work remained. He might have linked kingdom to kingdom under his authority, for the moment with a certain amount of success, but those kingdoms had still to be linked geographically. By means of communication, new roads, routes along rivers once used by plundering Norsemen, bridges across those rivers, Ireland might cease to be a land of impenetrable bogs and forests and travel might involve less dangers of not only physical but natural hazards.

Brian's eulogists talk of a network of roads growing out of the kingdom of Thomond into the very heart of Ireland, of bridges thrown across the Shannon at Athlone and Lanesborough — confusing the last, no doubt, with that built by Maoil-Seachlainn and Cathal of Connacht — aiding communication by road with the commercial centres. While men were thus employed there seemed little opportunity for war, but the fact that within three centuries Ireland was again a mass of pathless afforestation indicates how basic the improvements were. Doubtless they consisted of little more than mending or lengthening the great highways mentioned by the annalists, and known to be in existence as early as the sixth century (15). The most important were the five roads leading from Tara: Slighe Dhála, the south-western route to Osraighe; Slighe Asail, the western road in the direction of the southern Úi Néill seat at Dún na Sciath; Slighe Mhiodhluachra, leading to the north; Slighe Chualann, reaching in the direction of Dublin; and Slighe Mhór, the great western road into Connacht.

While Brian might have no use for Tara, the highways were an essential link between the four compass quarters of the island, and some, if not all, must have been maintained by the later Uí Néill — the apparent ease with which Maoil-Seachlainn had moved around the country bearing witness. If, as we learn from the source that provides their names, they were wide enough to allow two chariots to pass, they could also aid the passage of troops, hostile or friendly; and if Brian was to control movement upon them there can have been little time to create new highways. Elsewhere, a cursory clearance of forest trees near an existing trackway would have been sufficient if his army was to move with greater ease in the event of rebellion.

The threat of rebellion did not diminish as the years of comparative peace passed by, and as a safeguard Brian established well-garrisoned fortresses throughout Munster. Like the Normans of the following century, he was aware of the importance of one line of defence on which to retire. Cashel, too, was fortified and outlying fortresses guarded other royal residences. Thomas Moore might, in 'Rich and rare were the gems she wore', enthuse over a period in history in which a maiden might say:

> Sir Knight! I feel not the least alarm,
> No son of Erin will do me harm: —
> For though they love women and golden store,
> Sir Knight! they love honour and virtue more!

but Brian knew the reality and uncertainty of life, even though in 1006 he was able to march in Ulster and receive fresh hostages. It was doubtless the strength of his army — 'the men of Erin, both Irish and Foreigners' as the annalists termed it — that ensured the success of his mission; and although he might dismiss his troops on returning to Kincora, 1008 saw them recalled for an excursion into Armagh to settle a religious dispute. For the first time in history Ireland saw the nearest thing to a standing army.

During this period much of the general administration rested with Brian's eldest son, Murchadh, and here one can see another example of the old king's desire to found a secure dynasty. Normally an *Ardrí*, upon election, relinquished his own kingdom — Maoil-Seachlainn had done so in Aileach, and may have abdicated in Meath, which Brian restored to him — and the province throne passed to the eldest member of the family. Brian had one brother, at least, living in 1002, as well as nephews. The brother, Marcán, may have been passed over as a cleric — his career has already been referred to — but the nephews were numerous, at least three of them, Conaing, Longhargán and Cinnéide (16) being the sons of Brian's eldest brother, Donn Cuan, *tánaiste* of Thomond, who had died over half a century before. Their ages may have removed them from immediate succession to Mathghamhain, but by Brehonic tradition they were serious contenders for the throne of Thomond.

Brian appears to have renounced no titles when he became *Ardrí*, but he had little need to do so, for he was king of Ireland to an extent unparalleled in reliable history. Yet he had honoured and observed other traditions, and had left other dynasties to continue the tanistric system of succession. It seems that the exception to the rule was to be his own family, and the grooming of Murchadh, his eldest son but not eldest kinsman, as heir apparent must have been accepted by the Dál gCais, doubtless out of respect for that prince's abilities.

Certainly, alone among Irish sovereigns, Brian stands out virtually free from domestic strife. The one record of a family misdemeanour dates from 980 when Aodh, his nephew, was arrested on Brian's orders. The crown of Munster was scarcely on Brian's head, and he had just faced a

West end of the church at Tuamgraney

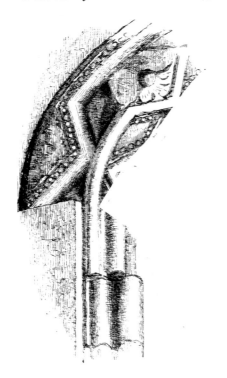
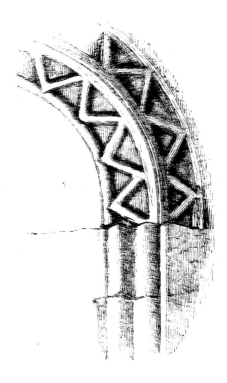

major rebellion led by the kings of the Decies and Leinster. Aodh, perhaps, did not share his uncle's pretensions to higher monarchy and saw his own rights to the throne of Thomond diminishing daily. While Brian was occupied in Leinster it would have been easier than usual for a prince to stir up dissidents, even among the Dál gCais. But the *Four Masters*, which provides the record, says nothing of the cause of Aodh's arrest, and we can only surmise the reason. Whatever happened, Aodh died a natural death in 1011, presumably reconciled to his uncle. That at the time of his death he was described as 'royal heir of Cashel' is misleading, for while *rídomna* (*ríoghdhamhna*), the word used in the original manuscript, means material for a king, it does not necessarily follow that the prince to whom it was applied was heir to the throne of his particular kingdom. Although of the blood royal, Aodh was not the *tánaiste*.

Of course, the principle of *tánaisteacht*, or tanistry, did mean that descendants of Donn Cuan and Mathghamhain were, in time and theory, senior to the descendants of Brian. But the hereditary system of succession, apparently instituted in Thomond by Brian, must have been accepted; for in 1054 the *Annals of Ulster* notes the death of another Aodh, a grandson of Donn Cuan and great grandson of King Cinnéide, who, while called the 'delight and glory' of the Dalcassians, was not even accorded the distinction of *ríoghdhamhna*.

But with the tanistric system operating elsewhere in Ireland, there was another prince who could have claimed the throne of Thomond after Brian's death, or at least the rank of *tánaiste* during Brian's lifetime. He was Conaing, eldest son of Donn Cuan, and he could have been only a few years younger than his uncle, certainly older than Aodh or Murchadh. There is no evidence, however, that he once opposed Brian's imperial march, or the increasing power of his cousin Murchadh. Indeed, he was to die at Clontarf, and his head was given the honour of burial near Brian in the precincts of Armagh cathedral.

The Dalcassians, or at least Brian and his immediate family, resemble more and more the Bonaparte clan as a dynastic group. Each son or son-in-law stood in the shadow of that one supreme being of their house, although unlike the Bonapartes they appeared to be longer contented with their lot. Sound marriages had been made by Brian for his daughters — one was queen of Dublin, another wife of the king of Desmond, a third wife of the king of Scotland — or Alba, as it then was — and, as a matter of interest, grandmother of the future King Macbeth (17), an irony when

*The Ranvaig Casket,
with the Runic
inscription, 'Ranvaig
owns this casket'*

one reads an anonymous play written about Brian a century ago, in which the Shakespearian characters of Macbeth and his wife are but lightly concealed in those of Brian and Gormfhlaith (18).

The Scottish marriage, arranged before Brian became *Ardrí*, was politically sound, for his son-in-law, who ascended the Scottish throne as Malcolm II in 1005, and who reigned for twenty-nine years until his murder at Glamis — a deed transferred by Shakespeare to the next reign — was an accomplished ruler. To Brian the alliance would prove useful should Ireland again be threatened by foreigners, as well as introducing Dalcassian blood into a kingdom that, although Celtic, was fast becoming dominated by one family. No alliance appears to have been contemplated with the English royal house at the time — in any case, Brian's contemporary there was Ethelred the Unready, and from 1002 the real master of England was Svein of Denmark. In later days, however, Brian's youngest son and eventual heir, Donnchadh, was to marry Driella, daughter of Godwin of Wessex and sister of Harold II, last of the Saxon kings (19).

Also, to compare the Dalcassians to the Bonapartes is not making so wild an analogy as might at first appear. By the eighteenth and nineteenth centuries princes were no longer killing or maiming their kinsfolk in order to gain a throne — at least not in Europe — but in the tenth and eleventh centuries fratricide, blinding and lack of family feeling characterised most, if not all, the royal houses of the continent and islands. The Uí Néill have already been cited as an example of unbrotherly love, while the annals of the kings of Leinster offer many instances of a prince slaying or blinding — and thereby disqualifying from kingship — his relation and sovereign. The house of Wessex was no better, although momentarily distracted by new Danish invaders.

Brian's sons — six at least were living when he became high king — were unusually loyal for their period in history, and in Murchadh we see not only loyalty but emulation. It was a rare case of a great man begetting a son who exhibited signs of similar accomplishment, and it was fortunate for Brian that the son, now middle-aged, was content to remain in second place. That both men were subject to sudden outbursts of temper — in the end, to cost them their lives and end Brian's dynastic aspirations — makes them more human; while for the moment any frustration that might have been rising in Murchadh's breast was latent. His power was certainly considerable — perhaps a reason for trouble with Aodh and the lack of it from Conaing.

Over the years of campaigning, Brian had retained the greatest affection for the wooded banks of the Shannon. Here had been his childhood home and now, in his declining years, he turned thither to seek the retreat so long denied him. As *Ardrí* he could have centred the government at Tara, rebuilding the long-deserted site and ruling from the middle of his kingdom. But as each Uí Néill had ruled from his own dún for at least five centuries, so Brian ruled from Munster. Cashel became the titular capital of sovereignty, but Brian returned to Kincora and, as the king and government were synonymous, so the Dalcassian fortress became the real capital. It was also near Limerick, which Brian opened up as a major commercial centre and to which, as time progressed, the centre of power gravitated.

Despite the uncertainty of the site of Kincora, I see no reason to doubt that it was from there that Brian ruled. While we must be wary of all traditional tales, that concerned with Brian's rebuilding of the fortress is so well-established that it almost certainly contains more than a grain of substance. The original building was, we are told (20), turned into offices and kitchens, and a new banqueting hall built at a distance, two long parallel galleries connecting the two sections of the palace. With Murchadh watching for possible disturbances from Dublin, Brian could afford to hold court with considerable magnificence, and 'here did this monarch entertain the princes and nobles in rotation, with a splendour and politeness unknown for at least two centuries. So exact was the etiquette of his court that the rank, station and places of his visitors were ascertained, so that no confusion could arise on account of precedence'.

Perhaps, after years of strife, even the slightest splendour would be regarded as a marvel, especially by lesser kings who had seen their own palaces burned to the ground and who, unlike Brian, did not have the wealth of Dublin or Limerick with which to rebuild them. The annalists did not deal in detailed accounts of royal entertainments, but there is one small vignette of the seating arrangements, although the original source is unknown (21). That two of the northern Uí Néill — the kings of Tír Eoghain and Tír Chonaill — are mentioned, makes one question the reliability of the account: one cannot imagine them accepting Brian's invitations to dine. The 'king of Ulster' mentioned — perhaps an allusion to the king of Aileach — is an equally unlikely guest. In the account, which is probably Dalcassian propaganda grafted on a story of a banquet in the high days of Tara, Brian sat at the head of the table with the king of Connacht at his right and the king 'of Ulster' at his left hand. The king of Tír Eoghain sat opposite him, and at the door on the side nearest Brian sat the king of Leinster. On the further side was Donnchadh, while Murchadh sat with his back to his father, next to Maoil-Seachlainn, invited in his role as king of Meath.

On either side sat Aonghus, a prince of Meath, and the king of Tír Chonaill; Tadhg, another of Brian's sons, sat with his namesake, king of Uí Mhaine in Co Galway, at the end opposite the door on Brian's right hand, while the chief of the southern Connacht tribe of Uí Fhiachrach Aidhne sat on Tadhg's right hand. For a banquet of this importance, the two galleries leading to the kitchens would be lined with one hundred servants, fifty on each side, one half to pass forward the steaming platters of meat, the other to return them emptied.

A double moat surrounded the palace in compliance with the Brehonic law, fed by the Shannon, the broad waters of Brian's trade route lying beneath the windows. On those waters the Irish fleet rocked at anchor, a tangible reminder of how the seemingly untameable enemies of Ireland had first penetrated the country, and how the man who proved them tameable had accomplished his objective. Maoil-Seachlainn, on a courtesy visit to Brian, probably regretted his own neglect in not gathering a fleet — although it would have been difficult to do so in the centre of Ireland. If it had been accomplished, would history have read differently for Maoil-Seachlainn?

And Brian himself, his white hair and beard framing the high forehead and ascetic features that have reappeared in many generations of his descendants: what were his thoughts as he gazed across the water and

Drawing of Noah from the Book of Ballymote

heard the lethargic evening sounds of the town beneath his walls? In the long, white twilight of an Irish summer did he relive, in memory, the long chain of events culminating in the dawn of peace? Did he recall the guerilla days in Clare, the taking of Limerick, the revenge at Bealach Leachta, the battle of Gleann Máma, as well as the days of defeat and impotent years of waiting until a new generation of fighters matured?

As the years of man lengthen there comes a time for more pleasant memories than those of war and hardship. Here at Kincora Brian was at home at last, here he could recapture the childhood that had been so often disturbed. He could indulge his grandchildren in their endless questions about life at Kincora in the old days; answering the inevitable youthful interrogation about long-dead members of the family and of the heroes in Ireland's golden age. As he moved towards his seventy-third year he must daily have expected death, and all signs indicated that he would avoid the traditional fate of so many Irish kings and would join his ancestors quietly from his bed at Kincora.

The monastic settlement at Glendalough

8

The Boru Tribute

AS a general, Brian was the epitomy of caution. With the exception of his encounters with Maoil-Seachlainn in Meath in 992 and 1000, and at Aonach Téide in 994 (when Ryan believes Brian himself was not present), each move he made was planned with a patience rare among Irish leaders; and his intelligence and determination were united in what, to his contemporaries, became a deadly war machine. That Maoil-Seachlainn thrice halted the machine is an example of how well-matched the rivals were — or how, perhaps on one occasion, Brian's absence gave Maoil-Seachlainn an easy victory. It is also an example of how lack of family support for Maoil-Seachlainn helped Brian gain the high throne with more ease than might have been expected.

As an administrator, Brian was perceptive and endeavoured to place Ireland, at least commercially, on a level with the known European nations. Through the pursuit of learning and, more prosaically, by the rebuilding of ruined walls, he rekindled the name of Ireland in the continental courts and monasteries. Indeed, restoration at Inis Cealtra or Clonmacnoise, for the time being free from assault, could be seen in striking contrast to the intrigues, factions and revolutions taking place in no less a city than Rome (1). Since the early part of the tenth century Rome and the Holy Roman Empire had been set on a collision course, exacerbated by the scandalous behaviour of popes such as John XII, deposed by the Emperor Otho I in 963; Benedict VI, attacked and strangled by followers of a rival faction in 975; or John XIV, murdered in 984. Brian became high king of Ireland in the year Emperor Otho III, who had made valiant attempts to resolve the papal squabbling, died; and by the time of Brian's death in 1014, fresh disorders had resulted in the intervention, in that very year, of the Emperor Henry II — later to be known as the Apostle of Hungary — and the restoration of the unworthy Benedict VIII to his see. The memory of Ireland's heyday as the 'land of saints and scholars', coupled with what has been termed (2) the 'extraordinary effectiveness' of Brian's reforms, suggested that once more the island would become a bastion of Christianity in a European world darkened by men who had abandoned the salvation of souls for the power and glory of temporal despotism.

Ireland did not return to its 'golden age', and within a century and a half of Brian's death Maolmhaodhóg Ó Morghair, better known to history as St Malachy of Armagh, had brought the island into line with a reformed Rome. Whether or not Brian's few short years of ecclesiastical restoration and building helped to lay the foundation for Ireland's happy amalgamation into the universal church is impossible to assess.

If the most powerful laymen, in the shape of the Uí Néill, were content to pay Brian lip-service while awaiting what they saw as the inevitable disintegration of Munster and a return to the days when one of their own house sat on the high throne, dissension simmered elsewhere in Ireland. The eastern kingdom of Leinster had seen with distaste the re-establishment of Leath Mogha as a territorial claim, and one can sympathise with Maol Mórdha, or at least with his better chieftains. Their kingdom had suffered more than any other during the five or six centuries before Brian's coronation as high king; anciently, part had been appropriated by the founders of the 'middle kingdom' of Meath, and with it had gone Tara. Whenever a high king from the north, or a powerful ruler of the Eoghanachta, was strong enough to press the claims of Leath Cuinn or Leath Mogha, Leinster suffered the horrors of invasion; and then there was the ever-dangerous presence of Norse Dublin on the northern border. Ravaged by north and south, tormented by the Norsemen, it is small wonder that from time to time Leinster formed an alliance with their oppressors in Dublin in an attempt to regain some form of national independence. Their pride of race, and traditions of the glories of the second century, when the legendary Cathaoir Mór of Leinster is said to have ruled Ireland (3), made any form of subjugation galling, but uneasy truces with Dublin were preferable to the yokes of Ulster or Munster.

The inability of the kings of Leinster to assert their independence before the Land Leapers became too firmly established, or during the reign of a week *Ardrí*, was due to the old problems of internal jealousy and distrust; the southern royal house of Uí Chinsealaigh, based at Ferns, hating the northern Uí Dhúnlaing, whose seat was at Naas. And for all their faults, the Uí Dhúnlaing, Gormfhlaith's family, who had ruled from north Leinster as overlords of all the province-kingdom since 738, presented an admirable picture of dynastic cohesion (4).

Although their kings might dislike the rule of Brian, it cannot be denied that for most inhabitants of Leinster, prosperity was returning after years of desolation. The rich trade brought into the sea ports, as well as the feeling of security from Norse or Danish attacks engendered by Brian's administration, cannot have failed to leave its mark on folk who, when not suffering invasion, were used as pawns in squabbles between their rulers. The revival of Eidirsceol by Brian was, if distasteful, a price the Lagenians had to pay for an ancestral mistake; and with the province-kingdom flourishing commercially it was a burden that could be borne with some degree of equanimity.

Such a state of affairs could have lasted indefinitely. Had Brian died in his sleep at Kincora, Murchadh was strong enough to hold Leath Mogha at least against a resurgence of Uí Néill supremacy in Leath Cuinn, and Maol Mórdha of Leinster would have thought carefully before matching his forces against the new king. It was Brian himself who made a fatal move, Brian himself who brought the simmering pot to boiling point.

In 1008 he had followed the usual approach to ensuring obedience by taking hostages from the Uí Néill. The method, like the institutions of high king and primacy of Armagh, was one which Brian recognised as advantageous; and as far as the hostages were concerned, they enjoyed a far more comfortable existence as permanent guests at Kincora than they might have done in an atmosphere of family feuds in their native territories. Three years earlier (5) just such a feud had broken into open warfare in the north, resulting in the deaths of Eocha, king of Ulaidh, and of Aodh of Aileach. The victorious army in the dispute, that of Tír Eoghain, had followed up its success with claiming as many victims from the other royal houses as possible; and Maoil-Seachlainn, more loyal to his kinsmen than they had been to him, raised a force to help Aileach resist the assailants.

But, as the annalists prosaically note (6), the king of Meath 'fell off his horse, that he was like to die'. For a man in his sixties the fall had been serious, but fortunately Maoil-Seachlainn did not die and two years later was helping to put down another quarrel in Aileach, this time without mishap.

It was probably to deter such slaughter in the future that Brian took the younger princelings from the royal nests to Kincora; and having hopefully settled Ulster, he began a circuit of the rest of Ireland, taking hostages and levying tribute. 'From Connaught came 800 cows and 800 hogs, from Tyrconnell 500 cloaks or mantles and 500 cows. From Tirowen 60 hogs and 60 loads of iron. The Clan Ruraighe of Ulster were bound to furnish 150 cows and 150 hogs. The people of the Oriels 160 cows. From Leinster 300 beeves, 60 hogs and 60 loads of iron. From Dublin 150 pipes or hogsheads of wine; and 365 pipes of red wine every year from the Danes of Limerick'. So says the *Four Masters*, and if we are to believe the account the tributes were of an extremely arbitrary nature. There is nothing in *Leabhar na gCeart* to show that Brian was entitled, either as high king or as king of Munster, to such quantities of cattle or goods; indeed the only *buadha*, or prerogatives, expressly stated as belonging to the high king, make very different reading:

> The fish of the Bóinn (Boyne) to eat; the deer of Luibneach (on the borders of ancient Meath and Munster, now obsolete as a place-name); the fruit of Manainn (unidentified, but not the Isle of Man as has been suggested); the heath-fruit of Brí Léith (Sliabh Calraighe in Longford); the cresses of the Brosnach (the Brosna river, rising in Westmeath and passing into the Shannon north of Banagher, Co Offaly); the water of the well of Tlachtgha (the ancient name of the Hill of Ward, near Athboy, Co Meath); the venison of Nás (Naas, seat of the kings of Leinster).

So that, apart from Eidirsceol, the only rights specifically due to Brian, as high king, from Leinster comprised the venison of Naas and, as king of Munster, the privilege of 'burning north Leinster' (7), a right he was shortly to put into practice.

Obviously the fragmentary nature of Irish manuscripts, the loss of much material and the endless additions and diplomatic erasions made throughout the centuries, as well as faulty nineteenth-century editing, turn the work of ascertaining the exact nature of the tributes into a virtually impossible task. In any case Brian, as successor of the Uí Néill at Tara (8), was entitled to tribute from the northern and western states, and no one appears to have questioned the account as given by the *Four Masters*. Not even Leinster's contribution seems unduly large, and Brian returned to Kincora, satisfied.

All was relatively peaceful until 1012. The previous year had seen the deaths, apparently of natural causes, of Brian's sometime dissenting nephew, Aodh, son of Mathghamhain, and also of Brian's own son, Domhnall. A son of the marriage to Eachraidh, granddaughter to the ruler of Uí Aodha Odhbha in Meath, and, if my theory of the order in which Brian's wives were married is correct, in his early thirties,

Domhnall is a completely faceless character. One is tempted to think that one at least of Brian's sons was of a less ambitious disposition than the father, less a warrior than Murchadh and less fractious than Tadhg and Donnchadh, both of whom were to lose their thrones. Was Domhnall of a more gentle and retiring nature than his brothers, emulating perhaps his ecclesiastical uncle, Marcán, who died in 1010? We shall never know, but to imagine one son as less distinguished, or less inclined to battle, than the others, makes Brian's family more human.

At any rate, Domhnall's death seems unconnected with the events of 1012, when, apparently without warning, Brian imposed a fresh tribute on Leinster: the bitterly resented Bóramha Laighean. The tribute, from which Brian gained a sobriquet that has endured to the present day, although commonly spelt in phonetic fashion, was a variation of the *Bóramha*, which means nothing more offensive than cattle tax. We have, in previous chapters, discussed the old Dál gCais fortress of Béal Bóramha, about a mile north of Killaloe (9), to which tribute due to the rulers of Thomond had long been driven. It was from the fortress that Brian's father, Cinnéide, had acquired a rather empty title, 'king of the populous realm of the Boru'; and while it was not a tax confined to Thomond or Munster, it was probably to this fortress that the men of Leinster were ordered peremptorily to drive their cattle.

Although a common enough tax in Ireland, the *Bóramha* as applied to Leinster had long caused a bitterness in kings and people, associated as it was with the loss of their ancient lands around Tara. Traditionally, the Bóramha Laighean was imposed by Tuathal Teachmhar, a legendary king of Connacht of the second century. Like so many of the early Irish kings, he belongs to the shadowy period of history, and while the *Four Masters* gives his death as taking place in 106 — O'Donovan, translator of those annals, says 160 — he may well have been one of those figures conjured up by the annalists to suit a particular role. But whether he existed or not, it is apparent that the tribute had been a point of grievance with Leinster for several centuries.

The *Annals of Clonmacnoise* record the Bóramha Laighean as being an annual tribute of 'one hundred and fifty cows; one hundred and fifty hogs; one hundred and fifty coverletts, or pieces of cloth to cover beds withal; one hundred and fifty cauldrons, with the passing great cauldron consisting in breadth and depress five fists, for the king's own brewing; one hundred and fifty couples of men and women in servitude, to draw water on their backs for the said brewing; together with one hundred and fifty maids, with the king of Leinster's own daughter, in like bondage and servitude.'

Of course, we have already seen that the *Annals of Clonmacnoise* cannot be taken too literally, and the fact that the king of Leinster's daughter was part of the tribute suggests that by the time the *Annals* were compiled in the seventeenth century the Bóramha Laighean had become confused with the tribute of Eidirsceol, levied by Munster. Such a suggestion becomes more probable when it is seen that the *Bóramha* was, allegedly, imposed by Tuathal Teachtmhar for the murder of two of his daughters — Eidirsceol was the result of the death of a Munster prince — an allegation that makes the origin of the tribute more romantic than likely. We can certainly discredit the statement that a total of three hundred men and women was part of the annual tribute — the impact on Leinster would have been serious, and, in time, the entire tribute had degenerated into nothing more than an attempt by each new *Ardrí* to assert his strength, and of each new king of Leinster to assert his independence.

Indeed, the demands were supposedly remitted altogether by Fíonnachta, *Ardrí* from 675 to 695, following a request by St Mo-Ling (10), the king discovering too late that he had remitted them until the Day of the Judgement.

Whatever the truth of this tale, Brian decided that the time had come to reimpose the Bóramha Laighean and it is not hard to see Gormfhlaith as a reason for his decision.

Dubhchobhlaigh died, as we know, in 1009, so that for three years Gormfhlaith could have been unrivalled queen at Kincora. Yet was she? Her obituary in 1030 refers to her as 'queen of Mumu', otherwise Munster, which suggests that she was the widow, rather than the secondary wife, of Brian. That she is not called 'queen of Ireland' is immaterial, for wives were never regarded by the annalists as the equal of their husbands. And while Brian was indisputably king of Munster, he was not recognised by every part of the island as king of Ireland. So that to term his widow queen of Munster was logical: it offended no-one and stated the truth.

But it is only too easy to visualise Gormfhlaith's position at Kincora. It must have been impossible from the beginning, with an elderly husband and the eyes of step-sons such as Murchadh upon her. Frustrated and isolated, queen only as a result of another woman's death and because of that, to her, pernicious Eidirsceol and the humiliation of her family, her pent-up feelings boiled over. We read much of Irish kings putting aside their wives, but there are few recorded accounts of wives leaving their husbands. If, taunted or snubbed by Murchadh and his brothers, Gormfhlaith found her position at Kincora untenable, and if she left suddenly and returned to her brother's court, swearing vengeance against the Dalcassians, we can see why Brian, prompted perhaps by Murchadh, reimposed the hated tribute.

No man, especially an old man, likes to be made into a fool, as we know from the story of Tíghearnán Ó Ruairc of Bréifne, whose middle-aged wife, Dearbhforgaill, left him for Diarmaid of Leinster over a century after Brian's death — and with such dire consequences for Ireland.

In an outburst of irritation and annoyance, Brian decided to humiliate Gormfhlaith's family before they could humiliate him. And he knew already that the princes and chieftains of Leinster, proud and obsessed with genealogy, looked down on him as an interloper in the matter of kingship. If Gormfhlaith did leave him, we can imagine the amusement and gossip it provided for men who traced their ancestry to the Flood and beyond.

The Bóramha Laighean, therefore, was suitable punishment for Lagenian snobbery and intrigue, and the province-kingdom was peremptorily ordered to send to Kincora 'thrice five thousand cows, thrice five thousand swine, thrice five thousand mantles, thrice five thousand silver chains, thrice five thousand wethers, thrice five thousand copper cauldrons, a great cauldron of copper which held twelve swine and twelve oxen, thirty cows with red ears, with calves of the same colour, with ties and tethers of bronze, and bronze pails as well ...'

We need not for a moment believe the numbers offered by the *Four Masters*. But it cannot be doubted that they were considerable and represented more than Leinster could afford without facing famine. Leinster heard the news with a mixture of fury and shock, but for the moment Brian was unrelenting. Murchadh was despatched with an army to Osraighe, one of the tributary kingdoms in Leinster, with instructions to enforce his father's orders, and his presence alone would have been gall to Maol Mórdha, remembering the incident of the yew tree at Gleann Máma.

The entry of Murchadh into Osraighe in 1012 enabled the prince to release some of the middle-aged energy he had built up in Brian's service. The whole province-kingdom of Leinster, as far as Glendalough and Kilmainham, was plundered, and Murchadh 'carried back with him great spoils and innumerable prisoners' (11).

Brian was quick to repent his hasty action, for he saw a violent storm on the horizon and fast approaching Kincora. A moment of frustration had risked his life's work, but there might yet be time to make amends and retain command of the situation. Maol Mórdha was summoned to Kincora with a request for three large masts for Brian's fleet — a considerable compliment to Maol Mórdha as the fleet was one of Brian's greatest joys in his old age. An appeal for a necessary part of its furnishings was intended as an honour to the recipient — and it was a brave attempt to mend the breach.

Maol Mórdha disliked and feared Brian, but with Murchadh laying waste to his kingdom and with the possibility of famine stalking the land, he had no choice but to meet Brian's appeal. Outwardly mollified, he set out for Kincora, the masts each carried by a principal Leinster clan. The rest of the story (12) is part of Irish folk-lore.

As they neared Kincora an argument broke out between the clans as to which should be first to present their mast to Brian. Maol Mórdha settled the dispute by taking first place at the mast carried by his own family, but in placing the timber on his shoulder caused a silver buckle or button to fly from his tunic. According to the story, he was splendidly received by Brian, but not by Gormfhlaith. Maol Mórdha handed her the buckle, asking her to sew it onto his tunic, but his sister recognised the buckle as a gift of Brian's, and threw it into the fire, cursing Maol Mórdha's inability to resist the *Ardrí*.

'You poltroon,' she said in effect, 'where is the spirit of your ancestors? Why do you yield service and vassalage to Brian? Did your father submit to Brian's father, or your grandfather to Brian's grandfather? Of course not, for they were men, unlike you. And now, no doubt, Brian's son will trample upon your son, just as Brian tramples upon you.' (13)

It was an unfair tirade — if we accept the essence of the translation — as Brian's father and grandfather had never been a threat to the nationalism of Leinster. It also raises the question of Gormfhlaith's whereabouts and strengthens our argument for the sudden imposition of the tribute.

If Gormfhlaith had returned to Leinster, we can imagine that Brian's initial anger had turned to fear of the intrigue in which she might be involved. Reconciliation with her brother was uppermost in his mind — but reconciliation with her? It is difficult to imagine Gormfhlaith returning to Kincora with her brother and the masts — or even for Brian to have requested her to do so — for both characters were too strong for that. If Brian could make friends with Maol Mórdha, he might still be well rid of Gormfhlaith; while she could never face a return to the isolation of Kincora and the snubs of the step-sons. Her reproaches to Maol Mórdha could have been made in Naas, and that the story has been set, traditionally, in Kincora, serves only to heighten dramatic effect: the ill-used or scheming wife at last showing her feelings during a visit by her brother.

Whether at Naas or Kincora, Gormfhlaith would have found sufficient material with which to abuse Maol Mórdha from the fact that he had responded to Brian's request for masts. But Maol Mórdha was to be irritated and intimidated enough while he was at Kincora, without worrying about a buckle. In the course of his first evening there, he was watching a game of chess between Murchadh and a young kinsman, and suggested a move that lost Murchadh the game. 'That,' said the loser (14), 'was like the advice you gave the Danes at Gleann Máma!' Maol Mórdha, aware that this was the prince who had pulled him, ignominiously, from a yew tree, replied angrily: 'I will now give them advice and they shall not be defeated.' The answer was obvious: 'Then you had better remind them to have a yew tree ready for your reception!'

It was the final reproach. In fury, Maol Mórdha left Kincora, refusing

Gaming board of yew wood, tenth century. Pins were inserted into the holes but the exact nature of the game is not known. The ornamentation is most closely comparable with that of a group of crosses on the Isle of Man

to attend a banquet held in his honour and without speaking to Brian. The *Ardrí*, seriously perturbed and until then perhaps unaware of Murchadh's lack of tact, sent a messenger after the king, asking him to return and to take leave formally and peacefully. But Maol Mórdha was not to be appeased. The luckless messenger was left at the side of the road with a fractured skull — vivid indication that Leinster and vassalage were to part company.

Alone, Leinster did not have the resources necessary for an outright attack, and Maol Mórdha knew that he must act with speed, for Murchadh would doubtless be on his heels — and he knew that next time they met the prince would not stop at pulling him from the branches of a convenient tree. To see Brian destroyed was Maol Mórdha's ambition — into this we can read Gormfhlaith's intrigues, too — and to achieve this he was to turn for help outside Ireland. To a point, one can sympathise with Maol Mórdha, but that he was willing to sell his kingdom simply to satisfy wounded pride loses him any chance of respect.

An assembly was convened immediately of the nobles and chieftains of Leinster, and the king described his treatment in Thomond, denouncing it as an insult not only to his person but to Leinster. The official submission to Brian was at once withdrawn and the eastern kingdom, preparing for battle, sought aid at first from the Uí Néill in Aileach and from other princes whose antipathy to Brian was known, but who would not act alone (15).

It is a testimonial to the character of Maoil-Seachlain that he did not seize this opportunity of trouncing his supplanter once and for all. Indeed, the former *Ardrí* stands out from the assembly of Irish kings as a man of courage, honour and infinite patience. A lesser man would have delighted in siding with the enemies of one who had taken his throne, but Maoil-Seachlainn must have made his position clear, for Maol Mórdha asked the king of Aileach, Maoil-Seachlainn's kinsman, Flaithbheartach, to attack Meath and ensure that Brian received no help from that quarter.

The men of Aileach, together with Ua Ruairc of Bréifne and Ua Ciardha of Cairbre Gabhra — the rulers of what is now Co Leitrim and the baronies of Tullyhunco and Tullyhaw in Co Cavan, and of the Granard area of Co Longford — ravaged Meath and one of Maoil-Seachlainn's sons was killed. Although retribution fell quickly upon the head of Ua Ciardha at least, Maoil-Seachlainn was in a desperate position. In what must have been an attempt to prove himself Brian's ally, and to show the undecided northern princes the potential strength of the alliance, he sent an expedition against Dublin, where Sitric had risen in support of his uncle. But at Draighen — now Drinan, near Kinsealy, Co Dublin — his army was all but annihilated and another son, Flann, fell before the combined forces of Dublin and Leinster.

So far Brian had made no move against Leinster. Doubtless he was shocked by the acceleration of events; doubtless, too, the Dál gCais were not prepared for immediate mobilisation — between 1010 and 1012 Murchadh had twice led forces against restless chieftains in Meath and Louth, and there may have been losses in his ranks, despite his success. At first, Brian may have hoped that Maoil-Seachlainn's support would be sufficient to show potential rebels that not all Ireland had rejected the Dalcassian ascendancy; more probably advancing years had weakened the old man's powers of decision.

Maoil-Seachlainn was in great danger and finally appealed for help from Brian. At last the Dál gCais rose and, together with a strong force from Connacht, marched into Osraighe, where Brian stayed for three months while Murchadh plundered southern Leinster (16). The support of Connacht was probably not so much an admission of support for Brian as a chance to take the field against the Uí Ruairc, kings of Connacht until reduced by the superior power of the Uí Concobhair (17).

Early in September, 1013, the entire army arrived before Dublin and for more than three months the city was blockaded. The Norse, who were in earnest, refused to give the traditional hostages and also refused to leave the city to give battle. In the depth of winter, with Christmas approaching, and provisions in the beseiging army diminishing, Brian found himself with the threat of mutiny on his hands. His army was not equipped to risk a full-scale assault on Dublin — Irish armies were rarely fitted for this sort of warfare, unlike continental armies. The only real 'cities' or fortified towns in Ireland, those built by the Land Leapers, were proving harder to capture than the *dúin* or traditional stockaded *ráthanna* of Irish kings. That they could be taken, especially by surprise, we have already seen — Brian had entered Limerick in the panic after Solchóid and Maoil-Seachlainn and Brian had sacked Dublin after Gleann Máma; but long seiges were almost unknown in Irish warfare.

Maoil-Seachlainn could not send any substantial relief and a prolonged absence from Munster could provide opportunities for dissidents to venture on rebellion of their own. It must have been with sadness of heart that the *Ardrí* turned south to Kincora: his empire was crumbling without the test of a major battle. But Munster remained loyal, and both

Sitric and Maol Mórdha were only too aware that it would not be long before Brian had collected a greater army and was investing Dublin with his old vigour. Sitric, with his uncle's support, turned overseas for help, first contacting Sigurd, Norse ruler of the Orkneys (18) and promising him the throne of Ireland and Gormfhlaith's hand in marriage if he would lend them his support. The 'kingdom of Ireland' may have referred to the overlordship of Dublin and Leinster, although we can hardly believe that Sitric and Maol Mórdha intended to surrender their own thrones or authority if Brian was dead. More probably it was as empty an honour as that offered by chieftains of the Uí Néill to Edward Bruce, brother of the King of Scots, in 1315.

Uncle and nephew were more concerned with gaining help in their struggle against Brian than in offering Sigurd a clearly-defined throne, and one wonders whether Sigurd was dupe enough to imagine that Brian's death would be sufficient excuse for a foreigner to become *Ardrí*.

The fact that Gormfhlaith, well past her prime, was part of the offer, was probably an indication of what was intended — overlordship of the eastern kingdoms, for it would bring matrimonial ties with the commercially-wealthy Dublin and Leinster. It also suggested that Brian was to die.

Hiberno-Norse coins of Sitric III, king of Dublin

At the same time there is no question that Sitric intended to surrender his own throne to the Orkneymen. The chances of Sigurd dying in battle before claiming his reward were high; and this became obvious when Sitric, urged on by his mother and uncle, offered the same prizes to a pair of notorious Scandinavian pirates. One of them, Brodar, who despite his description in the *Four Masters* as 'chief of the Danes of Denmark', was nothing more than a petty mercenary; and, according to another source (19), had been a 'mass-deacon, relapsed to paganism'. Both Sigurd and Brodar accepted the tempting offer and agreed to be in Dublin by Palm Sunday, 1014.

Brian, personally, was unprepared for this new confrontation. The years had left their mark upon him — seventy-three was a great age for the period — and the stalemate at Dublin had upset his confidence in his ability to subdue the rebels quickly. But the longer Leinster was allowed to bask in new-found independence, it was clear that the threat to Brian's rule elsewhere became greater.

The call to arms went out: from Loop Head to Limerick, across the limestone Burren and into the heart of the Connacht mountains; into the *tuatha* whose westerly neighbour was the wild Atlantic; up and down the Shannon and into the territories once ruled by Donnabhán and Maolmhuadh. The response was not as spectacular as the annalists would have us believe, and sweeping aside the romantic fiction that makes Ireland more united than ever it was, it is evident that Brian's principal support came from Munster itself, from the Uí Fhiachrach Aidhne — kinsmen of his first wife, Mór — and the Uí Mhaine of Galway, and from Maoil-Seachlainn of Meath. No help came from the *tuatha* of the north (20), and none can have been expected, although at least they did not renew their perfidy against Maoil-Seachlainn, of the previous year; and the king of Connacht refused to accompany Brian, perhaps remembering the frustration of sitting outside Dublin the last time he had taken the field with the *Ardrí*. Nor can we place any confidence in the story embodied in the Icelandic sagas, of how Ospak, a fellow-pirate of Brodar, refused to 'fight against so good a king' as Brian, and sailed to Ireland, where he was baptised and joined the *Ardrí*'s army at Clontarf (21).

But at least two of Brian's dynastic alliances proved of advantage. Cian of Desmond led the Eoghanacht troops to his side and from Scotland, another son-in-law, Malcolm II, despatched a small force under Domhnall, great steward of Mar. By the perversities of dynastic alliance, the Scottish king was himself father-in-law to Sigurd of the Orkneys (22), but with the eighteen-year-old Cnut of Denmark having succeeded his father on the English throne two months before, and the Saxon royal house seemingly exiled for good, Malcolm knew that fresh Scandinavian gains in Ireland, however small, could bode ill for the long-term safety of his own realm.

Although Brian's forces were probably smaller than those he had commanded at the time of his coronation, they were far superior to his enemies (23). Sitric and Maol Mórdha had to rely solely on their own armies and on two foreign allies, one of whom led a band of brigands. And as Easter, 1014, approached, and the final preparations for the ultimate battle in the life of Brian Boru were made, numerical supremacy at least seemed to be on his side.

9

The Weir of Clontarf

ON Palm Sunday, 1014, 'Sigurd came, and with the great Orkney earl a gathering of the chiefs and his followers, called to the war from every island on the Scottish main from Uist to Arran, beaten blades who had followed the descendant of Thorfinn, the skull-splitter, in many a roving cruise, half-heathen, half-Christian men who trusted perhaps to the Sign of the Cross on land and to Thor's holy hammer on shipboard . . .' (1)

Even without mention of the Norse of Dublin and the followers of Maol Mórdha this sounds a formidable foe, but it is well to remember that the Icelandic chroniclers, who provide us with this vignette, were as prone to exaggeration as their Irish counterparts. And the *Four Masters* went to town in no uncertain manner, not only on their own side: Brodar, the pirate, becomes 'chief of the Denmarckians' for example, while the *Annals of Loch Cé* created him earl of Caor Eabhrac (York), although there had been no Scandinavian ruler there since the middle of the previous century (2). Indeed, with hindsight, the *Annals of Loch Cé* decided that for Brian to 'attack Áth-Cliath on this occasion was not to attack a neglected breach. It was like putting a hand into a griffen's nest to assail it. It would not be evading conflict, but seeking great battles and contests, to advance against the multitude that had then arrived there; for the choicest brave men and heroes of the island of Britain had arrived there', while other accounts made Brodar one of the 'rulers of all the north of Saxonland' (3) and list among his supporters at Clontarf not only most of the Scandinavian population of Scotland and the Isles, but others from as far afield as Muscovy, where early Viking explorers from Sweden had founded trading centres and cities.

Looking back at Clontarf over nine centuries, obstructed with partisan eulogy, it is difficult to assess who exactly comprised the invading force. But it is certain that the followers of Sigurd and Brodar were numbered in hundreds rather than thousands, and that they were there to support

Sitric and Maol Mórdha rather than following in the bloodthirsty foot-steps of Turges. Both men had been promised a kingdom — presumably that of Dublin, with influence in Leinster as a result — but there is no proof that either sought anything more. They were certainly not leading a new invasion of Land Leapers, although a new work on the Vikings (4) seems to think differently:

> If Sigurd had won (it suggests) the result could have been a strong Norse domain extending from Shetland to Dublin, with Norse dominance in language and culture — a domain as strong as Norway proper and its neighbouring kingdoms. What repercussions that would have had is left to our imagination ... But it was not to be. Neither side could count itself the undisputed victor in the battle at Clontarf; yet it was nevertheless a historical turning point. A muster of the entire military strength of the Norse overseas settlements did not suffice to reverse a course of events already in full spate ...

To suggest that victory for Sigurd or Brodar would have resulted in the inclusion of Ireland as part of a Norse empire is hardly to be taken seriously. Had the king of Norway led the foreigners at Clontarf we might regard the battle in the light of Stamford Bridge, half a century later in England, when Harald Sigurdsson sailed with an armada to claim the Saxon crown. But the old days of Viking empire-building were on the wane: in England the young Cnut might have secured the throne on his father's death, but Danish influence had been paramount in that country for some time, and he was not to turn his eyes westwards, although he became one of the greatest of the Scandinavian rulers. By 1014 those who had built, or inherited, a kingdom were content to hold what they had unless, as in the case of Sigurd, a definite offer of additional territories had been made. As for dominance of Norse language and culture, nearly two centuries of Norse presence in Ireland had failed to replace Irish speech or culture. Norse and Saxon speech were similar enough to allow a high level of integration of the two races in England, but while, as we have seen in chapter three, certain ties, such as commerce, child fostering and eventually human nature drew the Norse and Irish together, the Irish language and culture were in no danger of being submerged. The fact that the language survived attempts in later centuries to annihilate it, and at a time when conquest by another foreign power appeared complete, shows how difficult it would have been for the heirs of a victorious Sigurd to turn Ireland into a new Scandinavian state.

The 'course of events already in full spate', the waning of the era of the

Land Leapers, is alone sufficient evidence to dispute the traditional magnitude of the 'invasion', and while Clontarf was certainly to be a turning point, it was one at which Ireland abandoned the concept of a strong central monarchy under the Dalcassians and returned to the old days of disunity and anarchy. That the Vikings did not seek fresh opportunities for conquest in the years after Clontarf shows how greatly their power had diminished.

Suddenly it is fashionable to applaud the Vikings, and to credit them with greater contributions to Irish history than is their due. Contemporary fashion should have no place in a critical examination of history and while, as we have seen, the Norsemen of Dublin, and elsewhere, did much for Ireland in trade and commerce, their legacy should be compared at all times with what has been left to us by native craftsmen, scribes and builders of the same time.

The power and the glory accorded men such as Brodar by Irish annalists should also be viewed dispassionately. Any honours attributed to them, as an enemy, reflected the greater honours of Brian. The greater the invading forces, the more notable the invading chieftains, the greater the glory of the Dál gCais in resisting them.

Accounts that the Irish army, or at least Brian's army, numbered twenty thousand, or that at the end of the day the enemy had lost an estimated fourteen thousand men (5) cannot be taken seriously. As we have already seen, the population of Ireland six centuries later was barely one and a half million, and even that figure was an estimate for the country controlled or settled by the English. In Brian's day the population must have been considerably smaller, and as much of Ireland was unrepresented in his army we can see how wildly exaggerated the annalists' figures were. Even at the battle of Hastings, half a century later, it has been reckoned that the Saxon and Norman armies totalled no more than nine thousand men. Clontarf was a smaller, less important battle, although the length of time it lasted and the fact that fighting consisted of encounters at close quarters, as well as the number of kings and princes slain, would suggest that altogether somewhere in the region of eight thousand men must have been engaged (6).

Clontarf was to be one of the fiercest engagements fought on Irish soil to that date. To Brian it represented a major threat to his authority and to the peace of the kingdom; to Maol Mórdha it represented an opportunity for revenge and a chance to reassert the independence of Leinster, for even if Sigurd had won the battle and assumed control in Dublin,

Leinster had known strong Norse kings before without falling completely into thraldom. To Ireland as a whole, it heralded a return to the days of internecine strife and, in time, paved the way for the next wave of invasion in 1169, an invasion, of course, impossible at the time of Clontarf.

Brian's most pressing concern was to contain the enemy within the area of Dublin, and to ensure that they did not infiltrate the countryside, receiving aid, willing or not, from the *tuatha* at the moment standing aloof. With the support of Maoil-Seachlainn his army outnumbered his foes (7) and the old king must have felt confident of a repetition of Gleann Máma. So confident, in fact, that on the eve of the battle he despatched a small force of Dalcassians and Eoghanachta southwards to Wicklow under the command of his youngest son, Donnchadh. The force was intended as a warning to any of the chieftains of southern Leinster, whose king was rival to Maol Mórdha and had ignored the call to arms, not to suddenly change their minds. It is also, incidentally, another indication that Donnchadh was not the son of Gormfhlaith. If my order of sequence of Brian's marriages is correct, a boy of little more than fifteen would hardly have been placed in command of a peace-keeping force, and more was to happen at Clontarf that suggests Donnchadh had grown to manhood.

Whether or not Donnchadh harried and plundered the country for good measure, as *Cogadh Gaedhel re Gallaibh* claims, and, missing the excitement of the coming battle, he may well have done so, the diversion apparently worked. No Uí Chinsealaigh chieftains fell at Clontarf, and doubtless the family hoped that if Maol Mórdha died they would stand a better chance of supplanting his family as overlords of the kingdom. In the event they had to wait until 1042 (8).

Brian fixed his headquarters north of Dublin, within sight of the city at what, today, is Phibsborough. Dublin, in 1014, lay south of the Liffey river, and on the sloping plain, north and east of the Tolka river and the sea, extending towards Clontarf and beyond, the Norse army encamped on Thursday, April 22. The Tolka flows from west to east, and to the west, near what is now Ballybough bridge, stood the little fishing weir of Clontarf. Despite the doubts and rather fruitless endeavours of some later historians to prove otherwise, all the available evidence points to the fact that the district known today as Clontarf was ever known by that name (9), and that there the battle was fought.

Arriving at what is modern Phibsborough, Brian held a council of war.

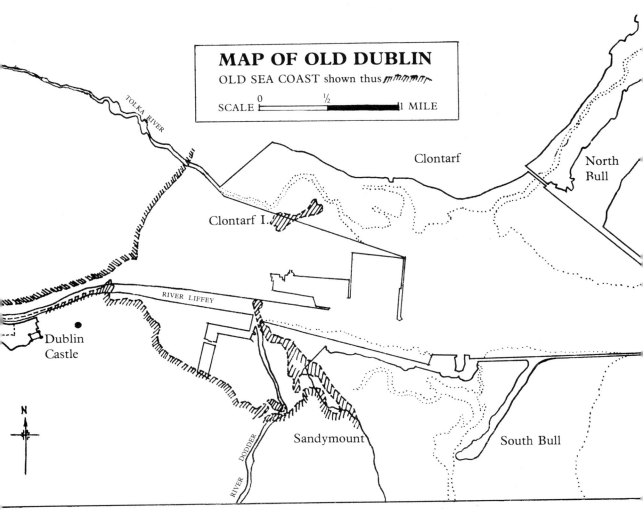

Clontarf

North Bull

Clontarf I.

TOLKA RIVER

RIVER LIFFEY

Dublin Castle

N

RIVER DODDER

Sandymount

South Bull

The Norse and early Norman city of Dublin

What took place is unknown, but it ended with Maoil-Seachlainn withdrawing his forces. This was indeed a bitter blow to Brian, numerically and personally, for with Donnchadh in southern Leinster he was at a serious disadvantage. Why, suddenly, did Maoil-Seachlainn desert the *Ardri*? It cannot have been due to jealousy or a sudden desire for revenge — we know enough about Maoil-Seachlainn's character to immediately refute such charges, and he did not join the enemy. Even had he nursed a secret hatred of his supplanter, is it likely that he would have gone this far, losing two sons in the process?

Everything points to a quarrel between Maoil-Seachlainn and Murchadh. Remembering Murchadh's rudeness during the visit of Maol Mórdha to Kincora, it is not too difficult to imagine the hot-tempered prince, now past middle age and no doubt anxious for his father and his kingdom, throwing an insult at Maoil-Seachlainn; perhaps reminding him of the unhappy position in which he had found himself when Aodh of Aileach witheld his support at the turn of the century. Carefully given advice may have been rejected with a suggestion that a high king who had lost his throne was incapable of offering serious comment. Murchadh, although a brilliant warrior, does not seem to have been a person to whom tact came naturally. Just as easy is it to imagine that Maoil-Seachlainn, grieving for his sons, would have been easily wounded or insulted. The annalists, more tactful than Murchadh, overlook the fact that he took no part in the conflict. The *Annals of Ulster*, the least unbiased, speaks of the 'hosting of Brian, son of Cinnéide, son of Lorcán, King of Ireland, and by Maoil-Seachlainn, son of Domhnall, King of Tara' to Dublin — the first time, as a matter of interest, that the work refers to Brian as king of Ireland; the *Four Masters* has a similar passage, and the *Annals of Clonmacnoise* mentions his hosting with Brian, albeit adding darkly that although 'he fought on Brian's side, was his mortall enemie'.

That last hint can be ignored, but as Ryan has pointed out in his essay on Clontarf, evidence to the fact that Maoil-Seachlainn took no part in the battle is that not one prince or chieftain from Meath was among the slain. The story that Maoil-Seachlainn watched the battle from a nearby hill can also be taken as an example of the calumny poured upon his head by Munster annalists. What is more likely is that, insulted and annoyed, the king of Meath returned home.

Whatever Brian thought of this unfortunate event there was little he could do to make amends. He was seventy-three years old, and had not wanted this new confrontation. Murchadh, himself advanced in years by the standards of his times — he must have been about fifty-three or four — was in command of the army, and all Brian could do was to send a messenger southwards asking for immediate reinforcements from Donnchadh. They came too late.

Throughout his life, Brian had shown prudence when it came to battle. Rarely had he attacked before his own force was sure of an advantage — the sorties into Meath in 992 and 1000 had been misjudged, but without lasting consequences — and if uncertain of his position had retired to await opportunities. But the presence of the long-boats in the wide and beautiful harbour beneath Sitric's capital, and the danger of internal risings in Munster made a speedy engagement with the enemy essential. If he retreated to Kincora he would face not only a loss of prestige but would leave the middle of Ireland open to fresh ravages from Maol Mórdha and his allies.

As Brian retired for his last night on earth his mind must have been in turmoil, and in a receptive state for the visitation of Aoibhinn, the *leannán sídhe*, or banshee, of the Dalcassians. Romantic accounts of Clontarf recount her nocturnal visitation to his tent and her prophecy that:

> Murchadh shall fall; Brian shall fall;
> Ye all shall fall in one litter;
> This plain shall be red tomorrow with thy proud blood ...

Different stories tell of her visit to Murchadh and of the appearance to a *giolla grádha* — aide-de-camp — of Brian of a phantom army of priests who likewise prophesied the old king's death. Foolishly, the story was repeated to Brian, or so *Cogadh Gaedhel re Gallaibh* tells us, although with superstition not far beneath the skin of any eleventh-century Irishman it is likely that omens were seen or heard throughout the camp on that last night.

Omens were rife on the Norse side, too. Before Brodar had left his piratical lair, superhuman ravens with iron beaks and claws had attacked his ships (10); the *doppelgänger* of Earl Sigurd had appeared to men in the Orkneys and dreadful prognostications of death had been received as far afield as Iceland. Of course, such tales added to the romance of Clontarf when they were introduced in later years. If they were to be believed, the Norsemen were fated, long before they reached Dublin, to be wiped from the face of the earth. But to those they left behind, the more overwhelming the odds, the greater the glory, the swifter the path to Valhalla.

Just as much part of romance may have been the tale in which Brodar, widely regarded as a wizard, attempted to divine the outcome of the battle. The rather perplexing result of his sorcery was a prophecy that, should they fight on Good Friday, Brian would die although his army would be victorious; should they fight before, all who opposed Brian would perish. The apologists for Sigurd and his friends certainly made the most of their superstitions, and the fact that circumstances made a battle on Friday inevitable have been overlooked. Ignoring omens, Sigurd and Brodar could not afford to wait until Donnchadh, summoned by his father, arrived with a fresh band of Dalcassians and Eoghanachta; while the news that Maoil-Seachlainn had parted company with the royal army provided an unforeseen opportunity for success. Brian and Murchadh, on the other hand, knew that delay on their part could give the enemy a chance of fanning out into the countryside. They could only pray that Donnchadh arrived quickly.

According to the *Annals of Loch Cé*, Donnchadh was actually present the night before the battle. The banshee, Aoibhinn, we are told, indicated to Brian that 'the first son [whom thou shalt see] shall be king after thee'. Brian ordered his servant to find Murchadh — this, despite the warning that Murchadh was also doomed — but Donnchadh appeared in the tent and asked his father whether he should go on a foraging expedition or remain in the camp. Brian, according to the story, answered roughly: 'I care not what thou doest, as it was not for thee I was seeking', and Donnchadh left the tent 'in anger'. The *Annals of Loch Cé* is probably based on the same source material used by the compilers of the *Four Masters*, who do not use the story. Had it been widely known at the time they would surely have seized upon it. We can certainly dismiss it, although it is interesting in the light of subsequent events involving Donnchadh.

That restless night over, Brian rode down from his vantage point near the Wood of Tomar, overlooking the battlefield, and in the cold dawn of Good Friday reviewed his troops. Because of his age he could obviously take no active part in the battle, but it would have been a matter of prestige for him to appear before his men, some of whom had served in his campaigns since boyhood. Whether or not he made the flowery, impassioned speech attributed to him by his eulogists (11) is unimportant; his presence must have been inspiration enough for those who had followed him this far.

Each army was composed of divisions. The place of honour in Brian's army was held by Murchadh with the Dalcassians, while Cian of Desmond commanded the chief section of the Eoghanacht contingent. Other commanders included Domhnall, king of the Cinéal Laoghaire branch of the Eoghanacht Uí Eachach, against whom Cian was to fall in battle later in the year; mac Beatha, king of Ciarraighe Luachra, and Mothla, king of the Decies. The contingent from Connacht was led by Tadhg, king of the Uí Mhaine, and Maol Ruanaidh na Paidre Ó hEidhin, 'of the Prayer', ruler of Uí Fhiachrach Aidhne and of the family from which Brian's first wife, the faceless Mór, had come over half a century earlier.

On the other side, Maol Mórdha, Sigurd and Brodar seem to have held command as a triumvirate, while Sitric remained in Dublin, ostensibly to hold the city against assault and to render assistance in the event of a retreat. There is no mention of Gormfhlaith in the chronicles, but one can imagine her standing on the wooden ramparts of her son's capital to watch the anticipated spectacle of the defeat of her husband.

It is unfortunate that, as with the pre-battle narratives, there is no reliable account of the conflict itself. Clontarf provided contemporary and later writers with the chance to indulge in a style reminiscent of the balmy days of Celtic chivalry, when a battle was a determined series of duels between one man and another. Murchadh in particular is singled out as a hero worthy of the old sagas. Regarding Sigurd as a personal foe — surely Maol Mórdha would have been first on his list? — he hacked his way through lines of Norse warriors, who thrust and stabbed from behind their long 'shield-walls' until courage or strength failed them. Sigurd died honourably, his head cut from his body, but not before he had wrapped the raven banner of the Orkneys around himself, every other bearer having been cut down by Irish swords (12).

His death prevented the introduction into Irish history of another dynasty of Land Leapers, perhaps fortunately so, for his youngest son, Thorfinn, known as the Black, was to prove himself, in the words of the *Orkneyinga Saga*, lucky in victory and skilful in battles and good in attack. That he had no claims to an Irish kingdom can indeed be seen as a blessing.

Aged about six when his father died, Thorfinn was brought up by his grandfather, Malcolm II. The Orkneys had been divided among his three half-brothers, Somerled, Brusi and Einar, and King Malcolm created the child Earl of Caithness, afterwards laying claim to a third of the Orkneys in his name. But if Malcolm hoped, through the child, to tame the Norse of the islands, he was to be disappointed.

Thorfinn, in time, was to obtain the whole of the earldom, as well as a considerable portion of Celtic Scotland. In 1040 he took arms against his cousin, Duncan, who had succeeded Malcolm II in 1034. The king was defeated at the battle of Torfness and, in the retreat, murdered at Bothna-gowan, now known as Pitgaveny, in Elgin, by his cousin and general, Macbeth. Macbeth and Thorfinn ruled Scotland between them, and while Thorfinn's prowess may have been exaggerated by the *Orkneyinga Saga* he was doubtless an able politician, gaining the friendship not only of the kings of Norway and Denmark but the German Emperor, Henry III, and Pope Leo IX who gave him 'absolution for all his misdeeds'. He died in 1057, the same year as Macbeth, and his heirs were able only to hold the Orkneys, but it is interesting to note that his grandson, Magnus

Erlendsson, was to be canonised as St Magnus after his murder in 1115.

Sigurd compares favourably with that other Norse king safe behind the walls of Dublin. Sitric, we are told, watched the proceedings of the day with his wife, daughter of Brian, beside him. The Dalcassian princess had inherited the spirit of her family (13), for as a party of Norsemen passed by the walls, pursued towards the harbour by Murchadh, she said; 'It appears that the foreigners have gained their inheritance — their natural inheritance — the sea. I wonder is it the heat that is upon them?' Sitric 'dealt her a rude blow, which knocked out one of her teeth', and while nothing else is heard of the queen, who seems to have been a true sister of Murchadh for speaking her mind, one imagines she survived to tell the tale.

The battle lasted all day — on this most of the annalists agree — with each side hacking and thrusting at each other with sword, short-shafted, wide-bladed axes and the javelin or dart. As far as bodily protection was concerned, the Norse were superior — unlike the Irish they had a military class — and wore the byrnie or *lúireach*, probably made of leather and reinforced with metal studs and rings (14). By the Irish armour of any sort was little used as late as the sixteenth century, when there is more than one reference in English sources to the Irishmen 'casting off their clothes except their shirts' when preparing to do battle. But if they lacked mail or leather shirts, the Irish were determined, and as the watery, chilling sun began to sink the enemy found themselves enclosed in a semi-circle. At one stage, probably late in the day, Sitric emerged from Dublin; but scores of his men were soon cut down and the king barely escaped with his life. Maol Mórdha did not escape — no yew tree was at hand this time — but at which point of the battle he fell is uncertain. Indeed, several of the annals ignore his death altogether; the *Four Masters* states laconically that 'there fell Maol Mórdha', while an unidentified source (15) maintains that he was 'slain returning from Clontarf, by Gilla Bairrine at Drehid Dubhgal'. It is unlikely, however, that the man responsible for the battle would have been allowed to leave the field alive.

Sadly, Murchadh was another to fall. As the sun began to sink he encountered Amrud, a Norse leader, and the two closed in a death struggle. Murchadh's right arm was paining him from continual use — the weight of his weapons was considerable — and although at a disadvantage he managed to prostrate Amrud and drive home his sword by leaning his breast upon it and pressing downwards. Amrud, with a dying effort, gave Murchadh a fatal thrust with a small sword or dagger.

The byrnie or lúireach *worn by Norse and Dane at Clontarf*

The future hope of the Dál gCais lingered until the following morning, when he made his confession and received the Sacrament (16).

As the evening came the retreat to Dublin was cut off for the Norse and Danes, and for those of Maol Mórdha's men who might have thought it was safer to flee to the city than towards their homeland. The only way open to them was by the sea, and thither they fled, many drowning in the high tide that prevented them from reaching the security of the long-boats. It was a disordered rout, Brian's army rushing headlong into the sea after their foe, and the sea claimed victors and vanquished with impartiality; among them Murchadh's fifteen-year-old son, Toirdheal-bhach, 'found near the fishing weir of Clontarf, with both his hands fast bound in the hair of a Dane's head . . .' Once it was obvious that the day was lost, Brodar decided to make his escape before the *Ardrí's* chieftains singled him out for retribution. Rather than risk crossing the battlefield, and trying to enter Dublin, he turned northwards, hoping to circuit the main retreat and to reach the coast above the city where, under cover of night, he could find means to return to his ships. His retreat, with a handful of followers, led him directly to the Wood of Tomar, the hillock on which Brian was stationed.

The old king had spent the day kneeling in front of a pavilion, praying for victory and receiving news of the battle. The progress of Murchadh's blue standard had cheered him, but the news that his son was mortally wounded must have been hard to bear, for on that son had been pinned the hopes of the infant dynasty. Impatient and tactless Murchadh may, from time to time, have been, but he had played a vital role in Brian's climb to power and in the administration of the kingdom; and there were none more suited among the Dalcassians to succeed Brian if the family was to maintain its power, at least in the south. Of Brian's other sons, those nearest Murchadh in age, Conchobhar and Flann, simply vanish from history. They are supposed to have fallen at Clontarf, but that might have been a convenient way for the chroniclers to dispose of them. The eldest surviving son of Brian's next marriage, Tadhg, had apparently remained at Kincora to manage affairs during his father's absence at Clontarf (17); Domhnall had died in 1012 and Donnchadh, as we know, was the only other son to take part in Brian's campaigns.

The fall of Murchadh brought consternation to Brian's attendants — his special bodyguard led by Niall Ó Cuinn of the Muintir Ifearnáin in Thomond — although the tales that they deserted him, either to join in the general pursuit of the enemy or to gain safety themselves cannot be taken seriously (18). Usually, the aged king is portrayed in his last moments as being attended only by a page-boy, a portrait intended no doubt to add greater lustre to his name in that he died virtually alone. The *Annals of Loch Cé* reports that Conaing, his nephew, son of the long-dead *tánaiste* of Thomond, Donn Cuan, was with him, kneeling in prayer. The idea is feasible, for Conaing must have been advanced in years — his father had been killed when Brian was still a child — and he would have been been able to take as little part in the battle as Brian. His age and experience would have made him a suitable counsellor for his uncle and together they would have watched the conflict in progress beneath them. Both would have needed a bodyguard, although it may have been small, for Brodar and his companions are supposed to have passed close to the royal pavilion without being challenged. Perhaps the guard had their eyes turned on the rout, and in that moment a follower of Brodar noticed the old king. He may have been a Limerick Dane, who would have seen Brian often enough, or even a Leinsterman, and he drew Brodar's attention to the figure kneeling by the pavilion. Brodar at first disbelieved what he was told, but his companion insisted and the Danish pirate saw the chance of striking one last blow against the Dál gCais (19).

Rushing at the bodyguard, he hacked his way through to where Brian and Conaing knelt. One version of the tale maintains that Brian managed to lift his sword and wound Brodar in the leg; but it is unlikely that a man of seventy-three, weary and mourning the loss of one or more sons, would have found the strength to protect himself against sudden assault. Brodar's axe fell upon his undefended head, then upon Conaing, and as the sun finally sank in the west, and its dying rays faded into shadows that encompassed the wide breadth of the island, the life-blood of the man who had devoted himself to Ireland stained the earth at the place where those shadows first gathered. As the sound of victory rang from Irish throats across the plain of Clontarf, and the flames of Leinster, Danish and Norse pavilions served to prolong the fading light, the cold sea breezes stirred branches in the Wood of Tomar and caressed the venerable locks, stained with scarlet, of the frail body that had so recently housed the soul of the greatest Irishman of his age.

Donnchadh and his Dalcassians arrived from Wicklow on the evening of Easter Sunday and found Cian of Desmond to greet them with the tragic news. Three generations of Donnchadh's family had perished, together with their allies, Tadhg of Uí Mhaine, Maol Ruanaidh of the Uí

Fhiachrach Aidhne, Mothla of the Decies, Domhnall, great steward of Mar, Scannlán, king of the Eoghanacht of Loch Léin and many other princes and chieftains. The total loss of men — Brian's and the enemy — cannot be estimated because of the gross exaggeration in the annals, but so far as the Dalcassians were concerned the blow was severe, and it was not until the last two decades of the century that anything like a revival of their power took place.

There was some satisfaction in the knowledge that the slayer of Brian had not escaped. As the king fell, Brodar and his band retreated to the wood and tried to conceal themselves. A number of trees had been felled to provide firewood for the *Ardrí*'s army, and branches lay about on every side. The remnants of the royal bodyguard — the *Annals of Ulster* says that Niall Ó Cuinn himself was slain, so that a fight to save the king must have been made — were augmented by troops from the battlefield, and taking the branches in their hands they formed a circle about Brodar's hiding place. Advancing steadily, they flung the branches upon the Danes before self-defence was possible (20); Brodar was captured alive and shortly paid the penalty for his deeds by having his entrails wound about a tree while he was living.

Brian is supposed to have made his will during the course of the battle (21), although evidence is unreliable. 'I bequeath my soul to God and to the intercession of St Patrick, my body to Armagh, and my blessing to my son Donnchadh ... convey my body to Duleek, sacred to St Ciarán, thence to Louth. And let Maol Muire, successor to St Patrick, together with his clergy, come thither for my remains ...' The interesting part of this will, as handed down, is Brian's blessing on Donnchadh. It makes the story of Donnchadh's appearance on the previous evening less likely than ever, but why a blessing for him and not for Tadhg? After Murchadh, Tadhg was the eldest son, apparently trusted enough to administer affairs at Kincora and, if Brian intended to institute an hereditary, rather than tanistric, principle of succession, the son most likely to succeed him. A blessing was tantamount to the nomination of a successor; was Tadhg of a disposition unsuited to continuing his father's work? Hardly, if Brian had given him duties which removed him from the risk of dying at Clontarf. Of course, the original account of the will, if indeed a will was made, could have been altered in later years to make Donnchadh's eventual succession — and suspected fratricide — appear legitimate; for while Murchadh would have found general support as Brian's heir, Donnchadh was the youngest of all the sons.

But the most immediate concern of the survivors was the burial of Brian's remains and those of the other dead. Easter Monday 'was spent in visiting the field of battle, for the purpose of burying the dead and succouring the wounded. The bodies of thirty chieftains were sent off to their territorial churches to be interred in their family burial grounds; and those who were still living among the wounded, were carried on biers and litters to the camp' (22). The bodies of Brian and Murchadh were carried to Swords, and thence escorted by the clergy to Armagh. With unprecedented ceremony, a tribute to his accomplishments and, more particularly, to his recognition of Armagh as supreme spiritual centre of Ireland, Brian was buried alone in a stone or marble coffin on the north-western side of the church — the side traditionally reserved for those slain in battle (23). Murchadh was buried in a coffin apart, together with the heads of his cousin, Conaing, and Mothla of the Decies, a special tribute to those two men, whose bodies, presumably, were returned for inter-ment in their own churches. For twelve days masses were said for the souls of father and son in churches and monasteries throughout the country; Brian had enabled the church to exist in relative peace and it now paid him the highest tribute. Never before had there been such a funeral in Ireland.

Memorial stone, Armagh Cathedral

And at Armagh Brian rests to this day; far from the woods and mountains of his beloved Thomond, far from the wild tracts where, as a youth, he had led a band of Dalcassians to harry the Danes. The exact location of his grave has been long forgotten — Armagh cathedral itself, a late nineteenth-century reconstruction and enlargement of a thirteenth-century shell, bears little resemblance to the structure of Brian's day; and indeed the building beside which the king was buried was destroyed by fire in the spring of 1020. Only a modern slab, set in the outside wall of the north transept commemorates the fact that he is buried there at all, but it is nevertheless a fitting resting place, in the grounds hallowed by the greatest figure inIrish spiritual history; a figure, like Brian, who rose from relative obscurity to cause his adopted country to be more than a fleeting shadow on the page of history. But while the work of the former slave-boy prospered and withstood the buffets of future centuries, the work of Brian Boru died with him.

Brian's tragedy is that he lived too long. Had he died quietly at Kincora in the midst of his 'notable reformation' there is a chance that Murchadh would have continued his work, in Leath Mogha if not elsewhere, with some success. His outbursts at Kincora and, presumably, before Clontarf, must have been due in considerable degree to frustration, albeit loyal frustration, at waiting so long to take his father's place. Had he gained the throne when Ireland was peaceful it is unlikely that he would have destroyed that which he had helped to build. Maol Mórdha would have posed a problem, but it is likely that the king of Leinster would have died violently before long, as two of his successors were to die within four years of Clontarf. Allies for Murchadh might always be found among the families of southern Leinster, and some form of peace assured in the east.

Had Murchadh survived Clontarf, he would have been able to rally the Dalcassians after the shock of Brian's death, but Tadhg and Donnchadh had not assumed the same heroic stature in the eyes of their clansmen. All Donnchadh could do was to turn towards Kincora with his own small band and the exhausted survivors of the battle. Their Scottish and Connacht allies returned to their own homes, while the Norsemen of Dublin and the followers of Maol Mórdha, as depleted as the victors, were unable to do more than lick their wounds behind the city walls. At least those walls were, for the moment, standing. Their friends from the Orkneys and Man had only to await low tide before regaining their long-boats.

Clontarf may have been a victory over the enemies of Brian's political schemes, but it also heralded the defeat of those policies. Unable to assail Dublin, hardly able to return to Munster, the Dál gCais and the Eoghanachta began once more to contest the provincial throne, Cian of Desmond reviving the old bitterness by claiming his rights as representative of generations of kings. O'Mahony maintains that he had 'never reconciled himself to the subordinate position that he was obliged to hold during the time of Brian's predominance'. This must be pure guesswork on O'Mahony's part, although we can imagine that Cian decided that Tadhg and Donnchadh were incapable of ruling with the force and vigour of their father; and with Brian and Murchadh dead there must have seemed little point, to Cian at least, of continuing the subjugation of his own family.

According to the *Leabhar Oiris*, the survivors of Brian's army camped at Kilmainham after the battle and began their homeward march as one army until they reached Mullaghmast, five miles east of present-day Athy in Co Kildare and some twenty-four miles from Kilmainham. There they separated into two camps, which gave Cian an opportunity of observing the diminished numbers in the Dál gCais ranks. This, says O'Mahony, encouraged the Eoghanacht prince to send Donnchadh a request for the restoration of the hostages, presumably taken by Brian before Clontarf to ensure the loyalty of the Eoghanachta, and for recognition of himself as king of Munster. Donnchadh refused the requests and, according to the romantic account in *Cogadh Gaedhel re Gallaibh*, prepared to give Cian battle, the Dál gCais warriors, sick and wounded as they were, stuffing their wounds with healing bog moss and binding those who could not stand, to vertical stakes. Cian, according to this story, retained his sense of honour, refusing to fight, and the two armies, once again men of Thomond and Desmond, went their separate ways. But before the Dál gCais reached their destination they faced another hostile gathering under Donnchadh mac Giolla Phádraig, king of Osraighe, who asked for hostages. The *Leabhar Oiris* tells us that Donnchadh, son of Brian, expressed his surprise — one imagines, rather scathingly — that 'such a demand should come from the men of Osraighe'.

Whether such a demand came from Osraighe is open to question. The Dál gCais could hardly have risked resisting the forces of mac Giolla Phádraig after suffering the loss of so many of their warriors at Clontarf, and one is tempted to suggest that the story was invented, or at least grafted onto the claims of Cian, by pro-Dalcassian annalists in an attempt to show that the Dál gCais, despite sickness and suffering in their ranks, could still put up a gallant resistance.

Whatever happened, it is obvious that Thomond and Desmond were to go their own ways after Clontarf; Brian, the binding factor, was dead and Cian, perhaps regarding his Dál gCais brothers-in-law as men incapable of maintaining the peace of Munster, saw that the only way of safeguard-

Cró-inis, where Maoil-Seachlainn died in 1022

ing Desmond was to assert his independence. Before long he was to face dissension within his own kingdom.

As far as the high throne was concerned, the only man worthy of succeeding Brian did so. Maoil-Seachlainn was restored, not as titular exponent of Uí Néill grandeur but with the courage he had exhibited in earlier days. In January of the following year (24), assisted by his kinsman, Flaithbheartach, king of Aileach, he carried on the work Brian and Murchadh had been prevented from completing. Marching on Dublin, he burned the city and turned south to Leinster, levying the *Bóramha* and receiving a 'great prey' of hostages. Munster he ignored, for like Cian he must have known Brian's surviving sons well enough to realise that, with their father's death, there would be no need to press claims on Leath Mogha. To Maoil-Seachlainn, to his kinsmen, the Dál gCais interlude was over, the old order restored, and those kinsmen, for whatever reason they had once deserted him, now welcomed him back. No Dál gCais were needed to show them how to subdue Leinster and the foreigners. Maoil-Seachlainn had been content to submit to Brian once, because he had recognised his rival's abilities. Before the battle of Clontarf he had found an old, white-haired, probably confused, man who, by the law of nature, could scarcely live much longer. Had Murchadh lived, Maoil-Seachlainn may have been prepared to allow that prince the chance of preserving his father's peace, but with both of them dead it was time to resume the reins of power. One cannot help but wonder if Brian had been defeated by Maoil-Seachlainn at the start of their fifteen-year rivalry, would Maoil-Seachlainn have achieved the same degree of 'notable reformation' himself. He may never have ruled Munster, as Brian never ruled the northern kingdoms, but he could, in those years before Gleann Máma, have rebuilt the power of the Uí Néill in something more than titular authority. Certainly, after Clontarf, he was the principal barrier to fresh Viking incursion.

In 1014, Maoil-Seachlainn was about sixty-six years of age, and the time for him to emulate Brian's successes was past. Before Brian's earthly remains had turned to dust it seemed as though his system of government of real hegemony over most of the states of Ireland had been no more than a dream. Maoil-Seachlainn lived on, respected and benevolent, until 1022 when, 'the pillar of the dignity and nobility of the west of the world' (25), he died at Cró-inis, an island retreat in Lough Ennell, within sight of his palace of Dún na Sciath. 'The Archbishop of Armagh, the *comharba* of St Colam Cille, and the *comharba* of St Ciarán being present, after he had received the Sacrament of Extreme Unction, he died a good death', reports the *Annals of Clonmacnoise*; and within a year of his burial at Armagh the forces of anarchy were again loose in Ireland.

Whatever his blessing to Donnchadh was intended to convey, Brian's eldest surviving son, Tadhg, had been proclaimed king of Thomond and, henceforth, the system of tanistry, in which the multitude of descendants of Donn Cuan and Mathghamhain might have claimed a right to the throne, was forgotten. And Tadhg found that throne difficult enough to retain. In 1019 there was a revolt among the Uí Chaisín — ancestors of the Macnamara clan — in Co Clare, in the course of which Donnchadh lost his right hand; and in 1023 Tadhg was slain by the Éile, a tribe whose territory was the present-day baronies of Ikerrin and Eliogarty in Co Tipperary, and Ballybritt and Clonlisk in Co Offaly. Donnchadh is generally believed to have been involved in his brother's death — although the more reputable annalists say nothing of this — and he certainly seized the throne of Thomond, driving his young nephew, Toirdhealbhach, into exile with his foster-father, Diarmaid mac Maoil na mBó, king of Leinster. That alliance, the one act of diplomacy from Tadhg's reign of which we know anything, was to stand the infant prince in good stead; but for the moment his supporters were without the strength to resist Donnchadh, who quickly proved himself a petty tyrant.

That he became king with only one hand is evidence both of his strength and of a weakening of the ancient codes surrounding monarchy. Under the Brehonic laws, a man with a physical blemish was automatically debarred from kingship, and there is no evidence that Donnchadh followed the example of the mythological Nuadhat Airgeadlámh, 'of the Silver Hand', a king of the Tuatha dé Danann whose missing extremity was replaced by the skill of his silversmith.

The death of Maoil-Seachlainn had left the high throne vacant, the electors of the Uí Néill unable to appoint even a puppet successor, although Flaithbheartach of Aileach would seem to have been an obvious choice. Donnchadh, who may have had the ambition but not the intelligence of his father, marched into Meath, and then into Leinster and Osraighe, taking in Dublin on the way. He 'carried off their pledges', say the annalists, and the hosting must have been undertaken in secrecy and with speed, for the Dalcassians, like their neighbours, were still waiting for the next generation of fighting men to mature after the losses at Clontarf.

In 1027 and 1031 Donnchadh again plundered the kingdom of Osraighe — the control of which was so vital to anyone who would rule Leath Mogha — but on both occasions met with heavy losses. He might style himself high king, but he achieved no more than Feidhlimidh mac Criomhthainn had done two centuries before. In Leath Cuinn, Flaithbheartach of Aileach proved himself an able monarch, while in Osraighe the rise of another Donnchadh — mac Giolla Phádraig — saw the king of Thomond's hopes blasted in that direction. Donnchadh of Osraighe overthrew the last of the heirs of Maol Mórdha in Leinster in 1036 and became king of the eastern kingdom until his death in 1039; Donnchadh of Thomond found his own wars degenerating to the old level of hostings against the Eoghanachta, by whom the crown of Munster was once again held. In 1045 and 1057 the reigning Eoghanacht sovereigns were killed, and in 1058 Donnchadh himself was expelled by his nephew, Toirdhealbhach, aided by Diarmaid mac Maoil na mBó, who sixteen years earlier had become king of Leinster.

Donnchadh was driven into exile and a monastery in Rome, and there he died in 1064, traditionally bequeathing the diadem and sceptre of the *Ardrí* to Pope Alexander II (26). His death removed from the stage of history the last of the principal characters involved in the events culminating at the fishing weir of Clontarf. Of the others, Sitric of Dublin, known in Norse chronicles by the nickname of Silkenbeard, continued to rule his kingdom, having for the third time in his life pledged lip-service to his step-father Maoil-Seachlainn. While Maoil-Seachlainn lived — and, then, during the reign of Flaithbheartach of Aileach — Sitric was unable to follow the pattern of his ancestors in remoulding Dublin as a major political centre in Ireland. Having rebuilt his city, he concentrated on wrangling with Leinster. In 1018 he blinded his cousin, Braon, son of Maol Mórdha, who had become king in 1016 after the deaths in quick succession of two other rulers of Leinster (27); but if he hoped to assert sovereignty over the kingdom he was unsuccessful. In 1021, the new king of Leinster, Úghaire, a monarch of very different mould to Maol Mórdha, defeated the Dublin army at present-day Delgany in Co Wicklow, and the influence of the dynasty of Ivar declined still more. In 1030 we find Sitric attacking the monastery of Kildare — achieved through the 'negligence of a wicked woman', as the annalists comment tantalisingly — and a victory over the Conaille Muirtheimhne, the Uí Dhorthain and the Uí Mheith at Inbhear Boinne — the mouth of the River Boyne — in 1035 was probably his military swansong.

In 1034 his son, another Olaf, was 'killed by Saxons' — perhaps while crossing England — journeying on pilgrimage to Rome, a journey Sitric himself had made in 1028, according to the *Four Masters*. In 1040 Sitric built the church of St Olaf, dedicated to that unlikely patron of Norway who had been slain, forcibly converting his subjects in 1030, and perhaps as a memorial to his dead son. The church, now replaced by Christ Church Cathedral, epitomised the sheathing of the Norse sword. Shortly afterwards Sitric was expelled from Dublin by Margrad of Waterford, who founded a new dynasty in the city-state, and he died in 1042 either on a final pilgrimage to Rome or, following in his father's footsteps, Iona. His daughter, Cailleach Fionáin, died in the same month, but the annalists fail to say where, or whether she was the daughter of the marriage to that Dalcassian princess who had watched the rout of Clontarf from the walls of Dublin.

One figure more remains — that of Gormfhlaith. She is said to have lived on until 1030, perhaps within the protecting walls of her son's kingdom, perhaps returning to Leinster and a quiet end within monastic walls — other women of her mould had done the same, notably the Saxon Elfrida, whose machinations had placed Ethelred the Redeless on the English throne in 978. The two women have a not dissimilar history, for both caused the death of kings — Elfrida by the knife and Gormfhlaith in a more spectacular way. Elfrida's murder of the young Edward 'the Martyr' at Corfe opened the way for Danish domination of her country; but Gormfhlaith's intrigues led to the weakening and, eventually, destruction of the power of her own family in Leinster and that of her son in Dublin.

Of all the descendants of Brian, who maintained the title of kings of Thomond until Henry VIII of England replaced it with an earldom in

1543, the one nearest to him in temperament and ability was Muircheartach Mór, his great-grandson. *Ardrí* from 1086 to 1119, he donated Cashel to the Irish church in 1101 and was, according to the historian Lanigan, 'an eminent prince, whose character ranked so highly in his lifetime that he was often consulted by the king of England, Henry I.' Muircheartach provided the timber for the original roof of Westminster Hall, and by St Anselm, Archbishop of Canterbury, was surnamed 'the Magnificent'.

Certainly, he alone among those who called themselves high kings, with or without opposition, after the death of Maoil-Seachlainn, showed signs of greatness. Was it merely a coincidence that his father, Toirdhealbhach, had married Mór, daughter of the ruler of Uí Fhiachrach Aidhne — a princess who bore the same name and blood as the first wife of Brian Boru? Muircheartach emulated his great-grandfather in many ways: he faced rivalry for the high throne from Domhnall Ó Lochlainn of Aileach and new threats from Dublin which, showing an inherent political sense, he avoided by marrying his daughter to Magnus, king of Dublin.

But the glory had passed with Maoil-Seachlainn in 1022 and, with the exception of Muircheartach, who had to wait until 1101 before general recognition as *Ardrí*, none of the Dalcassians and none of the Uí Néill who claimed the title were anything more than *go-bhfreasabhra*, never acknowledged and often resisted (28). After Muircheartach's death the political scene degenerated into a squabble between the Uí Conchobhair in the west and the Uí Lochlainn in the north; and the last prince of the Uí Néill to call himself *Ardrí*, Aodh Ó Lochlainn, was defeated and slain in 1166.

Brian Boru's hope of the high throne held by Dalcassian hands as a benefit to Ireland as a whole, died in 1014, and the battle at Clontarf has become the only reason that most people remember Brian at all; for the church has never taken seriously the inclusion in O'Hanlon's hagiology (29) of the life and works of the 'Blessed Brian Boru, King and Martyr'.

Such is the irony of history. But the aged *Ardrí* died not defending his kingdom against pagan invaders; he died, as other kings died, resisting those who questioned his authority. Clontarf simply brought to an end a remarkable reign of diplomacy and intellect, and halted a few short years of native regeneration. It should be remembered for that reason. Diplomacy and intellect so often took second place to brute force and violent cunning in Irish history before and after the time of Brian Boru.

Bibliography and Notes

CHAPTER ONE   *The Land Leapers*

(1) The Frankish chroniclers termed them Northmen, or Norsemen, a suitable sobriquet for the early invaders, as they included not only the inhabitants of Scandinavia but Picts from the wilds of what was to become Scotland. Later, Northmen identified the men of Norway only, as two separate peoples — Norwegians and Danes — settled in Ireland. In England the title 'Dane' was applied indiscriminately to all the invaders; and as J. M. Flood points out in *The Northmen in Ireland* (Dublin, date not given), 'Dane' or 'Danar' appears to have become synonymous with 'pirate'. To confuse matters more, the mediaeval romances referred to them as 'Africans' or 'Saracens', and Giraldus Cambrensis, historian of the Cambro-Norman invasion, alludes to Gurmundus — presumably Turges — son of an 'African prince', as 'conqueror of Ireland'. Such terms, perhaps, became synonymous with the opponents of Christianity as a result of the Crusades, but the position is best summarised by Stewart Oakley in *The Story of Denmark* (London, 1972): '... the records do not distinguish clearly between Danes and Norwegians any more than they probably did themselves ...'

(2) According to *The History of Ireland, Ancient and Modern*, by Martin Haverty (Dublin, 1867), '... it has been calculated that the ancient Irish monks had 13 monastic foundations in Scotland, 12 in England, 7 in France, 12 in Armoric Gaul, 7 in Lotharingia, 11 in Burgundy, 9 in Belgium, 10 in Alsatia, 16 in Bavaria, 6 in Italy and 15 in Rhetia, Helvetia and Suevia, besides many in Thuringia and on the left margin of the Rhine, between Gueldrea and Alsatia ...'

(3) The annalists record it as the 'burning of Reachrainn by the Gentiles, and its shrines broken and plundered', a statement that has caused several writers to identify the island with the present Rathlinn off the coast of Antrim. But both this island and Lambay were anciently called Reachrainn. Recognised authorities, including Liam de Paor contributing 'The age of the Viking wars' to *The course of Irish history*, edited by T. W. Moody and Fr F. X. Martin (Cork, 1967), are of the opinion that the attack was launched on Lambay Island.

(4) *A History of Denmark,* by Erik Kjersgaard (Copenhagen, 1974).

(5) *The Place Names of the Decies,* by the Very Revd P. Canon Power, DLitt, MRIA (Oxford, 1952). The history of the kingdom may serve to illustrate the elasticity of an Irish state, and the difficulty in locating present-day boundaries. As Canon Power says, 'Today the whole scheduled region is divided into eight complete baronies, with one almost complete and small portions of three others' in counties Cork, Waterford and Tipperary.

(6) *Irish Kings and High Kings,* by Francis John Byrne, Professor of early Irish history at University College, Dublin (London, 1973).

(7) *The Celtic Realms,* by Myles Dillon, late senior professor, Dublin Institute for Advanced Studies, and the late Dr Nora K. Chadwick, honorary Fellow, Newnham College, Cambridge (London, second edition, 1972). The kingdom of Midhe did not correspond to the present-day Co Meath, in which Tara stands. Tara appears to have been situated in the ancient Breagh — present Meath, south Louth and north Co Dublin, according to Dillon and Chadwick.

(8) *Early Irish History and Mythology,* by Thomas F. O'Rahilly (Dublin, 1971). See also *A History of Ireland,* by Edmund Curtis, MA, DLitt, late Lecky Professor of Modern History in the University of Dublin (London, 1961).

(8a) *Collectanea de Rebus Hibernicia,* edited by Charles Vallancey (1770), including the highly unreliable MSS of Sir Henry Piers of Tristernach Abbey, Co Meath (*obit* 1691), largely a collection of bad transcriptions from early chronicles. Dillon and Chadwick, in *The Celtic Realms,* suggest that the number was as small as ninety-seven, many of them corresponding with present-day baronies. For one of the simplest accounts of the settlement of Ireland, see *History of the Irish State to 1014,* by Alice Stopford Green (London, 1925). Haverty, in *The History of Ireland, Ancient and Modern,* writes: 'The Hy Nialls (Uí Néill) of the north were sub-divided into Kinel-Conell (Cinéal gConaill) and Kinel-Owen (Cinéal Eoghain). The former of these were excluded from the sovereignty since the death of Flahertach in 760; and the dignity of monarch alternated with tolerable regularity between the Kinel-Owen branch and the southern or Meath branch ... The Ulidians, or people of eastern Ulster, had their own king, and were rarely on amicable terms with their Hy Niall neighbours ...'

(9) Dillon and Chadwick, *The Celtic Realms.* But the *Annals of the Four Masters,* edited by John O'Donovan, MRIA, BL, second edition, (Dublin, 1856) records his death as taking place in 'The Age of Christ, 266'; while Byrne, in *Irish Kings and High Kings,* thinks AD366 a more realistic date, particularly as the 'chronology of the fifth-century Uí Néill dynasty has almost certainly undergone a deliberate process of pre-dating ...'

(10) Byrne, *Irish Kings and High Kings.* 'He [Cormac] is the only figure ... whose career one is tempted to regard as historical'. Dillon and Chadwick, on the other hand, regard the fifth century as the first reliable phase of Irish

history, although they admit that the chronology of the century is 'very uncertain' (*The Celtic Realms*, p. 55, note 3). Joan Newlon Radner, editing the *Fragmentary Annals of Ireland* (Dublin, 1978) maintains that recent research suggests that all the early chronicles represent the abridgement of a single text compiled under Uí Néill patronage up to, or about, the year 911.

(11) Alice Stopford Green, *History of the Irish State to 1014*.

(12) Byrne, *Irish Kings and High Kings*.

(13) *Historical Memoir of the O'Briens*, by John O'Donoghue, MA, BL (Dublin, 1860). A useful volume, much of which is based on O'Donovan's translation of the *Four Masters*.

(14) Byrne, *Irish Kings and High Kings*.

(15) Dillon and Chadwick, *The Celtic Realms*.

(16) See *Gaelic and Gaelicised Ireland in the Middle Ages* by Kenneth Nicholls (Dublin, 1972); also Byrne *Irish Kings and High Kings*.

(17) Byrne, *Irish Kings and High Kings*.

(18) *Ibid*. See also Professor Myles Dillon's paper, 'The taboos of the kings of Ireland' in *Proceedings of the Royal Irish Academy*, LIV (1951).

(19) *Leabhar na gCeart (The Book of Rights)* was edited with copious notes and translation by John O'Donovan, MRIA, BL (Dublin, 1847). O'Donovan noted that [in his day] 'two ancient vellum copies' were in existence, one in the *Book of Lecan*, supposedly compiled from another MSS in 1418; the other in the *Book of Ballymote*, compiled by various scribes from other MSS about the year 1390. O'Donovan felt that the stipends and tributes were of some antiquity, but emphasised that there were probably alterations made 'so as to agree with the tribes and sub-divisions of Ireland' at varying periods in history. The next, and latest, translation, by the late Professor Myles Dillon, appeared as *Lebor na Cert* (Dublin, for the Irish Texts Society, 1962); and while the text differs little from O'Donovan's version, Dillon regarded the first translation as unsatisfactory and not a straightforward assessment of the material as an historical document.

(20) Dillon, *Lebor na Cert*.

(21) Byrne, in *Irish Kings and High Kings*, cites Xenophon's *Anabasis* as providing a parallel from sixth-century [BC] Persia, with the pretender Cyrus winning submission from the ruler of Tarsus — the equivalent of an Irish *tuath* — and bestowing upon him gifts which it was the prerogative of the king to give.

(22) The account is that given by O'Donovan. Dillon replaces words such as 'matals' with 'cloaks', 'scings' with the completely different 'hides'.

(23) *Irish Battles*, by G. A. Hayes-McCoy (London, 1969).

(24) *History of Ireland*, by Stephen Gwynn (London, 1924).

(25) O'Donovan, in a footnote to *Leabhar na gCeart*, mentions a passage from the *Four Masters*, in which it is claimed that Tara was captured by the Uí Néill at the battle of Druim Deargaighe in 507AD. But this is in conflict with the theory, already mentioned, that the Uí Néill colonisation had

started in the previous century, probably from Tara itself. Traditionally, the last *Ardrí* to live at Tara was Diarmaid, who died in battle in 558, the place being deserted in fulfillment of a curse placed on the king by two monks, Bréanainn of Biorra and Ruadhán of Lothra. They prophesied Diarmaid falling in battle, a safe prediction for those days, and Ruadhán, himself a prince of Munster, the ascendancy of his own people. But, as Eoin MacNeill has pointed out in *Phases of Irish History* (Dublin, 1920), the real reason behind the desertion of Tara was due, in part at least, to the ending of military organisation in Ireland: in other words, the place could no longer be defended. The *ráthanna* or seats of the Uí Néill in the North and Meath could be better fortified although Tara was still used for ceremonial occasions, and held an important place in Irish life, as the *Annals of Ulster* for 779 suggest with the mention of 'an assembly of synods of Uí Néill and the men of Leinster in *the town of Tara*' (my italics). Professor R. A. S. Macalister, DLitt, LLD, FSA, suggests in *Tara: A Pagan Sanctuary of Ancient Ireland* (London, 1931) that the date from which the expression 'King of Tara' becomes merely a synonym for (titular) 'King of Ireland' is 839. There is no evidence to suppose that buildings remained at Tara by the time of Brian Boru.

(26) Canon E. A. Dalton, *The History of Ireland*, vol 1 (London, 1906), suggests that the *Fionnghaill* were 'the fair-headed inhabitants of Norway', the *Dubhghaill* complexion being 'of a darker tinge'. Haverty, in *The History of Ireland, Ancient and Modern*, adds that the *Dubhghaill* were 'probably the people of Jutland, and the southern shores of the Baltic Sea'.

(27) The Revd Geoffrey Keating, DD (1570–1650), a native of Clogheen, Co Tipperary, completed his *History of Ireland* about 1625, but he found it was impossible to have it published, perhaps because it was written in the Irish language and character. An English translation, by Dermod O'Connor, was first published in London in 1723, a second edition in 1726. But, according to P. W. Joyce in *A Social History of Ancient Ireland*, vol 1, 3rd impression (Dublin, 1920), O'Connor 'wilfully departed from his text and his translation is utterly misleading'. The complete text and translation, with notes, was issued by the Irish Texts Society of London, 1901–1914 in four volumes. But while O'Connor may be blamed for the dubious reputation Keating acquired, Keating himself believed in stories such as the arrival 'at the earliest period' in Irish history of the three daughters of Cain, no less. The original work is best summarised by Thomas D'Arcy McGee in *The Irish Writers of the Seventeenth Century* (Dublin, 1846) as 'a semi-bardic and semi-historical work ...'

(28) See 'The Vikings and the western world' by the late Dr Nora K. Chadwick, published in the proceedings of the International Congress of Celtic Studies held in Dublin, July 6 to 10, 1959, under the title *The impact of the Scandinavian invasions on the Celtic-speaking Peoples, c. 800–1100AD*, edited by Brian Ó Cúiv (Dublin, 1975). Dr Chadwick points out that the 'similarity of the high altar to the lofty incantation platform on which the

Norse magicians performed their magical rites must have been irresistible'.

(29) *North Munster Studies*, edited by Dr Etienne Rynne, MRIA, when Assistant Keeper, Irish Antiquities Division, National Museum of Ireland (Limerick; 1967): essay on 'The plundering and burning of churches in Ireland, 7th to 16th century' by A. T. Lucas, then director, National Museum of Ireland. He claims that between 695 and 1162 some sixty-eight clerics were slain, forty-one by the Irish, twenty-four by the Vikings. The number seems ridiculously small when he also states that in 816, according to the *Annals of Ulster*, four hundred 'persons' were killed in a contest between the communities of Taghmon and Ferns. The Durrow-Clonmacnoise contest has already been referred to; and while many of the 'persons' were doubtless laymen and servants attached to the monasteries, dead clerics would have numbered more than sixty-eight!

(30) *Ibid.*

(31) *Ibid.*

(32) Constitutions of the diocese of Ossory made at the Synod of Kilkenny in 1317 included the following clause: 'Those who in any way violently remove persons accused of crime who have fled for refuge to churches . . . or plunder goods deposited therein for safety, or who shall aid or abet others in so doing, shall *ipso facto* incur the greater excommunication . . .'

(33) For further reading on the round towers see the essay on 'The origin and usage of the round towers of Ireland', by George Petrie, RHA, VPRIA, in *The ecclesiastical antiquities of Ireland anterior to the Norman invasion* (Dublin, 1845); *Notes on Irish architecture*, vol II, by Edwin, third Earl of Dunraven, edited by Margaret Stokes (London, 1877); and the essay on round towers by Hodder M. Westropp in the *Ulster Journal of Archaeology*, vol 9 (Belfast, 1861–2).

(34) *Annals of the Kingdom of Ireland*, commonly called *Annals of the Four Masters*, compiled from earlier sources between 1632 and 1636 by (Brother) Mícheál Ó Cléirigh, OFM; Cú Choigcríche Ó Clérigh, Fear Fasa Ó Maoilchonaire and Cú Choigcríche Ó Duibhgeannáin. The original compilation was begun in the Franciscan convent of Dún na nGall (Donegal) and, when completed, was signed by the collectors and transcribers — except for Cú Choigcríche Ó Duibhgeannáin, who was absent on the day when the parchment was autographed. The *Annals* are dedicated to Fearghal Ó Gadhra, Lord of Moy and Coolavin in Co Sligo, 'the chieftain under whose patronage, and for whose use, the *Annals* were compiled', according to O'Donovan in his introduction to the 2nd edition of his translation (Dublin, 1856). According to Professor Eugene O'Curry, MRIA, author of *Lectures on the Manuscript Materials of Ancient Irish History* (Dublin, 1861), more than four worked on the *Annals*, including Muiris Ó Maoilchonaire, whose signature also appears on the copy, or part of one, which is today kept in the library of the Franciscan House of Studies at 'Dún Mhuire', Killiney, Co Dublin. But Muiris was only an associate of the 'four', as were Conaire Ó Cléirigh and Muiris

Ó Duinnshléibhe, two others who did not sign. The MS at 'Dún Mhuire' is part of one of the originals, the rest of which is in the library of the Royal Irish Academy, Dublin. Two copies of the MS were also made, one for Louvain Catholic University, the other for Fearghal Ó Gadhra. Part of the second copy is today in the library of Trinity College, Dublin.

(35) According to Dr Nora Chadwick ('The Vikings and the western world') Dublin was first occupied in 836 and a *longphurt*, or base from which to forage, was set up in 841. This does not invalidate the widely-held theory that an Irish settlement existed before these dates; indeed *Viking Settlement to Medieval Dublin: Daily Life 840–1540* (Dublin, for the Curriculum Development Unit, 1978) speaks of two settlements — Duibhlinn, a monastic enclosure of the sixth or seventh century — and Áth Cliath, a community of sorts on the ridge above the 'ford of the hurdles'. For further reading see *Dublin Before the Vikings, An Adventure in Discovery*, by Dr George A. Little (Dublin, 1957). A *longphurt* was also established, 840–1, at Anagassan in Co Louth.

(36) In his translation of the Revd John Lynch's *Cambrensis Eversus, seu potius Historica Fides in Rebus Hibernicis Giraldo Cambrensi Abrogata*, etc (Dublin, 1848–52), the Revd Matthew Kelly pointed out that ancient laws prescribed that 'all persons guilty of grevious crimes, and especially tyrants, traitors and parricides, should be sewn up alive in a sack and thrown into a river'. But the author, Lynch, was no less biased than Giraldus, although we must remember that the punishment for sacrilege in the time of Turges was drowning, with or without a sack, and it is probable that he met his death in such a way. In *A Social History of Ancient Ireland* (Dublin, 1920), P. W. Joyce, LLD, MRIA, says that the island fortress was known by the local inhabitants as Dún Tuirgéis, or Turges's Fort. It is also interesting to note that a modern writer, Magnus Magnusson, in *Viking Expansion Westwards* (London, 1973) doubts the existence of Turges, but does little to qualify his misgivings. He also compares Brian Boru to the 'obscure English war-leader called Arthur', and maintains that only through the pages of *Cogadh Gaedhel re Gallaibh* did Brian achieve the status of 'a peerless Christian emperor'. Such a sweeping dismissal is easy to make, but more difficult to qualify! For further reading see *The Placenames of Westmeath*, Rev Paul Walsh, MA, DLitt (Dublin, 1957); and *Annals of Westmeath*, James Wood (Dublin, 1907).

(37) Cionaoth II, surnamed mac Ailpín, a putative descendent of Fearghus mac Earca, assumed the throne in 834. By 850 he had destroyed Pictish power and united under his rule all but the Norse west coast of Alba. The *Annals of Ulster* and the *Four Masters* refer to him as 'king of the Picts', and it is not until the twelfth-century chronicler, Henry of Huntingdon, writes of him that we have the first mention of 'king of the Scots'. The last monarch of the Dál Riada race, Alexander III, died in a riding accident in 1285–6.

(38) *The Anglo-Saxon Chronicle*, a compilation of annals, was produced at the end of the ninth century in Wessex, under the supervision of Alfred the

Great. The events it describes were recorded often a century after they took place and are doubtless exaggerated. See also 'King Alfred, an eleventh centenary' by Timothy Wilson-Smith in *History Today*, Volume XXVIII (London, 1978).

(39) *The Scandinavian Kingdom of Dublin*, by Charles Halliday (2nd edition, Dublin, 1884).

(40) Dr Keating maintains that Cormac was 'egged on by some of the nobles of Munster, and in particular by Flaithbheartach, son of Ionmhainéan and abbot of Inis Cathaigh, who was of royal blood, to exact head tribute from the province of Leinster . . .' The story is given credence in *A History of the Diocese of Killaloe*, Part 1, 'The Early Period', by the Revd Aubrey Gwynn, SJ (Dublin, 1962). Keating claimed that he made use of a 'lost historical tract' entitled *Cath Bhealaigh Mughna* ('The Battle of Ballaghmoon') which may be identical with a tract published by O'Donovan for the Archaeological and Celtic Society.

(41) Several authorities, including the *Book of Ballymote*, the *Book of Lecan* and Dr Keating, place the battle at Magh Ailbhe in Uí Dróna (Moyabry in Idrone), miles further south of the place now called Ballaghmoon. But most writers, including O'Donovan in his translation of the *Four Masters*, and the Revd Canon O'Mahony writing 'A History of the O'Mahony Septs of Kinelmeky and Ivagha' in the *Journal* of the Cork Historical and Archaeological Society, Volume XIII, second series (1907), place it two and a half miles north of Carlow town and in the south of Co Kildare (Irish miles — no longer used — it should be noted, and equal to about four English miles). Cormac was buried in the monastic graveyard at Deseart Diarmada, now called Castledermot in Co Kildare, where, earlier in his life, he had been a student. Keating tells us that his dead body was 'assailed with javelins' by 'unruly folk' as it lay on the battlefield, and that his head was cut off and taken to the high king, Flann Sionna. But instead of commending the party which had mutilated Cormac's remains, the *Ardrí* 'reproached them severely for the deed . . . and the head was reverently taken from him to the body'.

(42) *Cashel of the Kings*, by the Revd John Gleeson, PP (Dublin, 1927).

(43) An example of 'Tara' being used as a synonym for 'Ireland'. Donnchadh lived at the southern Uí Néill seat of Dún na Sciath, the 'fort of the shields', on the western shores of Lough Ennell (Loch Ainnin of the ancient writers), about two miles south of present-day Mullingar. The circular fort still remains. See *Annals of Westmeath, Ancient and Modern*.

(44) *Four Masters*. 'Vengeance and destruction has descended upon the/race of the Clann-Cuinn for ever/As Murtough (Muircheartach) does not live; alas the country of/the Gael will always be an orphan'.

(45) Gwynn, *A History of the Diocese of Killaloe*.

CHAPTER TWO   *The Dalcassians and Munster*

(1)   Brian's birthdate is usually given as 926 or 941. The first is implied by the *Four Masters*, who claim that he was eighty-eight at the time of his death, and is accepted by many writers. But the Revd Professor John Ryan, SJ, MA, DLitt, accepts 941, the date given by the usually reliable *Annals of Ulster*, in his essay 'Brian Boruma, King of Ireland', *North Munster Studies* (Limerick, 1967) and in his paper, 'The Battle of Clontarf', in the *Journal* of the Royal Society of Antiquaries of Ireland, volume 68, part 1 (Dublin, 1938). The Ulster annalists had little reason to love Brian, but their general trustworthiness has long been acknowledged by scholars. As a minor prince of an obscure family, it is doubtful whether his birth would have attracted any great attention, and later panegyrists settled on 926 to lend strength to the tradition of his great age. But any age over seventy was a considerable achievement in the Ireland of 1014.

As far as defining the kingdom of Thomond is concerned, difficulties are encountered as the very name is a bastardisation of Tuadhmhumha, or north Munster. It would never have covered the whole of the north of that kingdom before the rise of the Dál gCais, and the name may have originally been adopted by the Dalcassians as a grandiose gesture designed to irritate the Eoghanachta. The researcher is not helped by statements such as that made by Samuel Lewis in *A Topographical Dictionary of Ireland* (London, 1837): 'The present county [Clare] formed from a very early period a native principality, designated Tuath-Mumhan, or Thomond, signifying 'North Munster ...' By no stretch of the imagination can Co Clare be considered 'North Munster' in the sense of a geographical division of the kingdom; and the real origins of that kingdom are as controversial as the real origins of Brian's family.

(2)   O'Mahony, 'A History of the O'Mahony Septs of Kinelmeky and Ivagha'. See also *West Cork and its story* by Jeremiah O'Mahony (Tralee nd, circa 1960).

(3)   Dillon and Chadwick, *The Celtic Realms*, 'With the fifth century we enter a new phase of history, and leave the Ireland of the ancient world behind ...' They also note that the reliability of the annals is a problem much debated at the time of writing — the same could still be said for the work of many contemporary historians. See also 'The Rise of the Dal Cais', by John V. Kelleher, Professor of Modern Irish Literature and History, University of Harvard, in *North Munster Studies*.

(4)   Writing of the depredations of the Land Leapers in *Ireland under the Normans 1169–1216* (London, 1911), Goddard Orpen says: 'The primitive literature of Ireland, which seems to have survived her Christianization, and even to have been preserved in the vernacular by Christian writers, was to a large extent lost ...'

(5)   Kelleher, 'The Rise of the Dal Cais'.

(6)   Ryan, in *North Munster Studies*, defines their ancient territory. The

suggestion that the Eoghanachta colonised much of Clare is made by F. J. Byrne writing the chapter on 'Early Irish Society' in Moody and Martin's *The Course of Irish History*.

(7) Ryan, *North Munster Studies*.

(8) *The Book of Lismore*, transcribed in 1480 for the daughter of the 8th earl of Desmond. Obviously, it was prejudiced in her Eoghanacht ancestors' favour.

(9) The quotation, given by Gleeson in *Cashel of the Kings*, is an interesting, if genealogically dubious, insight into the coronation of an Irish king.

(10) See *The Antiquities of Limerick and its Neighbourhood*, by T. J. Westropp, R. A. S. Macalister and G. U. Macnamara (Dublin, for the Royal Society of Antiquaries of Ireland, 1916). Westropp maintains that there 'is no true tradition' of the site of Kincora which was finally destroyed, as he admits, in the twelfth century; and although he suggests that the palace associated with Brian in later life was Béal Bóramha, he offers no qualifying evidence. For an account of the excavations at Béal Bóramha, under the direction of the late Professor Michael J. O'Kelly of the Department of Archaeology, University College, Cork, see the *Journal* of the Cork Historical and Archaeological Society, Vol LXVII, January-December, 1962.

The Hiberno-Norse silver pennies found at Béal Bóramha

(11) Cashel and Emly were united in 1569. See Gleeson, *Cashel of the Kings*, and for a description of the monastic system after St Patrick see Curtis, *A History of Ireland*. Mervyn Archdale, in his *Monasticon Hibernicum*, 'or An History of the Abbies, Priories, and other Religious Houses in Ireland' (Dublin, 1736), does not mention Marcán as abbot of Emly; nor does Gleeson, so it seems that the abbacy was a pro-Eoghanacht 'gift' assumed by the Dalcassians.

(12) There were at least two St Finnians — Finnian Cam, 'the hunchback', and Finnian the Leper. That the first-named built Inisfallen is the opinion of the Most Revd John Healy, DD, LLD, MRIA, in *Ireland's Ancient Schools and Scholars* (Dublin, 1893).

(13) O'Curry, *Lectures on the Manuscript Materials of Ancient Irish History*.

(14) *A Smaller Social History of Ancient Ireland*, by P. W. Joyce, LLD, MRIA (Dublin, 1908).

(15) *Ibid.*

(16) *Four Masters*.

(17) Gleeson, *Cashel of the Kings*.

(1)   *Viking Antiquities in Great Britain and Ireland*, Part 1, *An introduction to the Viking history of western Europe*, by Haakon Shetelig (Oslo, 1940).

(2)   *The Viking Achievement*, by P. G. Foote, Professor of Old Scandinavian in the University of London, & D. M. Wilson, Reader in archaeology of the Anglo-Saxon period in the University of London (London, 1970).

(3)   *The Story of England*, by Sir Arthur Bryant (London, 1953).

(4)   Foote & Wilson, *The Viking Achievement.*

(5)   *The Vikings*, by Allen Mawer, MA, Professor of English Language and Literature in Armstrong College, University of Durham (Cambridge, 1913).

(6)   *Irish Memories*, by E. OE. Somerville and Martin Ross (London, 1918).

(7)   Foote & Wilson, *The Viking Achievement.*

(8)   Shetelig, *Viking Antiquities.*

(9)   *Scandinavian Relations with Ireland during the Viking Period*, by A. Walsh (Dublin, 1922).

(10) Similarly, the Celtic invaders had adopted the gods and heroes of their Pictish ('Fir Bholg') predecessors. See *Celtic Myth and Legend,* by Charles Squire (London, no date but *c.*1904).

(11) Foote & Wilson, *The Viking Achievement.* See also the essay, 'The Vikings and the western world', by Dr Nora K. Chadwick, in the proceedings of the International Congress of Celtic Studies of 1959.

Thorgrimr's stone and Hiberno-Romanesque doorway, Killaloe Cathedral

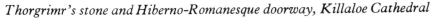

(12) See Daphne Pochin Mould writing on 'Iceland's Celtic Past' in the *Irish Times* of October 9, 1979; also *The Norsemen,* by Count Eric Oxenstierna, translated by Catherine Hutter (New York, 1965).

(13) This example comes from the Norse *Haraldsvaeði*, composed towards the end of the ninth century.

(14) Mawer, *The Vikings.*

(15) Foote & Wilson, *The Viking Achievement.*

(16) *The Celts,* by Nora Chadwick (London, 1970).

CHAPTER FOUR   *The wild huts of the desert*

(1) See N. Ó Cléirigh's essay, 'Clare's Roots — and the Northern Connection', in the *Claremens' Association Yearbook* (Dublin, 1979).

(2) Lewis, *A Topographical Dictionary of Ireland.* Although more intensively cultivated in his time than in Brian's, there is no reason to believe that Clare of the tenth century was entirely barren and unproductive.

(3) Pre-Milesian Tradraighe on the north bank of the Shannon, across the river from Danish Limerick, and in the present barony of Bunratty.

(4) *Ibid.* In 1837 Lewis was able to write: 'The numerous bays and creeks on both sides [of the Shannon] render it, in every wind, perfectly safe to the vessels navigating to Limerick ...' The Danes must have found the river equally useful.

(5) See the essay on the Battle of Knockdoe, 1504, in *Irish Battles,* by G. A. Hayes-McCoy (London, 1969). In *Ireland under the Normans 1169–1216,* Goddard Orpen suggests that the *lúireach* (from the Latin, *lorica*) supposedly worn by the 'Danes' at Clontarf in 1014 was 'probably of leather, reinforced with metal rings and studs', and not chain-mail. Even less protection is likely to have been worn half a century earlier. On the question of weapons in general, see *Early Christian Ireland,* by Máire and Liam de Paor (London, 1958). They conclude that, from manuscript drawings, the sword, spear and a small round shield were used in Ireland before the Viking times, and so, probably, was the throwing-axe, or *francesca.* After the ninth century, however, it seems that the Irish adopted the armaments of the Land Leapers, and on the high crosses of the early tenth century, Irish soldiers are portrayed with swords or spears of the type used by Vikings. Many Norse weapons, of course, must have been the spoils of war. The Viking cemetery at Islandbridge/Kilmainham, destroyed when the Great Southern Railway was built in the middle of the 19th century, was, according to the de Paors, the 'most considerable' cemetery of its kind in the Viking colonies. Numerous swords, spearheads, shield umbos and arrow heads were found — the bow and arrow does not seem to have been used widely by the Irish — and many of the swords reflected considerable craftsmanship. Pommels were highly ornamented, with 'silver strips beaten into grooves in the iron, chequer patterns in silver

and one very fine example richly gilt and decorated with small silver circles set in niells ...'

(6) Lewis, *A Topographical Dictionary of Ireland.*

(7) *Cogadh Gaedhel re Gallaibh (The War of the Gaedhil with the Gaill)*, edited by the Revd Dr J. H. Todd (Rolls Series, London, 1867). Most authorities, notably Fr John Ryan (in 'The Battle of Clontarf'), Eugene O'Curry (in *Lectures on the Manuscript Materials of Ancient Irish History*) and Professor F. J. Byrne (in *Irish Kings and High Kings*) recognise the work as containing considerable detail, but in varying degrees of reliability. Ryan and Byrne date the original from the first half of the twelfth century, O'Curry and Todd from before 1100. O'Curry believed that 'neither exaggeration nor falsehood would have been allowed to form part of so great a compilation'; Ryan, more sensibly, warns his readers of the 'romantic tale, in which heroes and villains play their parts and dramatic incidents are invented or exaggerated for the benefit of the reading public, all the while the interests of the Dal Chais are kept well before the writer's mind ...' Byrne, more bluntly, sees it as enshrining Brian's glory, 'but written in the reign of his great-grandson Muircheartach Ua Briain and reflecting the ambitions of that modernising king ...' Perhaps only by following Ryan's lead and neither completely accepting nor completely dismissing the text can we find some truth. Like the more reputable annals, it cannot be entirely disregarded, particularly if it *was* written at the earliest suggested date, when grandsons of the survivors of Clontarf were living. There would be some basis to the stories it contained, as there is basis to tales handed down to grandsons of those who fought in more recent conflicts. Canon O'Mahony virtually dismisses it as purely pro-Dalcassian, but then the worthy canon was pro-Eoghanacht.

(8) *Ibid.*

(9) *Ibid.*

(10) O'Mahony, 'A History of the O'Mahony Septs of Kinelmeky and Ivagha'.

(11) *Fragmentary Annals of Ireland*, under the year 850.

(12) *Four Masters.*

(13) O'Mahony, 'A History of the O'Mahony Septs of Kinelmeky and Ivagha'.

(14) In his edition of the *Four Masters*, O'Donovan points out that 'Some antiquaries say that [the murder] was at Leacht Mhathghamhna (Math-ghamhain's heap or memorial pile) on Muisire na Mona Moire, now Mushera mountain near Macroom, Co Cork ...' Canon O'Mahony maintains that Leacht Mhathghamhna is a name imposed later than 1749, as in that year the Cork historian, Smith, was told nothing of the name or of Mathghamhain's death in the area.

(15) *Cogadh Gaedhel re Gallaibh.*

(16) *Ireland before the Normans*, by Donncha Ó Corráin (Dublin, 1972). This is Ó Corráin's opinion, and he offers no proof that it was only a romantic story. He also rejects the suggestion that the Dál gCais owed their rise to Uí Néill patronage; maintaining that the Dál gCais were benefitted, instead,

by the 'general weakness' of the Eoghanachta. But, as I have pointed out in chapter two, Uí Néill intervention in the affairs of Munster was both logical and highly probable.

CHAPTER FIVE *Brian, King of Munster*

(1) The district is present-day Moyarta and Clonderalawin in south-west Clare. Among those to fall at Clontarf was Domhnall, son of Diarmaid, lord of Corca Bhaiscinn.

(2) O'Mahony, 'A History of the O'Mahony Septs of Kinelmeky and Ivagha'. Todd, editing *Cogadh Gaedhel re Gallaibh*, admits that Murchadh's exploit is not supported by historical evidence.

(3) For the location of Maolmhuadh's last stand see the opinions of Jeremiah O'Mahony in *West Cork parish histories and place names*, (Tralee, n.d., circa 1960). He suggests that it was on a hill on the north side of Moneycuskar, between the latter townland and that known as Mount Music, in the parish of Kilmichael, Co Cork. 'This part is now called Ballina, but it was known as Lackmalloe (Leacht Mhaolmhuaidh), the burial flag or monument of Maolmhuadh. When a king or chief was slain, a leacht or monument was raised on the spot where he fell. He may have been buried elsewhere, but the stone marked the place of his demise.' Canon O'Mahony in 'A History of the O'Mahony Septs of Kinelmeky and Ivagha' fixes the probable place of Maolmhuadh's burial as the Abbey of Kilbrennan, in the vicinity of Ráth Raithleann, about ten miles from the battlefield. Ráth Raithleann still exists in a good state of preservation. The site was excavated in the 'thirties by the late Seán P. Ó Ríordáin, then Professor of Archaeology in University College Cork. For an illustrated account of the excavation see *Proceedings* of the Royal Irish Academy, 47C (Dublin, 1942).

Dún Saidhbhe, Ráth Raithleann

(4) Gleeson, *Cashel of the Kings*. For information on the abbots of Emly see also Liam Ó Buachalla's essay, 'The Ecclesiastical Families of Cloyne', in the *Journal* of the Cork Historical and Archaeological Society, Vol VI, Part 2 (Cork, 1945).

(5) Ryan, in his essay 'Brian Boruma, King of Ireland'. Despite his argument, I do not believe that Brian took Gormfhlaith as a wife until after he entered Dublin, following Gleann Máma, and then principally as an implementation of Eidirsceol. Her relationship with Brian is discussed in more detail in the following chapter.

(6) *Four Masters*.

(7) *Annals of Clonmacnoise*. Although an unusually sober tome, its origins and connection with Clonmacnoise (in its heyday a far greater seat of learning and prayer than Armagh) are obscure; indeed, O'Curry, in *Lectures on the Manuscript Materials of Ancient Irish History*, found no reason why it should bear such a title. The translation was made six hundred years after Brian's death by Conall mac Eochagáin (1627) and claimed to trace Irish history 'from the earliest times' to 1408. But while this, as ever, is a fiction, and although mac Eochagáin makes no mention of the 'original' authors, it cannot be dismissed completely. Like *Cogadh Gaedhel re Gallaibh* and, in particular, the *Four Masters*, it contains important elements of fact. Annalists such as the *Four Masters* wrote what had been handed down by word of mouth, and they copied from existing manuscripts. While exaggeration was bound to appear in praise of a particular hero or event, there is no proof that the annalists were in any position to decide what was exaggerated. They seem to have regarded their job as writing down exactly what they heard, or read in older manuscripts, and it should be remembered that, without their writings, there would be no record of events on which later historians could work. Of course there was exaggeration, but with information uncovered by other means in the course of time, historians are able to separate fact from fancy.

(8) In 994 Olaf Trygvaeson returned with the king of Denmark, Svein Forkbeard (983–1014). After a further payment of Danegeld, Olaf returned to Norway to seize the throne and Svein went back to Denmark to mature plans for an English conquest. Ethelred's massacre of the Danes, including a sister of their king, in 1002 and his flight to Normandy in 1013, resulted in Danish colonisation of England and, from 1013 to 1035, the reign of the great Cnut, who brought the country twenty years of much-needed peace.

(9) *Annals of Clonmacnoise*.

(10) *Ibid.*

(11) *Ibid.*

(12) For a description of Maigh Adhair and the inauguration ceremony, see *The Antiquities of Limerick and its neighbourhood* by T. J. Westropp, R. A. S. Macalister and G. U. MacNamara (Dublin, 1916).

(13) Mawer, *The Vikings*.

(14) *Dermot, King of Leinster and the Foreigners* by Nicholas Furlong (Dublin, 1973). A long-awaited biography, clear and objective, of a much-maligned king who, like Brian, is usually remembered for the wrong reasons.

(15) Byrne, *Irish Kings and High Kings.*

(16) *Cogadh Gaedhel re Gallaibh.*

(17) This event is supposed to form the theme of Tom Moore's melody, 'Let Erin remember the days of old'. Tomar was evidently a chieftain of note. O'Donovan, in his introduction of *Leabhar na gCeart*, says that the earliest reference to a 'Danish prince' of this name occurs in the *Annals of Ulster* in 847, when he fell in battle against the men of Munster. Bearing in mind that dating in the annals is often erratic, Tomar could have been a follower of Turges, and his achievements obviously made an impression on his Norse successors in Dublin, his ring being kept as an heirloom. The wooded hill of Tomar, to figure in the last hours of Brian's life, was probably named after him. Carlus, says O'Donovan, was Tomar's contemporary.

(18) I do not believe the statement made by Curtis in *A History of Ireland*, and elsewhere, that Brian made Maol Mórdha king of Leinster. Had he been able to place a puppet on that throne, surely he would have chosen a prince from a rival dynasty — and secured an ally?

(19) Goddard Henry Orpen, writing on the 'Site of the Battle of Glen-Mama' in the *Journal* of the Royal Society of Antiquaries of Ireland, vol XXXVI (Dublin, 1906), says that 'all conditions would seem to be satisfied' by supposing this to have been the site. But he also suggests that the site could have been the mountainous defile between Blessington and Brittas, Co Wicklow, while rejecting the long-held theory that it was east of Dunlavin, Co Wicklow. Ryan, in 'Brian Borumha, King of Ireland', gives 997 as the date of the battle; the *Four Masters* 998 and the *Annals of Inisfallen* 999. Ryan apparently bases much of his dating on the various marriages of Brian, in which I suggest he is incorrect. The *Four Masters* dating is erratic, while according to Healy in *Ireland's Ancient Schools and Scholars*, the *Annals of Inisfallen* was most probably compiled by Maolsuthain Ua Cearbhaill, 'intimate friend and counsellor' of Brian. While Maolsuthain certainly accords Brian considerable attention in his writings, there is no reason to suppose that he invented, or made mistakes over, dates.

CHAPTER SIX *Emperor of the Gael*

(1) *Cogadh Gaedhel re Gallaibh.* Claen Conghair ('the slope of the path') appears to have been a position on the battlefield or on the retreat route; 'Not identified', says O'Donovan in his second edition of the *Four Masters* (Dublin, 1856).

(2) *Leabhar na gCeart.* In his introduction, O'Donovan quotes the *Annals of Clonmacnoise*, referring to the reign of a later king, Diarmaid mac Maoil na

mBó of Leinster, who in 1041 was 'reputed sufficient monarch of the whole' of Ireland because he 'command Leath Moye, Meath, Connaught and Leinster ...'

(3) See Orpen's article on the 'Site of the Battle of Glen-Mama' in RSAI *Journal*, vol. XXXVI.

(4) For example, the *Annals of Inisfallen* attributes the victory solely to Brian Lynch, in *Cambrensis Eversus*, to Maoil-Seachlainn.

(5) R. A. S. Macalister, in *The Archaeology of Ireland* (London, 1928).

(6) Dalton (*History of Ireland*) relies too heavily on the annalists and on *Cogadh Gaedhel re Gallaibh*, although little other source material was available for the period under discussion. But Dalton seemed unable to comprehend that the Irish Christians of the tenth and eleventh centuries were not the same as the Irish Christians of his own time.

(7) *History of Ireland*, by Edmund Campion (London, reprint, 1809).

(8) *Sylloge*, edited by Archbishop James Ussher (Dublin, 1632). His *Works* were edited by C. R. Elington (Dublin, 1847–62). See also the chapter on 'Morals' in *Irish Life in the Seventeenth Century*, by Edward MacLysaght, MA, DLitt, MRIA (Dublin, 1969).

(9) Orpen, in *Ireland Under the Normans 1169–1216*, claims in a footnote that Gormfhlaith was repudiated in succession by Olaf, Maoil-Seachlainn and Brian. There is no evidence as to the first repudiation, but it is feasible that it took place when Olaf went on his first and last pilgrimage to Iona. If Gormfhlaith had been intriguing while married to him, repudiation may have eased his conscience at least.

(10) See Orpen in *Ireland Under the Normans 1169–1216*.

(11) In the seventeenth century, marriage 'in its full sense was common at seventeen and eighteen, and sometimes the parties were brought together at a much earlier age' — MacLysaght, *Irish Life in the Seventeenth Century*. It is not unlikely that in Ireland of the tenth century fifteen was an unduly young age for a girl to marry. *The Annals of Inisfallen* referred to was edited with a translation by Seán Mac Airt, MA (Dublin, 1951).

(12) Ryan, in 'The Battle of Clontarf', states categorically that Gormfhlaith was the mother of Donnchadh. Certainly she had sons by Olaf and Maoil-Seachlainn, but it is possible that Donnchadh was accredited to her in a later editing of *Cogadh Gaedhel re Gallaibh* to account for his alleged fratricide and violent character. A case, perhaps, of sins of a parent being visited upon the son? It is not known who wrote *Cogadh*, although the early nineteenth-century historian, Dr Charles O'Conor, attributes it, without a scrap of proof, to mac Liag, Brian's bard or poet, who died in 1016, two years after his master. But O'Conor is alone among scholars in categorically attributing the work to him. Dr Todd, in his introduction to the London edition of *Cogadh*, 1867, 'has not discovered any ancient authority for attributing the work to mac Liag', and points out that no mention of the author's name is made by eminent scholars, such as Keating or the authors of the *Four Masters*, who have made use of the work. The

book is omitted from any list of mac Liag's works which, in any case, seem to have been purely poetic. Todd's edition was edited from three manuscripts. The first, and most ancient, was the *Book of Leinster*, which Todd says was written by Fionn, Bishop of Kildare, 'or at least during his lifetime' and while he was bishop from 1148–1160. The second, which Todd calls the *Dublin MS*, he believes to have been written about the middle of the fourteenth century. Both are fragments and both are in Trinity College, Dublin. The third MS is a paper copy in the handwriting of Ó Cléirigh, transcribed in 1635 and now in the Burgundian Library in Brussels. It was copied from the *Book of Cú Chonnacht Ó Dálaigh*, from which Ó Cléirigh had made a first copy in 1628, and which is now unknown. The original manuscript, which Todd admits was probably written during Brian's lifetime, or shortly afterwards while many of Brian's contemporaries were living, must be lost altogether.

(13) Kelleher, in 'The Rise of the Dal Cais' in *North Munster Studies*.

(14) It appears in *Cogadh Gaedhel re Gallaibh* and in many popular histories of more recent times. Ryan ignores it completely.

(15) Byrne, *Irish Kings and High Kings*.

(16) Ryan, in 'Brian Boruma, King of Munster'.

(17) 'This I have written in the sight of Brian, Emperor of the Scots'. The scribe was Maolsuthain Ua Cearbhaill of Loch Léin, friend and probably schoolmate of Brian, as Healy suggests in *Ireland's Ancient Schools and Scholars*. Ó Cearbhaill died in 1009, according to the *Four Masters,* in which he is described as *Saoi* (learned one) 'of the western world'. 'Scots' referred to the Irish, for it was not until the following century that the name Scotia was transferred to the land of Alba. See Macalister in *The Archaeology of Ireland*.

(18) *Phases of Irish History*, by Eoin MacNeill, Professor of Ancient Irish History in the National University of Ireland (Dublin, 1920). 'The title . . . is not a mere high-sounding epithet', he maintains. 'It means that, as Basil was then supreme temporal ruler in the East and Henry of Bavaria in the West, so was Brian in this island'. Or that, at least, is what Ua Cearbhaill was suggesting.

CHAPTER SEVEN   *A Notable Reformation*

(1) *Annals of Clonmacnoise*. Mac Eochagáin virtually dedicated his work to Brian because of the king's work in the scholastic field.

(2) See Healy's *Ireland's Ancient Schools and Scholars* for the original text. St Patrick is said to have founded Armagh in 445 — see *Historical Memoirs of the City of Armagh* by James Stuart, revised by the Revd Ambrose Coleman, OP, STL, MRIA (Dublin, 1900).

(3) Ryan, in *North Munster Studies*.

(4) Haverty, in *The History of Ireland, Ancient and Modern,* quotes

O'Donovan, but does not state from which source. In a footnote to his edition of the *Four Masters*, O'Donovan says that mac Liag was 'chief poet and secretary to Brian Bórumha, and is said to have written a life of that celebrated monarch, of which copies were extant in the last century; but no copy of this work is now known to exist . . .' Seemingly it did once exist, and it is mentioned by Edward O'Reilly in his *Irish Writers, commencing with the earliest accounts of Irish History* (Dublin, 1820). Yet O'Reilly does not include *Cogadh Gaedhel re Gallaibh* in the list of mac Liag's works.

(5)   *Surnames of Ireland*, by Edward MacLysaght, MA, DLitt, MRIA (Shannon, 1969).

(6)   *A View of the Present State of Ireland*, by Edmund Spenser (London, 1934).

(7)   MacLysaght, *Surnames of Ireland*.

(8)   See MacLysaght's article on the Lysaght family in the *Journal* of the Cork Historical and Archaeological Society, vol. 21 (Cork, 1915).

(9)   *Cogadh Gaedhel re Gallaibh.*

(10) *Four Masters.* The Conaille Muirtheimhne whose territory comprised that part of the present Co Louth, extending from the Cuailgne (Cooley) mountains to the river Boyne. Dundalk, Louth, Dromiskin, Faughart and Monasterboice are mentioned as in this territory, writes O'Donovan in a footnote to *Leabhar na gCeart.* The Cooley peninsula was the scene of the ancient Irish epic tale, *Táin Bó Cuailgne* ('The Cattle Raid of Cooley').

(11) Dillon, in his introduction to *Lebor na Cert.* Gleeson, in *Cashel of the Kings*, says: 'The original manuscript has been lost, but an imperfect copy taken from a 'dilapidated Psaltair' in 1451 is preserved in the Bodleian Library, Oxford. The word Psaltair in this case means political history, not religious, like the Psalter.'

(12) Healy, *Ireland's Ancient Schools and Scholars.* For the achievements of King Alfred see *England before the Norman Conquest*, by Sir Charles Oman, KBE (London, 1938).

(13) *Medieval Religious Houses: Ireland*, by Aubrey Gwynn and R. Neville Hadcock (London, 1970).

(14) *Four Masters.*

(15) O'Donovan, in his introduction to the first translation of *Leabhar na gCeart*, quotes as his authority the *Dinnsheanchas*, 'an ancient topographical tract', compiled, according to O'Curry (*Lectures on the Manuscript Materials of Ancient Irish History*), at Tara about 550 AD.

(16) O'Curry says that Longhargán and Cinnéide were ancestors of the families of O'Lonergan and O'Kennedy.

(17) Shakespeare makes no mention of the royal blood of Macbeth (mac Beatha). He was son of Finlaec, Great Steward of Moray, by Donada, a daughter of Malcolm II, and was first cousin to the unfortunate Duncan. In 1040 the north and west of Scotland were conquered by Norsemen under Thorfinn, and Macbeth joined forces with the invaders. Duncan was killed and Macbeth became joint ruler of the country with Thorfinn, his personal authority being confined to the land south and west of the Tay.

He is described in 1054, by the *Annals of Ulster*, as high king of Alba.

(18) *Brian Boru, A Tragedy*, by J. T. B. (London, 1879).

(19) Haverty, *The History of Ireland, Ancient and Modern*.

(20) *Cogadh Gaedhel re Gallaibh*. Westropp, Macalister and Macnamara, in *The Antiquities of Limerick and its Neighbourhood*, note the description but suggest Béal Bóramha, not Kincora, as the setting. In *History of the O'Briens* (London, 1949), the Hon Donough O'Brien makes the suggestion that Béal Bóramha was enlarged into the 'famous palace of Kincora', without evidence. The annalists, poets and local people have always made a distinction between the two, and it is Kincora, not Béal Bóramha, that has always been associated with Brian. There is not a shred of proof that the two forts were in fact the same place.

(21) Gleeson, in *Cashel of the Kings*, attributes this vignette to O'Halloran's *History of Ireland* (Dublin, 1819). But O'Halloran's source is unknown.

CHAPTER EIGHT *The Boru Tribute*

(1) See Fr John Ryan's essay, 'Ireland and the Holy See', in *Studies: An Irish Quarterly Review*, vol. L, no. 198 (Summer, 1961).

(2) *A Concise History of Ireland*, by Máire and Conor Cruise O'Brien (London, 1972).

(3) In *The History of Ireland, Ancient and Modern*, Haverty claims that Cathaoir Mór was 'the immediate predecessor of Conn of the Hundred Battles', whose reign he dates from 123 to 157 AD. But even if we accept the existence of either king, and they were probably no more than figures of legend and romance, it must be remembered that they were not high kings; simply the most powerful rulers in the country at that particular time. That the Bóramha Laighean was imposed first on Leinster after the conquest of its northern territories by the so-called 'Tara dynasty', is a point accepted by Dillon and Chadwick in *The Celtic Realms*.

(4) Byrne, *Irish Kings and High Kings*.

(5) *Four Masters*.

(6) *Annals of Ulster*, edited by William M. Hennessy (Dublin, 1887). Ryan pays tribute to the 'general trustworthiness' of these chronicles. The section to 1021, including a sober account of Clontarf, was derived by the compiler, Cathal mac Magnusa Mhéig Uidhir, from the *Book of Dubh dhá Léithe*, itself probably compiled by a prominent cleric at Armagh, who seemed less prone to exaggeration than his more humble brothers in religion. Cathal mac Magnusa Mhéig Uidhir, who died in 1498, was also eminent in religious affairs, being a *biatach* (hospitaller) at Seaṇadh, later Ballymacmanus Island and now Belleisle (private property) in Upper Lough Erne, between the present-day counties of Donegal and Fermanagh. He was also a canon chorister at Armagh, dean of the bishopric of Clogher, dean of Lough Erne, rector of Inis Caoin in the

lough, and died as vicar general of Clogher. After his death the annals were continued to 1541 by one Ruaidhrí Ó Caiside, who died in 1600; and a Dublin copy was continued to 1604 — to 1600 by Ruaidhrí Ó Luinín and for the next four years most probably by members of his family.

(7) If, as Professor Dillon has suggested, the *Book of Rights* was compiled after Brian became *Ardrí*, the authors exercised remarkable restraint in this section. More probably the *buadha* of the high king were anciently associated with the semi-legendary priest-kings of Tara.

(8) *Leabhar na gCeart*.

(9) See Westropp, Macalister and Macnamara in *The Antiquities of Limerick and its Neighbourhood*; and for a general study of the area, *A History of the Diocese of Killaloe*, by the Revd Aubrey Gwynn, SJ, and Dermot F. Gleeson (Dublin, 1962).

(10) Byrne, *Irish Kings and High Kings*. St Mo-Ling asked for remittance of the tribute until Monday (*Luan*). The Irish believed that the Day of Judgement would fall on a Monday. An account of the story appears under entry 67 IV for the year 677 in Joan Newlon Radner's *Fragmentary Annals of Ireland*.

(11) *The History of Clare*, by the Very Revd Patrick Canon White (Dublin, 1893).

(12) *Cogadh Gaedhel re Gallaibh*.

(13) Ryan, 'The Battle of Clontarf'.

(14) *Cogadh Gaedhel re Gallaibh*, quoted by Ryan.

(15) Ryan, 'The Battle of Clontarf'.

(16) *Cogadh Gaedhel re Gallaibh*.

(17) O'Donoghue, *Historical Memoirs of the O'Briens*. See also 'The Royal House of O'Connor', by James McGarry, in *Cara*, vol 5, no 2, April–June, 1972.

(18) *Saga of Burnt Njal*, translated by George Webbe Dasent from the Icelandic (London, 1861). 'A bald record of events,' says Ryan, 'but it gives some details of value.' Dasent (1817–1896) became interested in Scandinavian literature while in the diplomatic service in Stockholm. He became Professor of English Literature and Modern History at King's College, London, in 1853, but much of his finest work in translating the Norse sagas appeared between 1845 and 1870, while he was assistant editor of *The Times*. He was knighted in 1876. The account of Clontarf comes nearly at the end of *Burnt Njal*, and Gormfhlaith (Kormlode in the Norse) is blamed for the hosting against Brian, who is described as the 'best-natured of kings'. There are certain discrepancies in the work, notably the statement that Brian's eldest son was named Duncan — Dasent, or his source, presumably confused him with Brian's long-dead eldest brother, Donn Cuan. Brian is also accredited with a brother, 'the greatest champion and warrior', Wolf the Quarrelsome, and a Norse foster-son, Kerthialfad, whom he 'loved more than his own sons', and both of whom were, according to *Burnt Njal*, present at Clontarf.

(19) *Cogadh Gaedhel re Gallaibh.*

(20) Hayes-McCoy, *Irish Battles.*

(21) It is difficult to believe that a Viking pirate would have made so sweeping a change in his religion and allegiance, and is another example of the romance that surrounds Clontarf.

(22) The intricacies of genealogy also made Sigurd seventh in descent from Maoil-Seachlainn I, executor of Turges. See Pedigree II in *Loca Patriciana*, by the Revd John Francis Shearman (Dublin, 1882).

(23) Hayes-McCoy, *Irish Battles.*

CHAPTER NINE   *The Weir of Clontarf*

(1)   *Saga of Burnt Njal.*

(2)   See Ryan, 'The Battle of Clontarf'. The last Scandinavian king of York, Erik 'Bloodaxe', was expelled, and killed at the battle of Stainmore in 954. The *Annals of Loch Cé* were edited with a translation by William M. Hennessy, MRIA, when Assistant Deputy Keeper of the Records (London, 1871) and republished by the Stationery Office (Dublin, 1939). They begin in 1014 and, according to O'Curry, were continued to 1590 by Brian Mac Dermot of Carrick Mac Dermot, Co Roscommon. Earlier material could have been lost; what remains is probably based on the same sources as the *Four Masters* (see note 33, chapter one).

(3)   *Cogadh Gaedhel re Gallaibh.*

(4)   *West Over Sea*, by Jon Leirfall, translated by Kenneth Young from the Norwegian (Belfast, 1979).

(5)   *Four Masters*. Byrne, *Irish Kings and High Kings*, states that the total population of the country was probably 'well under half a million' at any given date between the fifth and twelfth century. In his *Political Anatomy of Ireland* (London, 1691), Sir William Petty, Surveyor-General of Ireland, estimated that the entire population of the country in 1169 was no more than 300,000 — surely less in 1014, assuming the estimate was reasonably made.

(6)   Compare the accounts of Clontarf (1014) and Knockdoe (1504) in *Irish Battles*, by Hayes-McCoy who concludes that, at Clontarf, 'the total strength of both sides together did not exceed 5000 men'.

(7)   Ryan, 'The Battle of Clontarf'.

(8)   Byrne, *Irish Kings and High Kings*.

(9)   Ryan, 'The Battle of Clontarf'.

(10) *Saga of Burnt Njal.*

(11) 'Long have the men of Ireland groaned under the tyranny of those sea-faring pirates, the murderers of your kings and chieftains, plunderers of your fortresses, profane destroyers of the churches and monasteries of God; who have trampled on and committed to the flames the relics of the saints. May the Almighty God, through His great mercy, give you strength

and courage this day to put an end for ever to the foreign tyranny in Ireland, and to revenge upon the tyrants their many perfidies and the profanation of the edifices sacred to His worship, this day on which Christ Himself suffered death for your redemption.' The fact that Brian himself had overcome the worst of the 'Norse tyranny', that the crimes attributed to the Norse were also practised by the Irish, and that Ireland was not facing a new invasion at the time unmask the speech for the fiction it most certainly is.

(12) *Saga of Burnt Njal.*

(13) *Cogadh Gaedhel re Gallaibh.* Todd says the original story appears in the Ó Cléirigh copy, preserved in the Burgundian Library, Brussels, which has the advantage of being intact. It is in the handwriting of the eminent Irish scholar and friar, Mícheál Ó Cléirigh, by whom it was transcribed in 1635. Another daughter of Brian, Bé Bhionn, died on pilgrimage to Armagh in 1073, according to the *Annals of Ulster.*

(14) Orpen, *Ireland Under The Normans 1169–1216.*

(15 The story, without source, appears in the *Journal* of the Royal Society of Antiquaries of Ireland, vol. III, 4th series (Dublin, 1874–5).

(16) *Cogadh Gaedhel re Gallaibh.*

(17) Ryan, 'The Battle of Clontarf'. In *A Brief Discourse in Vindication of the Antiquities of Ireland,* by Hugh Mac Curtin (Dublin, 1717), Tadhg is shown as being not at Kincora but 'in the Country of Cuailgne now the County of Louth, sent thither by his Father for Part of the Kingly Dues which that Country had neglected to pay ...' Mac Curtin, known in Irish as Aodh Buidhe mac Cruitín (Tawny Hugh Mac Curtin), was a distinguished scholar, but the *Discourse* is patently pro-Dalcassian and dedicated to William O'Brien, 3rd Earl of Inchiquin (1666–1719), tenth in descent from King Brian. It contains curious versions of the deaths of Brian and Murchadh and is as exaggerated as the annals and 'Authentick Irish Histories' to which the author referred.

(18) *Cogadh Gaedhel re Gallaibh.*

(19) *Ibid.*

(20) According to *Burnt Njal,* the chase of Brodar was led by 'Wolf of the Quarrelsome' and Kerthialfad, supposedly brother and foster-son to Brian. Canon O'Mahony, in 'A History of the O'Mahony Septs of Kinelmeky and Ivagha', presents a good argument for their being respectively Murchadh and Cian, the names and relationships corrupted in accounts of the battle transmitted to Scandinavia.

(21) *Cogadh Gaedhel re Gallaibh.* The content of the 'will', as handed down, implies that Brian made it after hearing that Murchadh had been mortally wounded. It is likely that the account is a pure example of Dalcassian invention.

(22) Todd, in his introduction to *Cogadh Gaedhel re Gallaibh.*

(23) Stuart and Coleman, *Historical Memoirs of the City of Armagh.* In England, early into this century, country people showed a strong disinclination to be

buried on the north side of a church — the area reserved traditionally for suicides and unknown victims of murder.

(24) *Annals of Loch Cé.*

(25) *Annals of Ulster.*

(26) Did the crown and sceptre ever exist? In his address to the AGM of the Royal Society of Antiquaries of Ireland, on 27 January, 1903, the president, J. R. Garstin, MA, MRIA, FSA, DL, referred to the possibility that Irish kings wore crowns of a 'sun-burst' design. This was the theory of Miss Margaret Stokes, the antiquarian, formed on the slender 'evidence' of fragments of bronze work, dating probably from the Iron Age, in the possession of the celebrated archaeologist, Sir Flinders Petrie. The fragments, which she maintained fitted round the top of a band, are preserved in the National Museum of Ireland. She conjecturally restored the 'crown' in an illustration that can be seen, together with Garstin's paper, in the RSAI *Journal*, vol. XXXIII, Consecutive series (Dublin, 1904). More recently, Professor G. A. Hayes McCoy, in *History of Irish Flags from earliest times* (Dublin, 1970), pointed out that the first pictorial representation of such a crown was in Keating's *General History of Ireland*, published in 1723, where an appalling 'artist's impression' of Brian Boru shows him wearing such a headpiece, for which there is no historical evidence whatever. The Irish Volunteer movement of 1780 and the Loyal National Repeal Association of 1840 both adopted a 'sun-burst' crown as an emblem. Wall paintings and an illustration in the *Book of Ballymote*, both 15th century, show kings wearing typical mediaeval crowns — with stylised leaf shapes rising from circlets.

What Brian wore we do not know, although it may have been a plain circlet of gold, a favourite decoration of the aristocracy of the time. The 'crown of Munster' referred to in this text is metaphorical in a sense, although it is unlikely that nothing was placed on his brow to distinguish him from the rest of the nobility.

There is an interesting footnote on p. 17 of *Limerick: Its History and Antiquities, Ecclesiastical, Civil and Military,* by Maurice Lenihan (Dublin, 1886): 'Two interesting relics supposed to have belonged to

The Petrie 'crown'

Mary Immaculate College
Issue Receipt

Customer name: Michael O'Halloran

Title: Brian Boru, King of Ireland
ID: 0100198109
Due: 09/04/2013 21:45

Total items: 1
3/26/2013 2:15 PM

Thank you for using the Self Service System
Please retain this receipt for Due Date

Brian Boru are still in existence — namely his harp and his sceptre. The latter was presented to the museum of the Royal Dublin Society ... by the Dowager Marchioness of Thomond ... in 1857. The harp, according to the statement given in the fourth volume of the *Collectane de Rebus Hibernicia*, remained, with the crown and other regalia of Brian Boru, in the Vatican, until the reign of Henry VIII, when that 'Defender of the Faith' received the harp with his new title. The Pope, it is said, kept the crown, which was of massive gold ...' Earlier tradition records the crown or diadem being presented to Henry II of England by Pope Adrian IV on the eve of the Anglo-Norman invasion. It is unfortunate that recent enquiries to the Vatican have failed to elicit whether or not such an item of regalia ever found its way to Rome; and the sceptre has been lost for many years.

The Hon Donough O'Brien, in his *History of the O'Briens*, adds that Henry VIII 'cared as little for the monasteries as he cared for the harp, for which he had no use as he could not play upon it ...' According to O'Brien, the king gave the harp, which is now believed to have belonged to a period much later than that of Brian, to Lord Clanricarde. Writing in the *Journal of the Royal Society of Antiquaries of Ireland*, vol. LXXVIII (Dublin, 1948), Professor Hayes-McCoy mentions a sword in the possession of Lord Inchiquin at Dromoland Castle, Newmarket-on-Fergus, Co Clare, and which had been owned by the O'Brien family 'from time immemorial'. Hayes-McCoy described it as resembling 'some of the early Continental hand-and-a-half or two-hander swords', 36 inches long in the blade and with a grip 11½ inches long. Whether or not this belonged to Brian cannot be proved, but it sounds as though it was nearer his period than the sword said traditionally to have been his, which was preserved at Rostellan Castle, Cobh, Co Cork — the principal seat of the O'Briens from 1662 — until the death of James, 3rd and last Marquis of Thomond in 1855. The sword, which Hayes-McCoy identified as a claymore, probably German, of the 16th century, was sold by Lord Thomond's trustees and eventually came into the possession of the Oulton and Vernon families at Clontarf Castle, Dublin. As early as 1820, Crofton Croker was told by a gatekeeper at Rostellan (demolished in 1944) that the claymore had belonged to Brian.

Another reputed relic of Brian was a bronze finger ring preserved by the descendants in the female line of the 2nd Marquis of Thomond until the 1930s, when it was given to the 16th Lord Inchiquin of Dromoland Castle.

(27) Braon died, a monk at Cologne, in 1052.
(28) See Kelly's edition of *Cambrensis Eversus*.
(29) See Ryan, 'Brian Boruma, King of Ireland'. 'The Blessed Brian Boru, King and Martyr' appears in O'Hanlon's *Lives of the Irish Saints*, vol. 4 (Dublin, 1886). There had been earlier attempts at beatification of Brian, the first in 1082 by an Irish priest at Mainz. As Ryan dryly notes: 'The patriotism of these men is inspiring, but the result has unfortunately not been ratified by the Congregation of Rites ... Brian is a saint the heroism of whose virtue is recognised only by his enthusiastic fellow-countrymen.'

Illustrations

THE author and publishers would like to thank the institutions and people who gave permission to use copyright material. The numbers before each entry refer to the page. The initials and names following indicate the source.

Photographs:

BFE   Bord Fáilte Éireann
CPW   Commissioners of Public Works
DMD   Denis MacDonald, Limerick
DNM   Danish National Museum
DPM   Daphne Pochin Mould, Co Cork
JQ   John Quaid, Co Cork
KC   Kevin Coleman, Tralee
MJOK   Professor Michael J O'Kelly

MM   Manx Museum
NM   Norman Morrison
NMI   National Museum of Ireland
RIA   Royal Irish Academy
SM   Sean Magee, Mullingar
SPOR   Professor Seán P Ó Ríordáin
TCD   Trinity College, Dublin
UOO   Universitets Oldsaksamling, Oslo

Drawings:

Bartlett   – W.H., from *Scenery and Antiquities of Ireland* by N. P. Willis and J. Stirling Coyne (London, n d)

Beauford   – T, from *Antiquities of Ireland* by Edward Ledwich (Dublin, 1790)

Dunraven   – Earl of, from *Notes on Irish Architecture*, (London, 1875)

Petrie   – George, from *The Ecclesiastical Architecture of Ireland Anterior to the Norman Invasion* (Dublin, 1845)

Warren   – H, from *History of Ireland*, vol 1, by Thomas Wright (London, n d)

Frontispiece Section of a page of vellum in the *Book of Armagh*, now in the library of Trinity College, Dublin, with the inscription 'Briain Imperatoris Scotorum' commencing fourth line from the end. (See also pages 128 and 203). *TCD*

12 Lambay Island, Ireland's Eye, and the sixteenth-century Howth Castle. *Bartlett*

15 Sceilig Mhíchíl is a rock rising some six hundred feet above the sea, nine miles off the Kerry coast. The monastery there was sacked by the Vikings in 812, the first of four recorded attacks during the ninth century. *Dunraven*

16 The Oseberg ship, discovered in a burial mound in Norway in 1904, measures 72½ feet in length. The combination of sail and oars gave Viking ships speed and manoeuverability, and they were equally effective in open sea or shallow river. *UOO*

18 The five kingdoms of Ireland, after MacNeill, *Celtic Ireland* (Dublin, 1921).

19 The seven kingdoms of Ireland, after Curtis, *Ireland* (Dublin, 1932).

21 The catstone on the hill of Uisneach in Co Westmeath is said to mark the spot where the

210

five ancient kingdoms of Ireland converged. *BFE*

24 The Grianán of Aileach is on the Inishowen peninsula, Co Donegal. It was largely reconstructed by Dr. Bernard of Derry in 1870. *DPM* **25** Aerial view of the Grianán. *DPM*

28 *Top* Reconstruction of a *crannóg*, drawn by W. F. Wakeman for *The Lake Dwellings of Ireland*, W. G. Wood-Martin (Dublin, 1886). *Crannóga* were the lake equivalent of the *ráthanna* or ring forts. Though some belong to pre-historic times, there is evidence that others were being used in the sixteenth century and even later. The larger *crannóga*, such as those of Ballinderry near Moate, Co Westmeath, and Lagore near Dunshaughlin, Co Meath, both of which belonged to the southern Uí Néill, were fortresses. See also *Antiquities of the Irish Countryside*, Séan P. Ó Ríordáin (London, 1942); Sir William Wilde's *A Descriptive Catalogue of the Antiquities in the Museum of the Royal Irish Academy* (3 vols, Dublin, 1857–62); *A Handbook of Irish Antiquities*, W. F. Wakeman (second edn. Dublin, 1891). *Below* Restoration of a *ráth*, drawn by W. F. Wakeman for *Traces of the Elder Faiths in Ireland*, W. G. Wood-Martin (London, 1902). The larger *ráthanna* were defensive structures, with high banks, deep fosses or well-built stone walls, usually with three ramparts around them. The great majority, however, had no military significance and were merely security structures around farmsteads. Estimates of numbers vary from thirty to over forty thousand, and they are found in almost every part of Ireland. See 'The Ancient Forts of Ireland', T. J. Westropp in *Transactions of the Royal Irish Academy*, 31 (Dublin, 1896–1901), 579; *The Archaeology of Ireland*, R. A. S. Macalister (London, 1928); *Pagan Ireland*, W. G. Wood-Martin (London, 1895); *Antiquities of the Irish Countryside*.

35. Clonmacnoise. The smaller of the two round towers seen through a window in the church Temple Finghin. *BFE*

39 Lough Owel, or Loch Uair of the ancients, where Turges was drowned. *BF*

39 Prisoner's chain and collar, found in the *crannóg* of Lagore. *NMI*

42 Holestone and ancient burial stone at Castledermot, Co Kildare. *CPW*

43 Monastic remains on Inis Cathaigh (Scattery Island) in the Shannon. *CWP*

46 Muircheartach's circuit of Ireland, after a map drawn for the Irish Archaeological Society in 1841 by John O'Donovan.

51 Móin na hInse, near Roscrea, Co Tipperary, has a finely decorated twelfth-century chancel arch at the east end (shown) and west doorway typical of the 'Irish Romanesque' style. The abbot's apartments were in the adjoining building. *CPW*

52 Western portal *top* and choir arch of Móin na hInse. *Beauford*

55 General plan of Béal Bóramha made by Professor Michael J. O'Kelly, at the time of excavations carried out under his direction in 1961. Habitation is securely dated by the discovery of two Hiberno-Norse silver pennies of 1035 and 1070 during the excavation, but occupation probably continued until the destruction of the place by King Toirdhealbhach Ó Conchobhair of Connacht in 1118. *MJOK*

56 *Top* Béal Bóramha from the west, overgrown by trees. *Below* The base of the rectangular house, outlined by post-holes and ranging rods. In the left background is the back of an unfinished Norman motte of the early thirteenth century, which had covered the original *ráth* and the house. *MJOK*

59 Inisfallen. The *Annals of Inisfallen*, now in the Bodleian Library, Oxford, was compiled here, at least in part. See also page 201. *Bartlett*

60 Monastic ruins on Inisfallen. *CPW*   **63** Inisfallen, from the lake. *KC*

66 Excavations at Wood Quay, 1974–81, directed by Patrick J. Wallace, Assistant Keeper of Irish Antiquities at the National Museum of Ireland, Dublin. *NMI*

67 Detail of eleventh-century post-and-wattle house at Wood Quay. *NMI*

68 Two armlets of gold ropes. Of Viking type, they were found together in a late tenth-century context during excavations at High Street and Christ Church Place, 1962–74, directed by Breandán Ó Ríordáin, Director of the National Museum of Ireland. *Right* Bone motif or trial piece used for casting metalwork. Scores were found at late tenth-, eleventh- and twelfth-century levels at Wood Quay. *NMI*

72 *Left* Wheel-headed cross from Lonan, Isle of Man, ninth or tenth century. Though Celtic in style, it probably marks the grave of a Norseman. *MM*

72 Memorial stone from Ballaqueeney, Isle of Man, with ogham inscription: '[The stone] of Bivaidu, son of the tribe of Cunava [li]', ie, the Conaille Muirtheimhne, a sub-kingdom north of the river Boyne, Co Louth. *MM*

75 Page from *Leabhar na hUidhri*, the *Book of the Dun Cow*, believed to be the oldest non-ecclesiastical manuscript entirely in the Irish language, now extant. The page (55) is a fine copy of the earliest surviving version of the *Táin Bó Cúailnge*, the plunder of the cows of Cooley. In the Royal Irish Academy Library. *RIA*

77 The knoll of Papataettur where Irish monks are believed to have settled in the eighth century. In the background are the mainland hills. *DPM*

78 The stone ruins of the Irish settlement. *DPM*

79 Miniature wooden ship of Viking type, and a ship with sail incised on a wooden plank, dating from the late eleventh or early twelfth century. *NMI*

81 The cliffs of Moher off the west coast of Co Clare. *BFE*

82 The Burren is a bare limestone upland covering fifty square miles. *BFE*

83 Lough Derg on the river Shannon, backed by the Slieve Bernagh mountains. *BFE*

87 Ráth Raithleann, royal *ráth* of the Cinéal Aodha branch of the Eoghanacht Uí Eachach and capital of Maolmhuadh's kingdom, is a triple-fossed *ráth* enclosing almost three acres, with an elaborate series of gates defending the king's *ráth*. Raithleann is the genitive case of Raithliu, the name of a queen according to Jeremiah O'Mahony in *West Cork Parish Histories*, of a nurse in the household of Corc, king of Munster, according to a traditional story. Corc was the first king of Munster to make Cashel his royal residence, in the second half of the fourth century. The place, now called Garranes, is about seven miles north of Bandon and three miles south-east of Crookstown, Co Cork. The map, from the *Journal* of the Cork Historical and Archaeological Society, vol XIII, p. 29 (Cork, 1907), shows Ráth Raithleann (1); Dún Saidhbhe (2), named after King Brian's daughter who was married to Cian mac Mhaolmhuaidh; the *ráthanna* of Cuileann, the harper (3); of Maolán (4); of the Ollamh, Poets, Women and Doorkeeper (nos. 5 to 8). Two eleventh-century poems attributed to Giolla Caomh give descriptions of Ráth Raithleann, called the *ráth* of Cian.

88 *Top* The entrance to Ráth Raithleann. *Anvil. Below* Section cut through the defences on the north side of Ráth Raithleann during the excavations conducted by Professor Seán P. Ó Ríordáin in 1937, showing workmen standing on the summits of the banks and bottoms of the fosses. *SPOR*

91 Viking silver coins buried at Mungret, Co Limerick, about 950AD and found in 1840. Fig. 1: Obverse and reverse of two-thirds of an Anglo-Saxon penny of Edward the Elder (899–924). Fig 2: Obverse and reverse of half a clipped penny of Athelstan (924–939).

157 Gaming board of yew wood, tenth century, found at Ballinderry *crannóg*, Co Westmeath, during excavations by a Harvard University team in 1932. The 'ring chain' interlaces in two corners are common in Viking art but rare in Irish. *NMI*

160 Hiberno-Norse coins of Sitric III. Coins were struck in Dublin in the name of Sitric in the years following the victory of Brian and Maoil Seachlainn at Gleann Máma.

162 The drawing of the death of King Brian is in accord with the *Book of Leinster* account that there was no one with the king except Latian, a page-boy. As an Irish manuscript, the *Book of Leinster* ranks next to *Leabhar na hUidhri* in age and importance. Marginal notes seem to indicate that transcription began in the middle of the twelfth century, about a hundred and thirty years after Clontarf, under the patronage of Diarmaid mac Murchadha, king of Leinster, and that additions were made in succeeding years. One hundred and seventy leaves are in Trinity College, and eleven in the Franciscan House of Studies, Killiney. *Warren*

167 The Norse and early Norman city of Dublin, based on de Gomme's map of 1673 AD. From the *Journal* of the Royal Society of Antiquaries of Ireland, Vol LXVIII, Part 1 (Dublin, 1938)

173 The byrnie or *lúireach* worn by Norse and Danes at Clontarf. *UOO*

177 King Brian's memorial stone at Armagh Church of Ireland Cathedral.

180 Cró-inis the island retreat on Lough Ennell where Maoil Seachlainn died. *SM*

182 Silver shrine of the 'Stowe' Missal, the oldest surviving mass-book of the Irish church. The missal was closely associated with the monastery of St. Ruadhán at Lorrha in north Tipperary and in all probability was written in the ninth century. The shrine was made at the initiative of Donnchadh, son of Brian Boru, king of Ireland, and of mac Raith Ua Donnchadha, king of Cashel. The middle Irish inscription on the face of the shrine reads: BENDACHT DE AR CECH ANMAIN AS A HARILLIUTH, 'a blessing of God on every soul according to its merit'; OR DO DONDCHAD MACC BRIAIN RIG HEREND, 'Pray for Donnchadh, son of Brian, king of Ireland; OCUS DO MACC RAITH HU DONDCHADA DO RIG CASSIL, 'and for mac Riath Ua Donnchadha, king of Cashel', OR DO DUNCHAD HU TACCAIN DO MUINTIR CLUANA DORIGNI', 'Pray for Donnchadh Ua Taccain of the community of Cluain Dorigni'. Mac Raith Ua Donnchadha was king of the Eoghanacht of Cashel and *tánaiste* of Munster. His death is recorded in the *Four Masters* at 1052. Donnchadh Ua Taccain, believed to have been a monk at Clonmacnoise, was the silversmith who made the shrine, probably between 1023 and 1052. It was redecorated in the second half of the fourteenth century. Both missal and shrine are in the Royal Irish Academy's collection in the National Museum, Dublin. *NMI*

194 Two Hiberno-Norse silver pennies, both fragmentary but of particular interest and importance, from the excavations of Béal Bóramha. Dr. R. N. H. Dolley, formerly of the Department of Coins and Medals, British Museum, is of the opinion that they were minted in Dublin, coin (a) c. 1035 and (b) c. 1070. *MJOK*

195 Portion of the shaft of a cross made by a Christianised Dane, unique in that it is the only stone in existence with a bilingual inscription – 'Thorgrimr erected this cross' in Viking Runic, and a blessing on Thorgrimr in Ogham. It is now inside the cathedral of Killaloe, founded about 1185 by Domhnall Mór O'Briain on the site of an earlier Romanesque church built by King Brian. *Right* Hiberno-Romanesque doorway from the earlier church at Killaloe, now inside the Cathedral. Thorgrimr's stone is in the foreground. *NM*

198 Dún Saidhbhe, Ráth Raithleann. *Anvil* **208** The Petrie 'crown'.

Glossary

THE following lists of Irish words and proper names are arranged in three columns: (1) Irish spellings (as opposed to the various anglicised or semi-anglicised alternatives usually employed in works of this nature), (2) rough guide to pronunciation for English speakers, (3) broad phonetic transcription.

Because of the lack of a spoken standard in modern Irish, the pronunciations indicated in columns (2) and (3) have of necessity been arbitrarily chosen in several instances. Stress is marked only in the case of words which may *not* be accented in the first syllable; in these cases the symbol ¹ precedes the syllable taking the main stress, e.g. *ardrí* (awrd'rē, /aːrd'riː/) is stressed in the second syllable.

For column (2) a system adapted from that used in the *Concise Oxford Dictionary of Current English* has been employed:

(i) **Vowels**

ā ē ī ō ū o̅o̅ *as in* mate mete mite mote mute moot

ă ĕ ĭ ŏ ŭ ŏŏ *as in* rack reck rick rock ruck rook

e̊ *as in* nakėd, re̊ly

Unmarked vowels are of neutral quantity, as in the second syllable of the word *reason*.

(ii) **Consonants**

Each consonant in Irish has both broad (velarised) and slender (palatalised) values and this cannot be adequately shown in English, but it is hoped that the use of '(w)' and '(i)' [not to be pronounced] after certain consonants may indicate the articulation of the preceding sounds.

Additional consonants:

ch as in German and in some words of Scottish origin

gh bearing the same relation to *ch* as *g* does to *c*

d̠ intermediate between the *d* of *dough* and the *th* of *though*

ṫ intermediate between the *t* of *tank* and the *th* of *thank*

Column (3) exhibits an adaptation of the International Phonetic Alphabet, palatalised consonants being followed by the symbol /′/ and unstressed short vowels being indicated by /ə/ or /e/.

Names of people and places

Spelling as in text	*pronunciation*	*broad phonetics*
Adhamhnán	ownawn	/əuna:n/
Agallamh na Seanórach	og alav na shănōrach	/agələ nə ʃano:rəx/
Aileach	ălach	/al'əx/
Áine Cliach	awne klēach	/a:n'e kl'iəx/
Airgeadlámh	arigedlawv	/ar'ig'ədla:v/
Airtre	ărtrė	/artr'ə/
Aodh	ā	/e:/
Aodh Buidhe mac Cruitín	ā b(w)ē mok kritēn	/e: bi: mak krit'i:n/
Aodh Finnliath	ā fĭn'lĕa	/e: f'in'l'iə/
Aodh Oirnidhe	ā ōrnē	/e: o:rn'i:/
Aoibhinn	é vin	/i: v'in'/
Aonach Téide	ānach tādė	/e:nəx t'e:d'ə/
Aonghus	ānēs	/e:ni:s/
Ardghal	awrdēl	/a:rdi:l/
Ard Mhacha	awrd vŏcha	/a:rd vaxə/
Áth Cliath	aw'klēa	/a:'kl'iə/
Áth Fhir-diadh	awhir'dēa	/a:hir'd'iə/
Bachall Íosa	bŏchal ēsa	/baxəl i:se/
Bé Bhionn	bā v(i)ūn	/b'e: v'u:n/
Béal Bóramha	bāl bōrōō	/b'e:l bo:ru:/
Bealach Mughna	b(ă)lŏch mōōna	/b'aləx mu:nə/
Bearna Dhearg	b(e)awrna yărag	/b'arnə ɣ'arəg/
Bóinn	bōn	/bo:n'/
Bóramha Laighean	bōrōō līn	/bo:ru: ləin/
Braon	brān	/bre:n/
Breagh	bră	/br'a/
Bréanainn of Biorra	brānin of bĭra	/br'e:nən'/ of /b'irə/
Bréifne	brā nhe	/br'e: nhe/
Brí Léith	brē lā	/br'i: l'e:/
Brian Bórumha	brēan bō'rōō	/br'iən bo:'ru:/
Brian mac Cinnéide	brēan mok ki'nāde	/br'iən mak k'ə'n'e:d'ə/
Brosnach	brŭsnach	/brosnəx/
Cailleach Fionáin	kolach fĭnawn	/kal'əx fina:n/
Caimín	kŏmēn	/kam'i:n'/
Cairbre Aodhbha	kăribr(e) ā	/kar'ibr'e:/
Cairbre Gabhra	kăribrė gowra	/kar'ibr'e gəurə/
Caiseal	kŏshal	/kaʃəl/
Caoilte	k(w)ēltė	/ki:lt'ə/
Caor Eabhrac	k(w)ār owrak	/ke:r əurak/
Cathair Chuain	kăhir chōōin	/kahər' xuən'/

Cathal	kŏhal	/kahəl/
Cathal mac Maghnusa Mhéig Uidhir	kŏhal mok mawnusa vāg ēr	/kahəl mak mainəsə v'e:g' i:r'/
Cathaoir Mór	kŏkēr mōr	/kahi:r' mo:r/
Ceallachán	k(i)ălachawn	/k'aləxa:n/
Ceann Coradh	k(i)own kŭra	/k'əun korə/
Ceannfaoladh	k(i)anˈf(w)āla	/k'ənˈfe:lə/
Ceannfhada	k(i)aˈnăḏa	/k'əˈnadə/
Cearbhall	k(i)ărōōl	/k'aru:l/
Cearbhall of Osraighe	k(i)ărōōl of ŭsarē	/k'aru:l/ of /osəri:/
Cian	kēan	/k'iən/
Ciarán	kēarawn	/k'iəra:n/
Ciarraighe Luachra	kēarē lōōachra	/k'iəriʔ luəxrə/
Cill mo Shámóg	kēl moˈhawvōg	/k'i:l məˈha:vo:g/
Cinéal Aodha	kĭnāl ā	/k'in'e:l e:/
Cinéal gConaill	kināl gŏŏnil	/k'in'e:l gunəl'/
Cinéal Eoghain	kināl ōn	/k'in'e:l o:n/
Cinnéide mac Lorcáin	kiˈnāḋe mok lŭrkawn	/k'əˈn'e:d'ə mak lorka:n'/
Cionaoth mac Ailpín	k(i)ŏŏnā mok alpēn	/k'une: mak alp'i:n'/
Clann Chonaill	klown chŏŏnil	/kləun xunəl'/
Clann Eoghain	klown ōn	/kləun o:n/
Colam Cille	kŭlam kĭlė	/koləm k'il'ə/
Colam mac Ciaragáin	kŭlam mok k(i)ēaragawn	/koləm mak k'iəraga:n'/
Conaille	kŏŏnile	/kunəl'ə/
Conaille Muirtheimhne	kŏŏnile m(w)ĭrhēvne	/kunəl'ə mi:r'hevn'e/
Conaing	kŏŏning	/kunəŋ'/
Conaire Ó Cléirigh	kŏŏnar(ė)ō klārė	/kunər'(ə) o: kl'e:r'ə/
Conall mac Eochagáin	kŏŏnal mok ŭchagawn	/kunəl mak oxəga:n'/
Conchobhar	knoˈchōōr	/knoˈxu:r/
Conghalach	kŏŏˈnēlach	/kəˈni:ləx/
Conn	kown	/kəun/
Conn Céadchathach	kown k(i)ādˈchăhach	/kəun k'e:dˈxahəx/
Connachta	kŏŏnachta	/kunəxtə/
Corca Bhaiscinn	kŭrka vŏshkin	/korkə vaʃkən'/
Corca Dhuibhne	kŭrka ghēnė	/korkə ɣi:n'ə/
Cormac Cas	kŭramok kŏs	/korəmək kas/
Cormac mac Airt	kŭramok mok ărt	/korəmək mak art'/
Cormac mac Cuileannáin	kŭramok mok k(w)ĭlenawn	/korəmək mak kil'əna:n/
Críth Ghabhlach	krē chŏvlach	/kr'i: xavləx/
Cró-inis	krōnish	/kro:n'əʃ/
Cruachain	krōōach(w)in	/kruəxin'/
Cú Choigcríche ó Duibhgeannáin	kōō choˈgrēh(ė)ō dīganawn	/ku: xəgr'i:h(ə) o: dəig'əna:n'/
Cúailnge	kōōelė	/kuəl'ə/
Cuarán	kōōarawn	/kuəra:n/
Cuileán	k(w)ĭlawn	/kil'a:n/

Dál gCais	ḍawl gŏsh	/da:l gaʃ/
Dál gCuinn	ḍawl g(w)ēn	/da:l gi:n'/
Dál Riada	ḍawl rēaḍa	/da:l riəḍə/
Dealbhna	dălona	/d'alənə/
Dearbhforgaill	daravŭrg(w)il	/d'arəvorgil'/
Deasmhumha (in)	dă'sōōn	/d'a'su:n'/
Déis Bheag	dāsh v(i)ŭg	/d'e:ʃ v'og/
Déis Deiscirt	dāsh dĕshkirt	/d'e:ʃ d'eʃk'ərt'/
Déis Tuaiscirt	dāsh tōōeshkirt	/d'e:ʃ tuəʃk'ərt'/
Déise Mumhan	dāshi mōōn	/de:ʃi mu:n/
Diarmaid	dēarm(w)id	/d'iərməd'/
Diarmaid mac Maoil na mBó	dēarm(w)id mok m(w)ēl na mō	/d'iərməd' mak m'i:l' nə mo:/
Diarmaid mac Murchadha	dēarm(w)id' mok mōōrachū	/d'iərməd' mak murəxu:/
Dinnsheanchas	dēn'hănachas	/d'i:n''hanəxəs/
Do-Chonna	ḍo'chōōna	/də'xunə/
Domhnall	ḍōnal	/do:nəl/
Donn Cuan	ḍown kōōan	/dəun kuən/
Donnchadh	ḍōōnacha	/dunəxə/
Draighean	ḍrīn	/drəin/
Droichead Dubhghaill	ḍrĕhaḍ ḍōōl	/drehəd du:l'/
Druim Deargaighe	ḍrēm dărag(w)ē	/dri:m' d'arəgi:/
Dubhchobhlaigh	ḍōō'chowlig	/du:'xəuləg'/
Dubh dhá Léithe	ḍōōv aw lāhe	/duv a: l'e:hə̇/
Dubhghaill	ḍōōvghēl	/duvɣi:l'/
Duibhlinn	ḍēlin	/di:l'ən'/
Eachraidh	ăch(a)ra	/ax(ə)rə/
Eidigeán	ādigawn	/e:d'əg'a:n/
Eidirsceol	ĕdirskōl	/ed'ir'sk'o:l/
Éireamhón	āravōn	/e:r'əvo:n/
Eocha(idh)	ŭcha	/oxə/
Eoghan	ōn	/o:n/
Eoghan Mór	ōn mōr	/o:n mo:r/
Eoghanachta	ōnachṭa	/o:nəxtə/
Feara Mhaighe Féine	f(i)ăra v(w)ē fāṅe	/f'arə vi: f'e:n'ə/
Fearghus mac Earca	fărēs mok ărka	/f'ari:s mak arkə/
Fear Gráidh	far graw	/f'ar gra:/
Feidhlimidh	fīlimė	/f'əil'əm'ə/
Feidhlimidh mac Criomthainn	fīlimė mok krĭf(w)in	/f'əil'əm'ə mak kr'ifin'/
Fianna	fēana	/f'iənə/
Fionn mac Cumhaill	f(i)ūn mok kōōl	/f'u:n mak ku:l'/
Fionn mac Gormáin	f(i)ūn mok gŭramawn	/f'u:n mak gorəma:n'/
Fíonnachta	fēnachṭa	/f'i:nəxtə/·

Fionnbharra	f(i)ūnvŏra	/f'u:nvarə/
Fionnghaill	fōōnghēl	/f'u:nɣi:l'/
Fir Bholg	fĭr vŭlag	/f'ir' voləg/
Flaithbheartach	flăharṭach	/flahərtəx/
Flann Sionna	flown shōōna	/fləun ʃuna/
Gleann Máma	gl(i)own mawma	/gl'əun ma:mə/
Gleannamhain	glă'nōōn	/gl'a'nu:n'/
Giolla Ciaráin	g(i)ōōla kēarawn	/g'ulə k'iəra:n'/
Glúiniarainn	glōōn'ēarin	/glu:n''iərən'/
Gormfhlaith	gŭromla	/gorəmlə/
Grianán	grēanawn	/gr'iəna:n/
Inbhear Bóinne	ĭnvar bōnė	/inv'ər bo:n'ə/
Inis Caoin	ĭnish k(w)ēn	/in'əʃ ki:n'/
Inis Cathaigh	ĭnish kăha	/in'əʃ kahə/
Inis Cealtra	ĭnish k(i)ălṭra	//in'əʃ k'altrə/
Ionmhainéan	ōōnv(w)inān	/invən'e:n/
Lachtna	lŏchna	/laxnə/
Laighin	līn	/ləin'/
Laoghaire	lārė	/le:r'ə/
Leabhar na hUidhri	lowr na hērė	/l'əur nə hi:r'i:/
Leabhar Oiris	lowr ĭrish	/l'əur ir'iʃ/
Leacht Mhathghamhna	l(i)achṭ vŏhōōna	/l'axt vahu:nə/
Leath Cuinn	lă'k(w)ēn	/l'a'ki:n'/
Leath Mogha	lă'mow	/l'a'məu/
Loch Ainninn	lŭch ănin	/lox an'ən'/
Loch Léin	lŭch lān	/lox l'e:n'/
Longhargán	lōōnargawn	/lunərga:n/
Lorcán	lŭrkawn	/lorka:n/
Mac Beatha	mok b(i)ăha	/mak b'ahə/
Mac Bruaideadha	mok brōōėdē	/mak bruəd'i:/
Mac Giolla Phádraig	mok g(i)ōōla fawḍrig	/mak g'ulə fa:drəg'/
Maigh Adhair	m(w)ī īr	/məi əir'/
Maigh Ailbhi	m(w)ī ălvė	/məi alv'ə/
Manainn	mŏnin	/manən'/
Maoil-Seachlainn	m(w)ēl'shăchlin	/mi:l'ʃʃaxlin'/
Maol Mórdha	m(w)āl mo:ra	/me:l mo:rə/
Maolmhaodhóg Ó Morghair	mu'lōō ōg ō morghir	/mə'lu:o:g o: morɣir'/
Maolmhuadh	m(w)ē'lōōa	/me:'luə/
Maol Muire mac Céileachair	m(w)āl m(w)irė mok kālachir	/me:l mir'ə mak k'e:l'əxər'/
Maol Ruanaidh na Paidre Ó hEidhin	m(w)āl rōōana na pŏdir(e) ō hīn	/me:l ruənə nə padər'(e) o: həin'/

Maolsuthain Ua Cearbhaill	m(w)āl'sōŏhin ōō k(i)arōōl	/me:l'suhən' u: k'aru:l'/
Marcán	morkawn	/marka:n/
Mathghamhain	mŏhūn	/mahu:n'/
Mícheál Ó Cléirigh	mēhāl ō klērė	/m'i:he:l o: kl'e:r'ə/
Midhe	mē	/m'i:/
Móin na hInse	mōna'hēnshi	/mo:n'ə'hi:nʃə/
Mo-Ling	mu'līng	/mə'liŋ'/
Mór	mōr	/mo:r/
Muintir Ifearnáin	m(w)ēntir ĭfernawn	/mi:nt'ər' if'ərna:n'/
Muircheartach	m(w)irihartach	/mir'əhərtəx/
Muircheartach mac Liag	m(w)irihartach mok lēag	/mir'əhərtəx mak l'iəg/
Muireagán	m(w)iragawn	/mir'əga:n/
Muirgheas	m(w)i'rēs	/mi'ri:s/
Muiris Ó Maoilchonaire	m(w)irish ō mul'chōŏnarė	/mir'əʃ o: məl'xunər'ə/
Muisire na Móna Móire	m(w)ishire na mōna mōrė	/miʃər'ə nə mo:nə mo:r'ə/
Mumha(in)	mōōn	/mu:n'/
Murchadh	mōŏracha	/murəxə/
Muscraighe	mōōskrē	/mu:skri:/
Muscraighe Tíre	mōōskrē tērė	/mu:skri: t'i:r'e/
Nás	Naws	/na:s/
Niall Caille	nēal kŏlė	/n'iəl kal'ə/
Niall Glúndubh	nēal glōōndŏŏv	/n'iəl glu:nduv/
Niall Naoighiallach	nēal nē'ghēalach	/n'iəl ne:'ɣiələx/
Niamh	nēav	/n'iəv/
Ó Briain	ō brēėn	/o: br'iən'/
Ó Caiside	ō kŏshidė	/o: kaʃəd'ə/
Ó Ciardha	ō kēara	/o: k'iərə/
Ó Cuinn	ō k(w)ēn	/o: ki:n'/
Ó Duinnshléibhe	ō dĭnhlāve	/o: din'hl'e:v'ə/
Ó Dúnlaing	ō dōōling	/o: du:ləŋ'/
Ó Fáilbhe	ō fawlė	/o: fa:l'ə/
Ó Faoláin	ō f(w)ālawn	/o: fe:la:n'/
Oilill Fionn	ĭlil f(i)ōōn	/il'əl' f'u:n/
Oilill Ólom	ĭlil ōlom	/il'əl' o:ləm/
Oirghialla	ūˈrēala	/ə'r'iələ/
Oisín	ĕshēn	/eʃi:n'/
Olchobhar	ŭlchowr	/olxəur/
Ó Lochlainn	ō lŭchlin	/o: loxlin'/
Ó Lorcáin	ō lŭrkawn	/o: lorka:n'/
Ó Luinín	ō līnēn	/o: lən'i:n'/
Ó Néill	ō nāl	/o: n'e:l'/
Órlaith	ōrla	/o:rlə/
Ó Ruairc	ō rōōėrk	/o: ruərk'/
Osraighe	ŭsarē	/osəri:/

Reachra(inn)	răchra *or* răchrin	/raxrə/ or /raxrin'/
Ruadhán of Lothra	rōōawn of lŭrha	/ru:a:n/ of /lorhə/
Ruaidhrí	rōōerē	/ruər'i:/
Sadhbh	sīv	/səiv/
Saingeal	sănggel	/saŋg'al/
Saltair Chaisil	sŏltir chŏshil	/saltər' xaʃəl'/
Scannlán	skownlawn	/skəunla:n/
Sceilig Mhíchíl	shkĕlig veˡhēl	/ʃk'el'əg v'iˡhi:l'/
Seanán	shănawn	/ʃana:n/
Seanchas Mór	shănachas mōr	/ʃanəxəs mo:r/
Sléibhín	shlāvēn	/ʃl'e:v'i:n'/
Sliabh Callraighe	shlēav kŏlarē	/ʃl'iəv kaləri:/
Sliabh Fuaid	shlēav fōōėd	/ʃl'iəv fuəd'/
Slighe Asail	shlē ŏsil	/ʃl'i: asəl'/
Slighe Chualann	shlē chōōalan	/ʃl'i: xuələn/
Slighe Dhála	shlē ghawla	/ʃl'i: ɣa:lə/
Slighe Mhiodhluachra	shlē vēˡlōōachra	/ʃl'i: v'i:ˡluəxrə/
Slighe Mhór	shlē vōr	/ʃl'i vo:r/
Solchóid	sŭlaˡchōd	/soləˡxo:d'/
Tadhg	ţīg	/təig/
Teamhair	towr	/t'əur'/
Tighernán	tēarnawn	/t'iəna:n/
Tír Chonaill	tēr chŏōnil	/t'i:r' xunəl'/
Tír dhá Ghlas	tērawˡghlas	/t'i:r' a:ˡɣlas/
Tír Eoghain	tēr ōn	/t'i:r' o:n'/
Tobar Gleathrach	ţŭbar glărhach	/tobər glarhəx/
Toirdhealbhach	ţrēlach *or* ţŭrlach	/tre:ləx/ or /turləx/
Tuadhmhumha(in)	ţōōen	/tuən'/
Tuathal Teachtmhar	ţōōhal tachvar	/tuəhəl t'axvər/
Tuirgéis	ţirgāsh	/tirg'e:ʃ/
Úghaire	ōōrė	/u:r'ə/
Uí Aodha Odhbha	ē ā ow	/i: e: əu/
Uí Chairbre Aodhbha	ē chăribr(e)ˡā	/i: xar'əbr'ˡe:/
Uí Chaisín	ē chăshēn	/i: xaʃi:n'/
Uí Chinsealaigh	ē chēnshala	/i: x'i:nʃələ/
Uí Dhomhnaill	ē ghōnil	/i: ɣo:nəl'/
Uí Dhortain	ē ghurhine	/i: vorhin'/
Uí Dhróna	ē ghrōna	/i: ɣro:nə/
Uí Dhúnlaing	ē ghōōling	/i: ɣu:ləŋ'/
Uí Eachach	ē ăchach	/i: axəx/
Uí Fhiachrach Aidhne	ē ēchrach īnė	/i: i:xrəx əin'ə/
Uí Fhidhghinte	ē ēntė	/i: i:nt'ə/
Uí Mhaine	ē vŏnė	/i: van'ə/

Uí Mhéith	ĕ vā	/i: v'e:/
Uí Néill	ĕ nāl	/i: n'e:l'/
Uí Ruairc	ĕ rōoérk	/i: ruərk'/
Uisneach	ĭshnach	/iʃn'əx/
Ulaidh	ŭla	/olə/

Irish words used in text

airigh	ărig	/ar'ig'/
ardrí	awrd¹rē	/a:rd¹ri:/
biatach	bēatach	/b'iətəx/
bó-airigh	bō ărig	/bo: ar'ig'/
breitheamhain	brehōon	/br'ehu:n'/
buadha	bōōa	/buə/
céadmhuintear dhlightheach	k(i)ād¹v(w)ēnter ghlīhach	/k'e:d¹vi:nt'ər ɣl'ihəx/
céile	kālė	/k'e:l'ə/
cloidheamh	klēv	/kli:v/
cloigtheach	klĭkăch	/klik'ax/
cna(i)p	knăp	/knap/ or /knap'/
cóigeadha	cōōgē	/ku:g'i:/
comharba	kōrba	/ko:rbə/
crann-tábhaill	krown¹tawl	/krəun¹ta:l'/
deirbhfhine	dĕrivĭne	/d'er'iv'in'e/
flaith	flŏ	/fla/
flatha	flŏha	/flahə/
gallán	gu¹lawn	/gə¹la:n/
garrdha	gŏrē	/gari:/
giolla grádha	g(i)ŏōla graw	/g'ulə gra:/
go bhfreasabhra	go vrăsōora	/gə vr'asu:rə/
leannán sídhe	li¹nawn shē	/l'ə¹na:n ʃi:/
longphuirt	lōōngf(w)irt	/lu:ngfirt'/
lúireach	lōōrach	/lu:r'əx/
mormhaor	mōrar	/mo:rər'/
mórthuath	mōrhōōa	/mo:rhuə/
ollamhain	ŭlōōn	/olu:n'/
ráthanna	rawhana	/ra:hənə/
ríoghdhamhna	rē¹ghowna	/ri:¹ɣəunə/
seanchaithe	shănachihe	/ʃanəxəhə/
tánaiste	ṭawnishtė	/ta:niʃt'ə/
tánaisteacht	ṭawn ishtechṭ	/ta:nəʃt'əxt/
trosc	ṭrŭsk	/trosk/
tuagh chatha	ṭōōa chaha	/tuə xahə/
tuarastal	ṭōōarasṭal	/tuərəstəl/
tuatha	ṭōōaha	/tuəhə/

Index